Hospitality Trends and Dimensions

HOSPITALITY TRENDS AND DIMENSIONS

Nandini Rajpal

CENTRUM PRESS
NEW DELHI-110002 (INDIA)

CENTRUM PRESS
H.O.: 4360/4, Ansari Road, Daryaganj,
New Delhi-110002 (India)
Tel: 23278000, 23261597, 23255577, 23286875
B.O.: No. 1015, Ist Main Road, BSK IIIrd Stage,
IIIrd Phase, IIIrd Block, Bengaluru-560085 (INDIA)
Tel: 080-41723429
Email: centrumpress@gmail.com
Visit us at: www.centrumpress.com

Hospitality Trends and Dimensions

First Edition, 2013

ISBN 978-93-81460-18-4

PRINTED IN INDIA

Printed at Balaji Offset, Delhi.

Contents

Preface

Globalization is essentially a process by which an ever tightening network of ties that cut across national political boundaries connects communities in a single, interdependent whole, a shrinking world where local differences are steadily eroded and subsumed within a massive global social order. Today's ever-expanding global economy has made travel the number one industry, boasting a customer base that is wealthier and more technologically savvy than ever. How can a hotel owner compete for the attention of this growing crowd?

A look at the latest trends in hospitality reveals what's hot – the convenience of technology and a more relaxed use of space. The latest word? Like everywhere else – wireless. Cell phones, laptops, PalmPilots – most of us would be lost without them. For business travelers in particular, access to e-mail and corporate networks is crucial. Generally, this connection is provided through dial-up access, but improvements in virtual private networks (VPNs) are changing that. VPNs provide reliable, secure Internet access to corporate data and messaging systems. For the business traveller who doesn't mind juggling a laptop in one hand and a plate in the other, restaurants are serving an enticing array of side dishes. Not only might you place your order at a kiosk, but you can offer suggestions to the establishment, send e-mail, surf the net or even access chat rooms – all during your meal.

In the guest room itself, a more homelike environment tops the list of trends. Designers are introducing features such as adjustable lighting, water fountains, more harmonious colour schemes and aromatherapy. Tired of hearing the sound of generic piped-in music? Soon, guests will walk into their hotel rooms and hear music characterizing the locale, such as jazz in a New Orleans' hotel. Fitness-conscious guests may even find a stretch bar or stationary bike in their rooms, a convenient and private option to the hotel's health club. Entertainment also has taken a step forward.

More guest rooms have CD players, and designers are encouraging hoteliers to replace awkward armoire-style entertainment centres with flat-screen televisions. This can cut an average of four inches (10 cm) off each individual room – an economically savvy choice for the owner of an 800-room hotel. New designs are creating a more open feeling in guest bathrooms. Doors remain open when the room is not in use and upper-floor bathrooms may even have windows. What could be more relaxing than a view of the ocean from a shower in a Miami high-rise hotel? Designers also are changing the way bathrooms and sleeping areas relate to each other visually. For instance, a shuttered opening may replace the typical wall. One unique idea uses a glass pane filled with magnetically-oriented particles. At the touch of a button, the pane alternates between transparent and opaque.

This book fulfills the long felt necessity of a text dealing with concepts of this subject. It can also prove to be a worthy companion and guide for the students, users and researchers.

—Author

1

Hospitality Laws, Education and Training

General Provisions

Article 1

This Law is based on Article 11 of Revolutionary Basic Principles and enforcements of Democratic Republic of Afghanistan and also to administer and develop Tourism of in Afghanistan.

Article 2

The defined terms used in this Law have the following meanings:

1. Tourist: a person who visits a country rather than his residential homeland, if he does not perform a job which he is paid regularly. This visit also used for the purpose of entertainment, relaxation, holidays, treatment, research, sporting, trading and visiting relatives and also includes panel visits and meetings and includes 24 hours of staying.
2. Tourist establishments: staying place, restaurants, bars, cafes, office that administers tours for tourists.
3. Staying place of tourist:
    1. Hotel
    2. Guest house
    3. Club
    4. Vila
    5. Entertaining centres
    6. Catripping

7. Caravan (parks)

4. Entertaining Centres: establishments which provide the tourist entertainment facilities.
5. Camping: area identified and used for tenting and garaging tourist's vehicle.
6. Caravanning: vehicle that has facilities for accommodation of tourist.
7. Touring areas: that are determined as touring areas by Tourism administration or other relevant government agency and areas that have natural beauties, cultural artists, and heritages, touring establishments, national and international exhibitions, national parks and other places.
8. Touring activities: that expand and develop tourism in the country.
9. Touring Services: provided by touring establishments for tourists.
10. Organization: Tourism Organization of Afghanistan.

Afghanistan Tourism

Article 3:

The Tourism Organization works under the framework of the Ministry of Transportation based on the relevant Charter as a state owned profitable enterprise by the name of (Tourism Organization of Afghanistan).

Article 4

The Charter of the Organization shall be prepared based on the provisions of State Enterprises Law and this Law.

Article 5

This organization has the following functions and authorities:

1. Administration of all relevant tourism activities in the government of Afghanistan.
2. Securing touring areas and providing touring services, and taking actions against those who destroys tourism industry of the Afghanistan.

3. Making publicities to attract tourists inside and outside the of Afghanistan and for this purpose provides guide books, brochures, posters, photos, slides, postcards, maps, movies, magazines and other paper, radio and TV advertisements.
4. Training of professional personnel required for tourism while this industry develops in the country.
5. Establishing unity with domestic and international tourism agencies of friend countries and attending in international gatherings and other tourism exhibitions by permission of the government.
6. Constructing tourism establishments in ancient areas with the agreement of relevant authorities.
7. Provision and implementation of tourism developing plans under framework of the Government.
8. Providing birds and other animals hunting programs for tourists and benefiting from such programs to strength economy of the Afghanistan with the agreement of Ministry of Agriculture and develop tourism.
9. Provision and publication of tourism estimates.
10. Other functions and authorities described in the agreement.

Tourism Establishments

Article 6

Owners of staying places, bars, restaurants and tea house of tourists are required to get a business license by paying the amount determined based on the grade of the business set by the Tourism Organization.

Article 7

Only registered accommodation places can accept tourists and this provision is not applicable on hosting government guests.

Anyone breaches this provision will be penalized for afs 500 per night of each tourist staying.

If the penalties increase from afs 3000 then based on the provisions of the law, the person shall be prosecuted.

Article 8

Tourism establishments shall be graded once in two years for the purpose of checking of domestic and international standards by the tourism organization. There is no ban for restaurants, bars and tea houses that are out of this grade and accepts tourists.

Tourism establishments shall be registered in the tourism organization after a registration fee is paid. The registration fee is not refundable after the issuance of a business license.

Article 10

Construction plans, location and programs of tourism establishments shall be provided by the Tourism organization. Any kind of activities which are contrary to this article shall cease until receiving such approval.

Article 11

The tourism organization gives the priority to those who have graduation documents from relevant educational entities which are accepted by the organization upon hiring of professional personnel.

Miscellaneous Provisions

Article 12

This organization is the only responsible entity in Afghanistan that practices tourism travel agency functions.

Article 13

A tourism visa (except for religious celebrations) for Afghan citizens and tourism visa renewal for foreign citizens shall be requested through the tourism organization.

Article 14

The required amount of the money for an afghan tourist to take outside of Afghanistan shall be determined by request of this organization and approval of the government. Official panels and tour for the religious purposes are exceptions from this provision.

Article 15

The minimum amount of currency that a tourist must have

upon entering the Afghanistan shall be determined by the request of this organization and approval of the government.

Article 16

This law is applicable after its publication in the official gazette. With the enactment of this Law, the Tourism Law of the year 1976 (1355) and its rules are cancelled

Visa Rules for India

About Visa

A Visa gives permission to the person who wishes to stay in a country for a specific period of time to fulfil a specific motive. It is usually attached or stamped in the individual passport. All travellers to India (except citizens of India going Nepal and vice versa) must possess visas.

Duration of Visa

Tourist visas are normally available for a duration of three months to six months for multiple entries (important for side trips to Nepal and other countries). Other options include a one-year student visa, journalist visa or business visa, or five years visa for non-resident Indians. When applying for a visa, make sure your passport is valid for 6 months beyond the date of intended return journey.

Getting the Visa

If you apply for a visa through the Indian embassy in your resident country the process becomes much fast. You are required to fill an application form providing your current passport with at least two passport size photographs. Applications can be sent through mail with the payment in the form of money orders. No cash or cheques are accepted. If applying in person, the consulates and embassies will usually accept cash otherwise only money orders are accepted. The visa formalities, cost of visa and the time lag between the application and issue of visa varies from country to country.

Special Permits

Certain regions of India require a special permit in addition to an Indian visa. Permits are issued by Indian High Commissions and Embassy of India abroad, by the Ministry of Home Affairs in Delhi, or by Foreigner's Registration Offices (FRRO's) in Indian cities.

These areas include:

Northeast India: The region of seven sisters in India except Assam, Meghalaya and Tripura states which are open for tourism. If visiting Assam then consult your embassy before starting your journey. Arunachal Pradesh, Nagaland, Manipur, and Mizoram require restricted area permits due to tribal insurgencies and fears of conflict with China.

A minimum of four people can travel together, and the group must be sponsored by a Government approved travel agency. These permits generally cost Rs. 300-400. Permits are valid for 15 days and renewable for next 15 days at the Foreigner's Registration Offices in each state capital. The permits are issued in 2 days-2 months depending on the state.

Sikkim: Sikkim borders China and is treated as a military buffer by the Indian Government. Foreigners need a permit to enter Sikkim and the maximum stay period cannot exceed more than 15 days an year. Permits are free of cost and readily available in the major Indian cities. The validity of permits can be extended at the Commissioner's Office in Gangtok under special circumstances, but then only for 3-5 days, and only once a while. For North Sikkim, an inner line permit is required. It is issued only through tour companies to the groups of four or more. A guide must accompany the group and the minimum charge is US$ 30-35 per day, including the guide. It is issued in a day but is available only in Gangtok.

Andaman and Nicobar Islands: The Nicobar Islands are off-limits. Leave plenty of time if applying for a permit for Andaman Islands from the Ministry of Home Affairs or from Indian Embassies abroad. Those arriving by air can obtain permits in Port Blair on arrival.

Lakshadweep: Only Bangaram Island of this archipelago is open to foreigners. The necessary free permit can be obtained through the Liaison Officer, Lakshadweep or at some of the hotels in Cochin. You'll need four passport size photographs. The permit can be obtained in a day or two.

New Visa Rules Hit Two Major Road Projects in HP

Press Trust of India / Shimla October 27, 2009, 11:07 IST

The Government's decision barring foreigners from working in the country on business visa has hit two major road projects in the apple belt of Himachal Pradesh.

Under the new visa rules which came into force in August this year, foreigners are not allowed to work in the country on business visa and they have to obtain work visa for the purpose.

The new rules have upset two World Bank funded major road projects in the hill state being carried by China-based firm Longjian Road and Bridge Company Limited. Some 80 Chinese engineers and workers engaged in the two projects left India before expiry of their business visa on September 30.

The road projects are –Theog-Kotkhai-Hatkoti-Rohroo and Mehtapur-Una-Amb. The first one falls in the apple producing area of Shimla district and completion of the road project would have facilitated faster movement of the crop to the market.

The halt of the project has dealt a severe blow to the Himachal Pradesh government.

"We have taken up the matter with the Centre and also drawn the attention of the World Bank to the same", state Public Works Department Minister Thakur Gulab Singh told PTI today.

The two projects awarded in May and June 2008 were to be completed by November 2010. However, so far only 7-8 per cent work has been completed, official sources said. Emphasising that major road projects worth Rs 1,365 crore would have been beneficial for apple cultivators, the HP government has written to the Centre for either extension of business visa or grant of employment visa to the Chinese workforce.

Principal Secretary PWD P C Kapoor, who recently met External Affairs Ministry officials on the issue, said we have requested the Centre that if granting visa to 80 Chinese was not possible, they should consider giving the same to 10 Chinese engineers "crucial for execution of the project".

Considering the seriousness of the situation, Chief Minister Prem Kumar Dhumal has also taken up the matter with the Centre, the PWD minister said.

He said if the matter is not resolved at the earliest, we would take up the issue with the World Bank seeking permission for cancellation of the contract to the Chinese company and giving it to somebody else for early completion.

A letter has also been written to the Chinese company asking it to complete their contractual obligation of completing the projects on time, the Minister said. Kapoor said the matter is under consideration of the Union government and they have assured the state positive action on the same.

Revised Visa Rules May Hit Vital Projects

Special Correspondent

New Delhi: The Union Home Ministry's move to streamline the visa system without consulting other stakeholders has claimed collateral damage in the form of up to 1,000 Russian scientists and engineers working in critical sectors such as defence undertakings and nuclear power plants.

The Ministry's decision to ask all foreigners working on business visas to get them converted into employment visas means these Russian engineers will have to return to Moscow and apply afresh. As a result, projects with tight timeliness such as the Koodankulam nuclear power project could be hit by delays unless a "more flexible" system is worked out, according to official sources. They admitted to having been "taken by surprise" by the Ministry's move to end the "misuse" of business visas. Officials said two rounds of talks were held in Moscow and Delhi. Other Ministries whose projects could be affected are in touch with the Home Ministry, given the "close friendship" with Russia and the fact that its engineers are carrying out "important projects."

It all began when the Home Ministry, concerned at the practice of foreigners taking up employment in India on business visas, decided to set a deadline for converting them into employment visas. As the process sometimes took up to a year, it was decided to set a timeline of 60 days for accepting or rejecting employment visa applications.

While there will be minimal impact on sensitive projects if other foreigners return, Russians are known to be working in impossible-to-replace positions such as the development of a cruise missile and a fifth generation fighter, setting up of nuclear power plants, naval projects and catering to the fighters being imported by India.

"The rule is being applied across the board regardless of who is asking for the visa. The intention is good and sufficient notice was given," the sources said.

"If the Russians go back, some projects could suffer delays. So we believe there should be a flexible approach," they said.

Biological Diversity and Tourism

Rainforests are an example of biodiversity on the planet, and typically possess a great deal of species biodiversity. This is the Gambia River in Senegal's Niokolokoba National Park.

Biodiversity is the variation of life forms within a given ecosystem, biome, or for the entire Earth. Biodiversity is often used as a measure of the health of biological systems. The biodiversity found on Earth today consists of many millions of distinct biological species, which is the product of nearly 3.5 billion years of evolution.

Etymology

The term was used first by wildlife scientist and conservationist Raymond F. Dasmann in a lay book advocating nature conservation. The term was not widely adopted for more than a decade, when in the 1980s it and "biodiversity" came into common usage in science and environmental policy. Use of the term by Thomas Lovejoy in the Foreword to the book credited with launching the field of conservation biology introduced the term along with "conservation biology" to the scientific community.

Until then the term "natural diversity" was used in conservation science circles, including by The Science Division of The Nature Conservancy in an important 1975 study, "The Preservation of Natural Diversity." By the early 1980s TNC's Science program and its head Robert E. Jenkins, Lovejoy, and other leading conservation scientists at the time in America advocated the use of "biological diversity" to embrace the object of biological conservation.

The term's contracted form *biodiversity* may have been coined by W.G. Rosen in 1985 while planning the *National Forum on Biological Diversity* organized by the National Research Council

(NRC) which was to be held in 1986, and first appeared in a publication in 1988 when entomologist E. O. Wilson used it as the title of the proceedings of that forum.

Since this period both terms and the concept have achieved widespread use among biologists, environmentalists, political leaders, and concerned citizens worldwide. The term is sometimes used to equate to a concern for the natural environment and nature conservation. This use has coincided with the expansion of concern over extinction observed in the last decades of the 20th century.

A similar concept in use in the United States, besides natural diversity, is the term "natural heritage." It pre-dates both terms though it is a less scientific term and more easily comprehended in some ways by the wider audience interested in conservation. "Natural Heritage" was used when Jimmy Carter set up the Georgia Heritage Trust while he was governor of Georgia; Carter's trust dealt with both natural and cultural heritage.

It would appear that Carter picked the term up from Lyndon Johnson, who used it in a 1966 Message to Congress. "Natural Heritage" was picked up by the Science Division of the US Nature Conservancy when, under Jenkins, it launched in 1974 the network of State Natural Heritage Programs. When this network was extended outside the USA, the term "Conservation Data Center" was suggested by Guillermo Mann and came to be preferred.

Definitions

A Sampling of fungi collected during summer 2008 in Northern Saskatchewan mixed woods, near LaRonge is an example regarding the species diversity of fungi. In this photo, there are also leaf lichens and mosses.

Biologists most often define "biological diversity" or "biodiversity" as the "totality of genes, species, and ecosystems of a region". An advantage of this definition is that it seems to describe most circumstances and present a unified view of the traditional three levels at which biological variety has been identified:

* genetic diversity
* species diversity

* ecosystem diversity

This multilevel conception is consistent with the early use of "biological diversity" in Washington. D.C. and international conservation organizations in the late 1960s through 1970's, by Raymond F. Dasmann who apparently coined the term and Thomas E. Lovejoy who later introduced it to the wider conservation and science communities. An explicit definition consistent with this interpretation was first given in a paper by Bruce A. Wilcox commissioned by the International Union for the Conservation of Nature and Natural Resources (IUCN) for the 1982 World National Parks Conference in Bali The definition Wilcox gave is "Biological diversity is the variety of life forms...at all levels of biological systems (i.e., molecular, organismic, population, species and ecosystem)..." Subsequently, the 1992 United Nations Earth Summit in Rio de Janeiro defined "biological diversity" as "the variability among living organisms from all sources, including, 'inter alia', terrestrial, marine, and other aquatic ecosystems, and the ecological complexes of which they are part: this includes diversity within species, between species and of ecosystems". This is, in fact, the closest thing to a single legally accepted definition of biodiversity, since it is the definition adopted by the United Nations Convention on Biological Diversity.

The current textbook definition of "biodiversity" is "variation of life at all levels of biological organization".

For geneticists, *biodiversity* is the diversity of genes and organisms. They study processes such as mutations, gene exchanges, and genome dynamics that occur at the DNA level and generate evolution. Consistent with this, along with the above definition the Wilcox paper stated "genes are the ultimate source of biological organization at all levels of biological systems..."

Measurement

A variety of objective measures have been created in order to empirically measure biodiversity. Each measure of biodiversity relates to a particular use of the data. For practical conservationists, measurements should include a quantification of values that are commonly-shared among locally affected organisms, including humans. For others, a more economically defensible definition should allow the ensuring of continued possibilities for both adaptation and future use by humans, assuring environmental sustainability.

Distribution

Selection bias continues to bedevil modern estimates of biodiversity. In 1768 Rev. Gilbert White succinctly observed of his Selborne, Hampshire "all nature is so full, that district produces the most variety which is the most examined."

Nevertheless, biodiversity is not distributed evenly on Earth. It is consistently richer in the tropics and in other localized regions such as the Cape Floristic Province. As one approaches polar regions one generally finds fewer species. Flora and fauna diversity depends on climate, altitude, soils and the presence of other species. In the year 2006 large numbers of the Earth's species were formally classified as rare or endangered or threatened species; moreover, many scientists have estimated that there are millions more species actually endangered which have not yet been formally recognized. About 40 percent of the 40,177 species assessed using the IUCN Red List criteria, are now listed as threatened species with extinction-a total of 16,119 species.

Even though biodiversity declines from the equator to the poles in terrestrial ecoregions, whether this is so in aquatic ecosystems is still a hypothesis to be tested, especially in marine ecosystems where causes of this phenomenon are unclear. In addition, particularly in marine ecosystems, there are several well stated cases where diversity in higher latitudes actually increases. Therefore, the lack of information on biodiversity of Tropics and Polar Regions prevents scientific conclusions on the distribution of the world's aquatic biodiversity.

A biodiversity hotspot is a region with a high level of endemic species. These biodiversity hotspots were first identified by Dr. Norman Myers in two articles in the scientific journal *The Environmentalist*. Dense human habitation tends to occur near hotspots. Most hotspots are located in the tropics and most of them are forests.

Brazil's Atlantic Forest is considered a hotspot of biodiversity and contains roughly 20,000 plant species, 1350 vertebrates, and millions of insects, about half of which occur nowhere else in the world. The island of Madagascar including the unique Madagascar dry deciduous forests and lowland rainforests possess a very high ratio of species endemism and biodiversity, since the island separated from mainland Africa 65 million years ago, most of the species and ecosystems have evolved independently producing unique species different from those in other parts of Africa.

Many regions of high biodiversity (as well as high endemism) arise from very specialized habitats which require unusual adaptation mechanisms. For example the peat bogs of Northern Europe.

Evolution

Biodiversity found on Earth today is the result of 4 billion years of evolution. The origin of life has not been definitely established by science, however some evidence suggests that life may already have been well-established a few hundred million years after the formation of the Earth. Until approximately 600 million years ago, all life consisted of archaea, bacteria, protozoans and similar single-celled organisms.

The history of biodiversity during the Phanerozoic (the last 540 million years), starts with rapid growth during the Cambrian explosion—a period during which nearly every phylum of multicellular organisms first appeared. Over the next 400 million years or so, global diversity showed little overall trend, but was marked by periodic, massive losses of diversity classified as mass extinction events.

The apparent biodiversity shown in the fossil record suggests that the last few million years include the period of greatest biodiversity in the Earth's history. However, not all scientists support this view, since there is considerable uncertainty as to how strongly the fossil record is biased by the greater availability and preservation of recent geologic sections. Some argue that, corrected for sampling artifacts, modern biodiversity is not much different from biodiversity 300 million years ago.Status Report on Classification Estimates of the present global macroscopic species diversity vary from 2 million to 100 million species, with a best estimate of somewhere near 13–14 million, the vast majority of them arthropods.

Most biologists agree however that the period since the emergence of humans is part of a new mass extinction, the Holocene extinction event, caused primarily by the impact humans are having on the environment. It has been argued that the present rate of extinction is sufficient to eliminate most species on the planet Earth within 100 years.

New species are regularly discovered (on average between 5–10,000 new species each year, most of them insects) and many, though discovered, are not yet classified (estimates are that nearly 90% of all arthropods are not yet classified). Most of the terrestrial diversity is found in tropical forests.

Human Benefits

Biodiversity also supports a number of natural ecosystem processes and services. Some ecosystem services that benefit society are air quality, climate (both global CO_2 sequestration and local), water purification pollination, and prevention of erosion..

Since the stone age, species loss has been accelerated above the geological rate by human activity. The rate of species extinction is difficult to estimate, but it has been estimated that species are now being lost at a rate approximately 100 times as fast as is typical in the geological record, or perhaps as high as 10 000 times as fast. To feed such a large population, more land is being transformed from wilderness with wildlife into agricultural, mining, lumbering, and urban areas for humans.

Non-material benefits that are obtained from ecosystems include spiritual and aesthetic values, knowledge systems and the value of education.

Agriculture

The economic value of the reservoir of genetic traits present in wild varieties and traditionally grown landraces is extremely important in improving crop performance. Important crops, such as the potato and coffee, are often derived from only a few genetic strains. Improvements in crop plants over the last 250 years have been largely due to harnessing the genetic diversity present in wild and domestic crop plants. Interbreeding crops strains with different beneficial traits has resulted in more than doubling crop production in the last 50 years as a result of the Green Revolution.

Crop diversity is also necessary to help the system recover when the dominant crop type is attacked by a disease:

* The Irish potato blight of 1846, which was a major factor in the deaths of a million people and migration of another million, was the result of planting only two potato varieties, both of which were vulnerable.
* When rice grassy stunt virus struck rice fields from Indonesia to India in the 1970s. 6273 varieties were tested for resistance. One was found to be resistant, an Indian variety, known to science only since 1966. This variety formed a hybrid with other varieties and is now widely grown.
* Coffee rust attacked coffee plantations in Sri Lanka, Brazil, and Central America in 1970. A resistant variety was found in Ethiopia. Although the diseases are themselves a form of biodiversity.

Monoculture, the lack of biodiversity, was a contributing factor to several agricultural disasters in history, the European wine industry collapse in the late 1800s, and the US Southern Corn Leaf Blight epidemic of 1970.

Higher biodiversity also controls the spread of certain diseases as pathogens will need to adapt to infect different species

Biodiversity provides food for humans. Although about 80 percent of our food supply comes from just 20 kinds of plants, humans use at least 40,000 species of plants and animals a day. Many people around the world depend on these species for their food, shelter, and clothing. There is untapped potential for increasing the range of food products suitable for human consumption, provided that the high present extinction rate can be stopped.

Human Health

The diverse forest canopy on Barro Colorado Island, Panama, yielded this display of different fruit

The relevance of biodiversity to human health is becoming a major international political issue, as scientific evidence builds on the global health implications of biodiversity loss. This issue is closely linked with the issue of climate change, as many of the anticipated health risks of climate change are associated with changes in biodiversity.

Some of the health issues influenced by biodiversity include dietary health and nutrition security, infectious diseases, medical science and medicinal resources, social and psychological health, and spiritual well-being. Biodiversity is also known to have an important role in reducing disaster risk, and in post-disaster relief and recovery efforts.

One of the key health issues associated with biodiversity is that of drug discovery and the availability of medicinal resources. A significant proportion of drugs are derived, directly or indirectly, from biological sources; Chivian and Bernstein report that at least 50% of the pharmaceutical compounds on the market in the US are derived from natural compounds found in plants, animals, and microorganisms, while about 80% of the world population depends on medicines from nature (used in either modern or traditional medical practice) for primary healthcare.

Moreover, only a tiny proportion of the total diversity of wild species has been investigated for potential sources of new drugs. Through the field of bionics, considerable technological advancement has occurred which would not have without a rich biodiversity.

It has been argued, based on evidence from market analysis and biodiversity science, that the decline in output from the pharmaceutical sector since the mid-1980s can be attributed to a move away from natural product exploration ("bioprospecting") in favour of R&D programmes based on genomics and synthetic chemistry, neither of which have yielded the expected product outputs; meanwhile, there is evidence that natural product chemistry can provide the basis for innovation which can yield significant economic and health benefits.

Marine ecosystems are of particular interest in this regard, however unregulated and inappropriate bioprospecting can be considered a form of over-exploitation which has the potential to degrade ecosystems and increase biodiversity loss, as well as impacting on the rights of the communities and states from which the resources are taken.

Business and Industry

A wide range of industrial materials are derived directly from biological resources. These include building materials, fibers, dyes, resirubber and oil. There is enormous potential for further research into sustainably utilizing materials from a wider diversity of organisms.

In addition, biodivesity and the ecosystem goods and services it provides are considered to be fundamental to healthy economic systems. The degree to which biodiversity supports business varies between regions and between economic sectors, however the importance of biodiversity to issues of resource security (water quantity and quality, timber, paper and fibre, food and medicinal resources etc) are increasingly recognized as universal. As a result, the loss of biodiversity is increasingly recognized as a significant risk factor in business development and a threat to long term economic sustainability. A number of case studies recently compiled by the World Resources Institute demonstrate some of these risks as identified by specific industries.

Other Ecological Services

Biodiversity provides many ecosystem services that are often not readily visible. It plays a part in regulating the chemistry of our atmosphere and water supply. Biodiversity is directly involved in water purification, recycling nutrients and providing fertile soils. Experiments with controlled environments have shown that humans cannot easily build ecosystems to support human needs; for example insect pollination cannot be mimicked by human-made construction, and that activity alone represents tens of billions of dollars in ecosystem services per annum to humankind.

The stability of ecosystems is also related to biodiversity, with higher biodiversity producing greater stability over time, reducing the chance that ecosystem services will be disrupted as a result of disturbances such as extreme weather events or human exploitation.

Leisure, Cultural and Aesthetic Value

Many people derive value from biodiversity through leisure activities such as hiking, birdwatching or natural history study. Biodiversity has inspired musicians, painters, sculptors, writers and other artists. Many cultural groups view themselves as an integral part of the natural world and show respect for other living organisms.

Popular activities such as gardening, caring for aquariums and collecting butterflies are all strongly dependent on biodiversity. The number of species involved in such pursuits is in the tens of thousands, though the great majority do not enter mainstream commercialism.

The relationships between the original natural areas of these often 'exotic' animals and plants and commercial collectors, suppliers, breeders, propagators and those who promote their understanding and enjoyment are complex and poorly understood.

It seems clear, however, that the general public responds well to exposure to rare and unusual organisms—they recognize their inherent value at some level. A family outing to the botanical garden or zoo is as much an aesthetic or cultural experience as it is an educational one.

Philosophically it could be argued that biodiversity has intrinsic aesthetic and spiritual value to mankind *in and of itself*. This idea can be used as a counterweight to the notion that tropical forests and other ecological realms are only worthy of conservation because they may contain medicines or useful products.

An interesting point is that evolved DNA embodies knowledge, and therefore destroying a species resembles burning a book, with the caveat that the book is of uncertain depth and importance and may in fact be best used as fuel.

Number of Species

According to the Global Taxonomy Initiative and the European Distributed Institute of Taxonomy, the *total* number of species for some phyla may be much higher as what we know currently:

* 10–30 million insects; (of some 0,9 we know today)
* 5–10 million bacteria;
* 1.5 million fungi; (of some 0,4 million we know today)
* 1 million mites

Due to the fact that we know but a portion of the organisms in the biosphere, we do not have a complete understanding of the workings of our environment. To make matters worse, according to professor James Mallet, we are wiping out these species against an unprecedented rate. This means that even before a new species has had the chance of being studied and classified, it may already be extinct.

Threats

During the last century, erosion of biodiversity has been increasingly observed. Some studies show that about one eighth of known plant species are threatened with extinction.Some estimates put the loss at up to 140,000 species per year (based on Species-area theory) and subject to discussion. This figure indicates unsustainable ecological practices, because only a small number of species come into being each year. Almost all scientists acknowledge that the rate of species loss is greater now than at any time in human history, with extinctions occurring at rates hundreds of times higher than background extinction rates.

The factors that threaten biodiversity have been variously categorized. Jared Diamond describes an "Evil Quartet" of habitat destruction, overkill, introduced species, and secondary extensions. Edward O. Wilson prefers the acronym HIPPO, standing for Habitat destruction, Invasive species, Pollution, Human Over Population, and Over harvesting. The most authoritative classification in use today is that of IUCN's Classification of Direct Threats adopted by most major international conservation organizations such as the US Nature Conservancy, the World Wildlife Fund, Conservation International, and Birdlife International.

Destruction of Habitat

Most of the species extinctions from 1000 AD to 2000 AD are due to human activities, in particular destruction of plant and animal habitats. Raised rates of extinction are being driven by human consumption of organic resources, especially related to tropical forest destruction. While most of the species that are becoming extinct are not food species, their biomass is converted into human food when their habitat is transformed into pasture, cropland, and orchards.

It is estimated that more than a third of the Earth's biomass is tied up in only the few species that represent humans, livestock and crops. Because an ecosystem decreases in stability as its species are made extinct, these studies warn that the global ecosystem is destined for collapse if it is further reduced in complexity.

Factors contributing to loss of biodiversity are: overpopulation, deforestation, pollution (air pollution, water pollution, soil contamination) and global warming or climate change, driven by human activity. These factors, while all stemming from overpopulation, produce a cumulative impact upon biodiversity.

There are systematic relationships between the area of a habitat and the number of species it can support, with greater sensitivity to reduction in habitat area for species of larger body size and for those living at lower latitudes or in forests or oceans. Some characterize loss of biodiversity not as ecosystem degradation but by conversion to trivial standardized ecosystems. In some countries lack of property rights or access regulation to biotic resources necessarily leads to biodiversity loss (degradation costs having to be supported by the community).

A September 14, 2007 study conducted by the National Science Foundation found that biodiversity and genetic diversity are dependent upon each other—that diversity within a species is necessary to maintain diversity among species, and vice versa. According to the lead researcher in the study, Dr. Richârd Lankau, "If any one type is removed from the system, the cycle can break down, and the community becomes dominated by a single species."

At present, the most threathened ecosystems are those found in fresh water. The marking of fresh water ecosystems as the ecosystems most under threat was done by the Millennium Ecosystem Assessment 2005, and was confirmed again by the project "Freshwater Animal Diversity Assessment", organised by the biodiversity platform, and the French Institute recherche pourle development (MNHNP).

Exotic Species

The rich diversity of unique species across many parts of the world exist only because they are separated by barriers, particularly large rivers, seas, oceans, mountains and deserts from other species of other land masses, particularly the highly fecund, ultra-competitive, generalist "super-species". These are barriers that couldn't have been easily crossed by natural processes, except through continental drift. However, humans have invented transportation with the ability to bring into contact species that they've never met in their evolutionary history; also, this is done on a time scale of days, unlike the centuries that historically have accompanied major animal migrations. As these species that never met before come in contact with each other, the rate at which species are extincting is increasing still.

The widespread introduction of exotic species by humans is a potent threat to biodiversity. When exotic species are introduced to ecosystems and establish self-sustaining populations, the endemic species in that ecosystem that have not evolved to cope with the exotic species may not survive.

The exotic organisms may be either predators, parasites, or simply aggressive species that deprive indigenous species of nutrients, water and light. These invasive species often have features, due to their evolutionary background and new environment, that make them highly competitive; able to become well-established and spread quickly, reducing the effective habitat of endemic species.

Exotic species are introduced by human, either unwillingly or intentionally. Examples on unwilling introduction are fore example ladybugs,... These were bred to help in combating pests in agriculture (for greenhouses).

Other examples of unwilling introduction are species that are unknowingly brought in by vessel or automotive. These include eg certain bacteria, spiders, seeds of certain plants,... Examples of intentional introduction are the planting of exotic plants in gardens.

It is clear that with simple measures the preventing of the spread of exotic plants, yet as of present, trying to reduce the inflow of exotic species has remained low on the political agenda. Also, the intentional planting of species that are marked as "indiginous", yet are from a non-indigenous strain can be considered exotic and create problems in the ecosystem. For example in Belgium, Prunus spinosa (an indigenous species) that originates from Eastern Europe has been introduced. This has created problems, as the this tree species comes into leave much sooner than their West European counterparts, bringing the Thecla betulae butterfly (which feed on the leaves) into trouble.

As a consequence of the above, if humans continue to combine species from different ecoregions, there is the potential that the world's ecosystems will end up dominated by relatively a few, aggressive, cosmopolitan "super-species". At present, several countries have already imported so much exotic species, that the own indigenous fauna/flora is greatly outnumbered. For example, in Belgium, only 5% of the indigenous trees remain.

In 2004, an international team of scientists estimated that 10 percent of species would become extinct by 2050 because of global warming. "We need to limit climate change or we wind up with a lot of species in trouble, possibly extinct," said Dr. Lee Hannah, a co-author of the paper and chief climate change biologist at the Center for Applied Biodiversity Science at Conservation International.

Genetic Pollution

Purebred naturally evolved region specific wild species can be threatened with extinction through the process of genetic pollution i.e. uncontrolled hybridization, introgression and genetic swamping which leads to homogenization or replacement of local genotypes as a result of either a numerical and/or fitness advantage of introduced plant or animal. Nonnative species can bring about a form of extinction of native plants and animals by hybridization and introgression either through purposeful introduction by humans or through habitat modification, bringing previously isolated species into contact. These phenomena can be especially detrimental for rare species coming into contact with more abundant ones. The abundant species can interbreed with the rarer, swamping the entire gene pool and creating hybrids, thus driving the entire native stock to complete extinction. Attention has to be focused on the extent of this under appreciated problem that is not always apparent from morphological (outward appearance) observations alone. Some degree of gene flow may be a normal, evolutionarily constructive, process, and all constellations of genes and genotypes cannot be preserved. However, hybridization with or without introgression may, nevertheless, threaten a rare species' existence.

Hybridization and Genetics

In agriculture and animal husbandry, the green revolution popularized the use of conventional hybridization to increase yield by creating "high-yielding varieties". Often the handful of hybridized breeds originated in developed countries and were further hybridized with local varieties in the rest of the developing world to create high yield strains resistant to local climate and diseases. Local governments and industry have been pushing hybridization which has resulted in several of the indigenous breeds becoming extinct or threatened. Disuse because of unprofitability and uncontrolled intentional and unintentional cross-pollination and crossbreeding (genetic pollution), formerly huge gene pools of various wild and indigenous breeds have collapsed causing widespread genetic erosion and genetic pollution. This has resulted in loss of genetic diversity and biodiversity as a whole.

A genetically modified organism (GMO) is an organism whose genetic material has been altered using the genetic engineering techniques generally known as recombinant DNA technology. Genetically Modified (GM) crops today have become a common source for genetic pollution, not only of wild varieties but also of other domesticated varieties derived from relatively natural hybridization.

Genetic erosion coupled with genetic pollution may be destroying unique genotypes, thereby creating a hidden crisis which could result in a severe threat to our food security. Diverse genetic material could cease to exist which would impact our ability to further hybridize food crops and livestock against more resistant diseases and climatic changes.

Climate Change

The recent phenomenon of global warming is also considered to be a major threat to global biodiversity. For example coral reefs -which are biodiversity hotspots- will be lost in 20 to 40 years if global warming continues at the current trend.

Conserving Biodiversity

A schematic image illustrating the relationship between biodiversity, ecosystem services, human well-being, and poverty. The illustration shows where conservation action, strategies and plans can influence the drivers of the current biodiversity crisis at local, regional, to global scales.

Conservation biology matured in the mid- 20th century as ecologists, naturalists, and other scientists began to collectively research and address issues pertaining to global declines in biodiversity. The conservation ethic differs from the preservationist ethic, historically lead by John Muir, who advocate for protected areas devoid of human exploitation or interference for profit. The conservation ethic advocates for wise stewardship and management of natural resource production for the purpose of protecting and sustaining biodiversity in species, ecosystems, the evolutionary process, and human culture and society.

Conservation biologists are concerned with the trends in biodiversity being reported in this era, which has been labeled by science as the Holocene extinction period, also known as the sixth mass extinction. Rates of decline in biodiversity in this sixth mass extinction exceeds the five previous extinction spasms recorded in the fossil record. In response to the extinction crisis, the research of conservation biologists is being organized into strategic plans that include principles, guidelines, and tools for the purpose of protecting biodiversity.

Conservation biology is a crisis orientated discipline and it is multi-disciplinary, including ecological, social, education, and other scientific disciplines outside of biology. Conservation biologists work in both the field and office, in government, universities, non-profit organizations and in industry. The conservation of biological diversity is a global priority in strategic conservation plans that are designed to engage public policy and concerns affecting local, regional and global scales of communities, ecosystems, and cultures. Conserving biodiversity and action plans identify ways of sustaining human well-being and global economics, including natural capital, market capital, and ecosystem services.

Means

One of the strategies involves placing a monetary value on biodiversity through biodiversity banking, of which one example is the Australian Native Vegetation Management Framework. Other approaches are the creation of gene banks, as well as the creation of gene banks that have the intention of growing the indigenous species for reintroduction to the ecosystem (eg via tree nurseries,...) The eradication of exotic species is also an important method to preserve the local biodiversity. Exotic species that have become a pest can be identified using taxonomy and can then be eradicated.

This method however can only be used against a large group of a certain exotic organism due to the econimic cost. Other measures contributing to the preservation of biodiversity include: the reduction of pesticide use and/or a switching to organic pesticides..

These measures however, are of less importance than the preserving of rural lands, reintroduction of indigenous species and the removal of exotic species. Finally, if the continued preservation of native organisms in an area can be guaranteed, efforts can be made in trying to reintroduce eliminated native species back into the environment.

This can be done by first determining which species were indiginous to the area, and then reintroducing them. This determination can be done using databases as the Encyclopedia_of_life, Global Biodiversity Information Facility,... Extermination is usually done with either (ecological) pesticides, or natural predators.

Strategies

As noted above (Distribution), biodiversity is not as rich everywhere on the planet. Regions as the tropics and subtropics are considerably much richer in biodiversity than regions in temperate climates.

In addition, in temperate climates, allot of countries are located which are already vastly urbanised, and require -in addition- great amounts of space for the growing of crops.

As rehabilitating the biodiversity within these countries would again require the clearing and redeveloping of spaces, it has been proposed of some that efforts are best instead directed unto the tropics. Arguments include economics, it would be far less costly and more efficient to preserve the biodiversity in the tropics, especially as many countries in these areas are only now beginning to urbanise.

However, only directing the efforts unto these areas would not be enough, as many species still need to migrate at certain times of the year, requiring a connection to other regions/countries. In the more urbanised countries in temperate climates, this would mean that wildlife corridors need to be made. However, making wildlife corridors would still be considerably cheaper and easier than clearing/preserving entirely new areas.

Judicial Status

Biodiversity is beginning to be evaluated and its evolution analysed (through observations, inventories, conservation...) as well as being taken into account in political and judicial decisions:

* The relationship between law and ecosystems is very ancient and has consequences for biodiversity. It is related to property rights, both private and public. It can define protection for threatened ecosystems, but also some rights and duties.
* Law regarding species is a more recent issue. It defines species that must be protected because they may be threatened by extinction. The U.S. Endangered Species Act is an example of an attempt to address the "law and species" issue.
* Laws regarding gene pools are only about a century old. While the genetic approach is not new (domestication, plant traditional selection methods), progress made in the genetic field in the past 20 years have led to a tightening of laws in this field. With the new technologies of genetic analysis and genetic engineering, people are going through gene patenting, processes patenting, and a totally new concept of genetic resources. A very hot debate today seeks to define whether the resource is the gene, the organism itself, or its DNA.

The 1972 UNESCO World Heritage convention established that biological resources, such as plants, were the common heritage of mankind. These rules probably inspired the creation of great public banks of genetic resources, located outside the source-countries.

New global agreements, now give sovereign national rights over biological resources (not property). The idea of static conservation of biodiversity is disappearing and being replaced by the idea of dynamic conservation, through the notion of resource and innovation.

The new agreements commit countries to conserve biodiversity, develop resources for sustainability and share the benefits resulting from their use. Under new rules, it is expected that bioprospecting or collection of natural products has to be allowed by the biodiversity-rich country, in exchange for a share of the benefits.

Sovereignty principles can rely upon what is better known as Access and Benefit Sharing Agreements (ABAs). The Convention on Biodiversity spirit implies a prior informed consent between the source country and the collector, to establish which resource will be used and for what, and to settle on a fair agreement on benefit sharing. Bioprospecting can become a type of biopiracy when those principles are not respected.

Uniform approval for use of biodiversity as a legal standard has not been achieved, however. At least one legal commentator has argued that biodiversity should not be used as a legal standard, arguing that the multiple layers of scientific uncertainty inherent in the concept of biodiversity will cause administrative waste and increase litigation without promoting preservation goals.

Analytical Limits

Taxonomic and Size Bias

Less than 1% of all species that have been described have been studied beyond simply noting its existence. Biodiversity researcher Sean Nee points out that the vast majority of Earth's biodiversity is microbial, and that contemporary biodiversity physics is "firmly fixated on the visible world" For example, microbial life is very much more metabolically and environmentally diverse than multicellular life. Nee has stated: "On the tree of life, based on analyses of small-subunit ribosomal RNA, visible life consists of barely noticeable twigs.

The size bias is not restricted to consideration of microbes. Entomologist Nigel Stork states that "to a first approximation, all multicellular species on Earth are insects". Even in insects, however, the extinction rate is high and indicative of the general trend of the sixth greatest extinction period that human society is faced with. Moreover, there are species co-extinctions, such as plants and beetles, where the extinction or decline in one is reciprocated in the other.

Definition

1. Biodiversity is the variety of life: the different plants, animals and micro-organisms, their genes and the

ecosystems of which they are a part. It is home to more than one million species of plants and animals, many of which are found nowhere else in the world.

2. "Biodiversity" is often defined as the variety of all forms of life, from genes to species, through to the broad scale of ecosystems (for a list of variants on this simple definition see Gaston 1996). "

Responsible Tourism

Responsible Tourism is tourism '*that creates better places for people to live in, and better places to visit*'. The 2002 Cape Town Declaration on Responsible Tourism in Destinations defines Responsible Tourism as follows:

"Responsible Tourism is tourism which:

- minimises negative economic, environmental and social impacts
- generates greater economic benefits for local people and enhances the well being of host communities
- improves working conditions and access to the industry
- involves local people in decisions that affect their lives and life chances
- makes positive contributions to the conservation of natural and cultural heritage embracing diversity
- provides more enjoyable experiences for tourists through more meaningful connections with local people, and a greater understanding of local cultural, social and environmental issues
- provides access for physically challenged people
- is culturally sensitive, encourages respect between tourists and hosts, and builds local pride and confidence"

Responsible tourism is fast becoming a global trend. Operators, destinations and industry organisations in South Africa, the United Kingdom, United States, the Gambia, India, Sri Lanka, are already practicing Responsible Tourism, and this list is growing. Recognising the global significance of Responsible Tourism World Travel Market, one of the world's largest travel exhibitions, has created World Responsible Tourism Day, to be celebrated annually during November. World Responsible Tourism Day is endorsed by the World Tourism Organisation and World Travel and Tourism Council.

Things That Responsible Tourism is Not

* Responsible Tourism is not another form of 'niche tourism' – Responsible Tourism is about the legacy and the consequences of tourism – for the environment, local people and local economies.
* Responsible Tourism does not only take place in protected natural environments – Any tourism business, whether located in a thriving metropolis, a desert, rural village, sub-tropical island, medieval town – can be a Responsible Tourism operation.
* Responsible Tourism is the responsibility of big business- The smallest of owner managed tourism businesses are already practicing Responsible Tourism.

How Responsible Tourism Differs from Sustainable Tourism

Responsible tourism and sustainable tourism have an identical goal, that of sustainable development. The pillars of responsible tourism are therefore the same as those of sustainable tourism – environmental integrity, social justice and maximising local economic benefit. The major difference between the two is that, in responsible tourism, individuals, organisations and businesses are asked to take responsibility for their actions and the impacts of their actions. This shift in emphasis has taken place because not much progress has been made on realising sustainable tourism since the Earth Summit in Rio.

This is partly because everyone has been expecting others to behave in a sustainable way. The emphasis on responsibility in responsible tourism means that everyone involved in tourism – government, product owners and operators, transport operators, community services, NGO's and CBO's, tourists, local communities, industry associations – are responsible for achieving the goals of responsible tourism. GITPAC International is the first implementing agency of Responsible Tourism in four destination in kerala for Department of Tourism Government of Kerala.

The Forces that are Driving the Growth in Responsible Tourism

Other than the fact that Responsible Tourism is the right thing to do, the following reasons should motivate tourism destinations businesses to adopt responsible tourism practices.

Planet Panic

Globally, concerns about global warming, destruction of the environment, erosion of cultures and lifestyles, and millions of people still living in poverty, are increasing. The number of initiatives aimed at saving some part of the environment, or improving the living conditions for the world's vulnerable people, increases by the day. This heightened awareness of the earth's crisis is spilling over into the way people behave in their homes, how they spend their money and the way businesses are run. Driven by changing personal ethics, individuals contribute financially or otherwise to environmental and humanitarian initiatives. They are also changing their buying patterns. There is a major upswing in responsible or ethical consumerism in the UK and in other major European markets. In the UK, the market share for ethical products grew by 22% between 1999 and 2004.

Customers Increasingly Demand It

Increasing numbers of consumers are looking at the reputation and responsibility of the companies they buy from; they want to have "guilt free" holidays. This affects their direct purchases from companies in tourism destinations and it influences the choices of source market companies too. UK and other European and Australian companies and increasingly American companies are asking about the responsibility of their suppliers and introducing check lists which rate the sustainability of their practices.

Responsible Tourism Makes Business Sense

A significant, and growing, number of tourists are looking for a better experience, a better quality product. They are looking for experiences which enable them to get closer to the "real" living culture of countries and to experience our diverse natural and cultural heritage. This is a global trend in the established markets as consumer expectations of their holidays change, people are taking more, shorter trips, and they expect to get more from them. In commercial market research UK holidaymakers were asked whether or not they would be more likely to book a holiday with a company if they had a written code to guarantee good working conditions, protect the environment and support charities in the tourist destination. In 1999 45% said yes, when the question was asked again in 2001 52% said yes.

It is a market trend that any tourism business cannot ignore. Responsible Tourism makes business sense because a growing proportion of consumers are looking for a better product. This trend implies that tourism businesses that practice Responsible Tourism will have a powerful competitive advantage over other tourism products.

Objectives of Tourism Development

Tourism Development – Can be defined as the process of providing facilities and services for visitors to a destination in order to gain economic and other benefits.

Responsible Tourism is about "making better places for people to live in and better places for people to visit." Responsible Tourism requires that operators, hoteliers, governments, local people and tourists take responsibility, take action to make tourism more sustainable.

This forum has been established to enable businesses, national and local governments, destinations, NGOs and individuals to share information and identify and debate best practices-its purpose is to advance Responsible Tourism.

The World Travel Market has adopted the Cape Town Declaration definition of Responsible Tourism for its World Responsible Tourism Day which encourages the industry to take responsibility for making tourism more sustainable and demonstrate their responsibility.

The Cape Town Declaration recognises that Responsible Tourism takes a variety of forms, it is characterised by travel and tourism which:

1. "minimises negative environmental, social and cultural impacts;
2. generates greater economic benefits for local people and enhances the wellbeing of host communities, by improving working conditions and access to the industry;

3. involves local people in decisions that affect their lives and life chances;
4. makes positive contributions to the conservation of natural and cultural heritage and to the maintenance of the world's diversity;
5. provides more enjoyable experiences for tourists through more meaningful connections with local people, and a greater understanding of local cultural and environmental issues;
6. provides access for physically challenged people; and
7. is culturally sensitive and engenders respect between tourists and hosts."

Behaviour can be more or less responsible and what is responsible in a particular place depends upon environment and culture. The Artyfroum provides a space where businesses and individuals can report there initiatives, share best practice and engage in discussion.

The forum contains links to many documents hosted on websites around the world – follow the hotlinks in the forum listings.

The Kerala Declaration on Responsible Tourism in Destinations March 2008

Responsible Tourism is about "making better places for people to live in and better places for people to visit." Responsible Tourism requires that operators, hoteliers, governments, local people and tourists take responsibility, take action to make tourism more sustainable.

This forum has been established to enable businesses, national and local governments, destinations, NGOs and individuals to share information and identify and debate best practices-its purpose is to advance Responsible Tourism.

The World Travel Market has adopted the Cape Town Declaration definition of Responsible Tourism for its World Responsible Tourism Day which encourages the industry to take responsibility for making tourism more sustainable and demonstrate their responsibility.

The Cape Town Declaration recognises that Responsible Tourism takes a variety of forms, it is characterised by travel and tourism which:

1. "minimises negative environmental, social and cultural impacts;
2. generates greater economic benefits for local people and enhances the wellbeing of host communities, by improving working conditions and access to the industry;
3. involves local people in decisions that affect their lives and life chances;
4. makes positive contributions to the conservation of natural and cultural heritage and to the maintenance of the world's diversity;
5. provides more enjoyable experiences for tourists through more meaningful connections with local people, and a greater understanding of local cultural and environmental issues;
6. provides access for physically challenged people; and
7. is culturally sensitive and engenders respect between tourists and hosts."

Behaviour can be more or less responsible and what is responsible in a particular place depends upon environment and culture. The Artyfroum provides a space where businesses and individuals can report there initiatives, share best practice and engage in discussion. Each year the International Centre for Responsible Tourism publishes Advances in Responsible Tourism The forum contains links to many documents hosted on websites around the world – follow the hotlinks in the forum listings.

Tourism Destination Management

Managing tourism destinations is an important part of controlling tourism's environmental impacts. Destination management can include land use planning, business permits and zoning controls, environmental and other regulations, business association initiatives, and a host of other techniques to shape the development and daily operation of tourism-related activities.

The term "destination" refers broadly to an area where tourism is a relatively important activity and where the economy may be significantly influenced by tourism revenues. Destination management is complicated by the fact that a single, recognizable destination may include several municipalities, provinces, or other government entities-in island environments it may be the entire country.

Participating governance structures led by local authorities, with the involvement of local NGOs, community and indigenous representatives, academia, and local chambers of commerce, make up what are known as "Destination Management Organizations" (DMOs). Often DMOs take the form of local tourism boards, councils, or development organizations. The network of local tourism businesses (hotels, attractions, transportation services, service providers such as guides and equipment rentals, restaurants, etc.) are also a significant part of a destination.

Destination Management Approach

The needs, expectations and anticipated benefits of tourism vary greatly from one destination to the next, and there is certainly no "one size fits all" approach to destination management. As local communities living in regions with tourism potential develop a vision for what kind of tourism they want to facilitate, a comprehensive planning framework such as Local Agenda 21 has proved useful and is being used more and more often. Promoting sustainable tourism within Local Agenda 21 processes is a way to strengthen local stewardship of the environment.

Destination Management Company

A Destination Management Company (DMC) is a term for a professional services company possessing extensive local knowledge, expertise and resources, specializing in the design and implementation of events, activities, tours, transportation and program logistics.

A DMC provides a ground service based on local knowledge of their given destinations. These services can be transportation, hotel accommodation, restaurants, activities, excursions, conference venues, themed events, gala dinners and logistics, as well as helping with overcoming language barriers. DMCs are able to provide preferential rates based on the buying power they have with their preferred suppliers. A DMC is an incoming tour operator catering for both corporate and leisure clients. DMCs differ from tour operators in that DMCs do usually not deal directly with end-clients, but trade through agents, which may be tour operators.

Destination Management Companies

What does a Destination Management Company (DMC) do? And why may you need one? If you are organizing a destination wedding, meeting, or other event, finding your way through the maze of possibilities can be daunting and confusing. This is where a Destination Management Company can be very useful.

Destination Management Companies specialize in the organization and logistics of destination events by finding the perfect venues and suppliers to suit your vision and travel/ transportation needs. Destination Management Companies are experienced in organizing events for your company destination event, destination wedding, or any other destination event you might have. The keyword when working with a DMC is "customized". No matter what the event or occasion, Destination Management Companies will always find creative and tailor-made solutions.

Besides organizing company meetings, company incentives and events, and destination weddings, companies offering Destination Managers can arrange venues for your events. Other special services include catering, dinners and entertainment. If you wish, a DMC will even make hotel selections/reservations, arrange transportation to and from the airport and provide travel coordination and management, guides and hostesses.

Your Destination Manager can coordinate VIP transfers, motor coaches for transportation and limousine and car rentals that can take you and your party wherever you need to go. DMCs design unique and creative itineraries for your destination event. Destination Management Companies remain behind the scenes while ensuring that everything runs according to plan.

When choosing a DMC for your wedding or company event, look for one that is knowledgeable about your chosen destination. Ask them lots questions and look at sample itineraries from their past events to ensure you're comfortable with their work.

Castillo Sightseeing Tours and Travel Service

Castillo Sightseeing Tours & Travel Services, Inc, now a full destination management company specializes in servicing incentive travel as well as corporate meetings in Puerto Rico has been in operation on the Island since 1975 when Joe and Irene Castillo first established it. The inception of Castillo Watersports back in those days was designed to provide deep-sea fishing, snorkeling, catamaran day sails, scuba and various other Watersports activities for most major hotels. Today, their business has expanded and they can claim to be the only DMC on the island who owns and operates all of their own equipment guaranteeing quality and excellence in service that is expected in a popular destination such as Puerto Rico. Watersports Division-Two state of the art 46' Gold Coast Catamarans, the "Barefoot III" and "Stampede". Tour Department & Operating to service all your groups ground transportation needs with its own ground transportation equipment. Group Sales Department & Our in house management staff is trained to assist you in the development and implementation of customdesigned program and venues to meet all your needs, a "One-stop-shop" while in Puerto Rico.

* Coordination for site inspections
* Enhanced airport meet and greet service
* Hospitality desk assistance
* Team Building, Boat Building and Beach Olympic Activities
* Custom designed dine-around evenings
* Selection and coordination for off-site venues
* Private and Specialized Tours and Activities
* Spouses Programs
* Entertainment and Catering Arrangements

That's where our destination management company comes in as we have the local knowledge, contacts and of course professional skills to ensure that your event in Ireland goes off without a hitch.

Our destination management company has offered a destination management service in Ireland since 1996 with many clients from UK, USA, and continental Europe.

Outbound

We also manage custom overseas events for the corporate market. With our international contacts and affiliations we can provide the expertise to any destination worldwide. You may have a particular destination in mind or like us to suggest options but the end product is that we devise and manage a detailed travel program based on your requirements. It's often the little things that make an incentive trip so memorable so let us inspire you with our ideas.

Destination Managment Services

Our destination management company offers a professional service which can include management of:

- Accommodation
- Transportation
- Itinerary planning
- Team Building
- Innovative Events & Concepts
- Sporting and leisure activities
- Social programmes
- Venue selection and management
- Themed events
- Registration & Database Management
- Specialist events and sub contractors
- Conference Materials
- Audio Visual Requirements
- Staging & Branding

2

Ethical Issues in Hospitality Business

Preamble

The Tourism Phenomenon

Tourism is a worldwide phenomenon affecting human society and the environment. While tourists and people working in the tourism industry may benefit, people in tourist receiving areas experience a threat to their self-determination and dignity. Against the dynamics of globalisation the vital rights of local communities have been threatened.

The Need for Change Towards Sustainable Development

Recognizing the urgency to raise awareness about the complex nature of tourism, its ambivalent role in the strive towards sustainable development and especially about its inherent dangers, representatives of groups, initiatives and organisations from around the world met in Stuttgart, July 6th to 9th, 1998, to discuss ways for constructively shaping tourism development.

This has been done in the conviction that change in tourism is necessary and possible, however, requiring a positive self-commitment of all stakeholders involved.

NGO Input in WTO Process

Guided by the WTO decision makers in the public and private sector are in the process of elaborating a 'Global Code of Ethics for Tourism'. From this code ethical norms can be evolved, representing the autonomy and sovereignty of pluralism that exists in the world, we suggest that the following be considered a useful foundation from which ethical standards for tourism can be defined:

A Challenge for All Actors Involved

The development of tourism and its related impacts present a challenge to all actors involved-tourists, receiving communities, employees, employers, managers, investors, journalists and politicians etc.-to assume responsibility and to act accordingly.

Global Ethics

All cultures and societies are committed to specific ethical values within which common areas of concern have been accepted. These values draw upon secular traditions and regulations which guide the interaction of individuals, communities and societies as well as to the different beliefs of the religions of the world.

Representations of these ethics can be found, for example, in various UN conventions and declarations, e.g. the Universal Declaration of Human Rights adopted by the UN General Assembly, the International Convention on the Rights of the Child, the Rio Declaration on the Environment and Development and the recommendations of Agenda 21. They have also been expressed as fundamental principles by the Parliament of the World's Religions. These principles embody the inviolable dignity of every human being as the very first fundamental ethical principle, which means that every person has a responsibility to treat all people everywhere and at all times in a humane way. These principles imply broad guidelines for human behaviour, such as the commitment to a culture of:

* non-violence and respect for all life;
* solidarity and a just economic order;
* sustainability of consumption with respect for fragile environments and scarce resources
* tolerance and a life of truthfulness;
* equal rights and partnership between men and women,
* protection of the rights of children

Ethics in Tourism

In the same way as ethical principals apply to all individuals, communities and societies, they also apply to all actors in tourism in their respective specific roles. This entails both rights and responsibilities. Concrete and specific ethical standards for behaviour and practises in tourism must follow these broad principles as outlined above.

This means for example:

* democracy and peace in the management and resolving of conflicts connected with tourism, which includes the openness and preparedness for a reciprocal understanding and the observance of the general principle of justice;
* solidarity with those who are directly and strongly affected by tourism and who suffer from unjust structures connected with tourism, and solidarity with those who need material or political and philosophical support in defending their interests and rights which are threatened by tourism development or which are ignored in decision making processes;
* justice in a world tourism order, an aim which intends to change all structures of injustice that exists in the fields of economics, politics, social and cultural life;
* respect of diversity in the various areas of life-societies, environment, cultures, religions and politics-which calls for sensitivity to difference and the practice of tolerance.
* authentic information for all people involved or interested in tourism. Such authentic information is a basic need for a just world tourism order. This places a particular responsibility on the media to be objective, fair and truthful when reporting on tourism. Professionals engaged in tourism education should also promote need for authentic research and information to develop sensitised and aware personnel in tourism.
* equal rights for all, women and men, children and old people, at home and abroad;

Demands

In order to improve the present situation in tourism and to minimize its negative impacts, we urge all actors involved to contribute the best of their knowledge, abilities, and skills towards a tourism that is in line with these ethical principles. We appeal to the international community and all actors involved in tourism, such as governments, other public authorities, decision makers and professionals in the field of tourism, public and private associations and institutions whose activities are related to tourism, tourists and local communities to adopt the following principles and work towards the following objectives:

Political

* the recognition and protection of political diversity;
* the control of tourism development in line with sustainability criteria-for the sake of the world of today, its present inhabitants and future generations;
* to adopt the principle of subsidiarity presupposing decentralisation, so that preference is given to local participants in decision-making rather than global, supranational and centralised institutions. They should be brought in only when problems cannot be resolved by local actors themselves.
* the participation of all persons involved, an aim which presupposes the freedom to participate and the duty to use this freedom responsibly;
* the empowerment of local communities who are affected by, involved in, engaged in and concerned with tourism development;
* protection of decision making structures of minorities and marginalized people/groups and the right to fight for their rights;
* the principle of good governance.

Economic

* the recognition and protection of economic diversity;
* the observance of labour rights;
* the fair sharing of profits and redistribution of income
* the restriction of non-resident ownership;
* the responsibility connected with ownership;

* the protection of local economies against displacement and disruption;
* the training for local entrepreneurship and support of local investment;
* the protection of the informal sector and its values;
* the protection of attractions against free consumption.

Environmental

* the recognition and protection of ecological diversity;
* protection of natural resources
* the provision just access to natural resources
* the implementation of special programmes to save endangered species

Social

* the recognition and protection of social diversity;
* The principle of self-reliance;
* gender equality;
* the right of children to childhood;
* the stabilisation of communities;
* the protection from exploitation or dependence;
* education and information skills;
* the participation in the setting up of master plans;
* the principle of accountability;
* the local/public definition of infrastructure standards;
* the integration of the local elite, investors and tourism
* the abolition of child prostitution
* local access to and sharing of all facilities between tourists and hosts

Cultural

* the recognition and protection of cultural diversity/multiculturalism
* tradition vs. modernisation

* the protection of local culture as opposed to tourist culture
* the protection of basic values
* the avoidance of zoo syndromes

Principles

The Code includes nine articles outlining the "rules of the game" for destinations, governments, tour operators, developers, travel agents, workers and travellers themselves. The tenth article involves the redress of grievances and marks the first time that a code of this type will have a mechanism for enforcement.

Why Do We Need an Alternative Code of Ethics for Tourism?

The member countries of World Tourism Organization (WTO) at its 13th General Assembly in Santiago, Chile adopted the new Global Code of Ethics for Tourism on 1 October 1999. Acclaimed for its lofty goals and coverage, the Code soon became the reference point for debates on a wide spectrum of issues relating to tourism such as sustainable development, equity and protection of local cultures.

The formulation of the Code was the culmination of a process of debates and deliberations within the global civil society as well as tourism industry on the negative impacts of tourism on environment and on cultural heritage and growing doubts on the claims that tourism benefits the residents of tourism destinations.

According to the Secretary General of WTO, "the Global Code of Ethic for Tourism sets a frame of reference for the responsible and sustainable development of world tourism at the dawn of the new millennium.

It draws inspiration from many similar declarations and industry codes that have come before and il adds new thinking that reflects our changing society at the end of the 20th century". He also describes the process of formulating the guidelines.

The code was first called for in a resolution of the WTO General Assembly meeting in Istanbul in 1997. Subsequently, a special committee for the preparation of the Global Code of Ethics was constituted. The Secretary-General and the legal adviser to WTO in consultation with WTO Business Council,

WTO's Regional Commissions, and the WTO Executive

Council Prepared a Draft Document. The United

Nations Commission on Sustainable Development meeting in New York in April 1999 approved the concept of the Code. WTO was also asked to seek further inputs from the private sector, civil society organizations and labour organizations. The Secretary-General remembers, "Written comments on the code were received from more than 70 WTO Member States and other entities. The resulting 10 point Global Code of Ethics for Tourism-the culmination of an extensive consultative process was approved unanimously by the WTO General Assembly meeting in Santiago in October 1999."

A close look at the process of formulation of the Code, however reveal that the role of the civil society has been marginal. It was initially drafted by entities known to safeguard the interests of the industry and at the instance of CSD, a notional participation was elicited from member states and civil society organizations. This is not surprising given the fact that the structure and processes of international consensus building often undermine the essential principles of democratic debate.

Nevertheless, if we consider the fact that the overwhelming demand for restructuring tourism practices had in the past and present emerged from individuals and organizations of the global the civil society, it is remarkable\ how hard it is to find their imprint in the text of the

Code. WTO has in its turn tried to project that the Code is a comprehensive document capable of addressing the complex web of tourism issues both in the developed and in the underdeveloped world. According to them, the formidable challenge is in the implementation of the Code and they refuse see any whiff of tensions or contradictions within the Code that could come in the way of its easy acceptance and implementation.

Hence, it is suggested by the secretary General of WTO that it "is intended to be a living document. Read it. Circulate it widely. Participate in its implementation. Only with your cooperation can we safeguard the future of the tourism industry and expand the sector's contribution to economic prosperity, peace and understanding among all the nations of the world".

The civil society organizations at the local and global levels have been upholding an unequivocal opposition to the processes and practices of mass tourism in the past decades which had resulted in the massive destruction of local cultures, livelihood of Indigenous People deterioration in environmental quality and depletion of natural resources, uneven economic gains, growth of exploitative commercial sex, child abuse, trafficking and an overall escalation of resource drain from the third world through under pricing as well as surplus extraction.

The need for a code of Ethics in Tourism emanated from the urgency of combating these maladies as well as setting new rules of the game for the industry practitioners. Nonetheless, it is surprisingly clear that the text of the Code does not reflect the wide set of concerns and issues that triggered the demand by the civil society organizations to set new rules.

It appears that the Code was formulated simply to provide legitimacy and to shore up the ailing travel industry whose global operations still smack of the very same nefarious practices condemned by the civil society. The acceptance of the Code by 106 member countries have not, according to reports from various local and global organizations working the area of sustainable development, equitable tourism, trafficking and child abuse, resulted in any mitigation of the exploitative character of tourism industry particularly in the developing world. When confronted by this contradiction, the official response is profoundly indifferent to the conflicting and contradictory' nature of the text of the Code itself.

Instead these problems are often counted as emanating from floppy implementation of the Code of Ethics. The failure of the respective national, regional or even local governments in sincerely adhering to and implementing the Code of ethics is highlighted as the major reason for the continued ill effects of tourism in the third world.

However in this discourse, the most important fact that is overlooked is the failure of the Code to reflect the aspirations and concerns of the marginalized communities and political and economic questions raised by the civil society. As a consequence of this official indifference to the larger questions of development, redistribution and ethics in the process of formulation of the Code, there are at least two important aspects of the Code that calls for a critical reassessment of its usefulness. One pertains to the limitations of the assumptions and principles of the code. Second pertains to the tension between the assumptions and principles of the code. We shall here discuss these two points. These conflicts are rooted in the gross negligence of the issues raised by the civil society as incorporated in the "Position Paper for further discussion on the issue of a Global Code of Ethics for Tourism" submitted to WTO by Equations, Tourism European Ecumenical Network (TEN) and Ecumenical Coalition on Third World Tourism (ECTWT).

Let me begin by taking a close look at some of the major the assumptions of the Code. These assumptions are detailed in the preamble of the code. In its eagerness to paint an exceedingly rosy picture of tourism practices the code at the outset itself argues a case for understanding tourism as an instrument for peace. The preamble of the Code asserts, "Through the direct, spontaneous and non-mediated contacts it engenders between men and women of different cultures and lifestyles, tourism represents *a vital force for peace* and a factor of friendship and understanding among the peoples of the world".

While we have reports from the grassroots about the conflicts over resources and cultural practices consequent on the increased flow of tourists into relatively quiescent regions of the world, the case for tourism as a tool for peace or conflict resolution has been very weekly argued. Its role in mediating for increased international understanding has never been worth considering. The geo-politics of the evolution of many of the tourism destinations is intertwined with economic aggression, occupation, colonization and war. As Eredric Jameson points out in his *Postmodernism, or the Cultural Logic of Late Capitalism,* "the underside of culture is blood, torture, death and horror".

Another major assumption of the Code of ethics is regarding the free market economy and its benefits. The code looks at the issue of marketization from the perspective of the industry and ignores the diverse views of local communities and the pangs of their integration into its fold. Hence it is argued, "World tourism industry has much to gain by operating in a market economy and environment of free trade". The Code is calloustyinsensitive to the enormous problems created as a result of the incorporation of local communities into the market economy.

As a corollary to this, and in gross violation of the position held by the representatives of the civil society, the Code asserts that tourism is compatible with the liberalization of the conditions governing trade in services. In one stroke it disowns the concerns of the local communities and takes a pro-GATS approach while it is denounced by majority of the developing countries and the global civil society for its exploitative character. The Code hence argues that 'responsible and sustainable tourism' is *"by no means incompatible with the growing liberalization* of the conditions governing trade in services and under whose aegis the enterprises of this sector operate and that *it is possible to reconcile in this* sector economy and ecology, environment and development, openness to international trade and protection *of social and cultural identities"*. The worldwide practice of mass tourism has in fact been a telling example of the failure of the modern sectors of the economy to achieve this blissful state of harmony so easily claimed by the Code.

The major Principles outlined in the code also fail to do justice to the set of issues that the civil society had been careful enough to take up with WTO. The Code at its best is trying to translate an ideal average of imagined benefits of tourism into its Principles.

Thus it is varyingly presented as providing a platform for mutual understanding and respect between peoples and societies, a vehicle for individual and collective fulfilment and an important factor of sustainable development. These goals are never met and the likelihood of such harmony and peace are increasingly challenged in the new context of globalization and market liberalization that WTO uncritically embraces.

Some of the Principles of the Code such tourism ought to be a contributor to the enhancement of cultural heritage, it should be a beneficial activity for host countries and communities; stakeholders have obligations in tourism development etc., do emphasize the need for upholding an equitable approach and perspective in tourism promotion activities as well as tourism practices. In this sense, the Code has been successful in appealing to the various actors in the field to mitigate the negative effects and strive to maximize the benefits. Nevertheless, the Code openly legitimize the excessive urge of the global capital to explore and exploit the quiescent areas and integrate them fully into market economy when it argues, "the planet's resources are equally open to all the world's inhabitants".

Moreover, this line of reasoning also undermines the right of autonomy and self-determination of local communities. In the name of a vague and inept concept of "Tourism Rights", the Code strikes at the very core of the demand of the marginalized and underprivileged communities for the rights to exercise their control over their own land and resources. Another principle, which runs as a corollary to this position, is the demand for liberty of tourist movements that states, "visitors should benefit from the same rights as the citizen of the country visited". Redistributive policies such as differential pricing for tourists from developed countries etc., which forms the core of the resource management and sustainable strategies of many of the third world destinations, are threatened by this principle.

The Code is very eloquent about the rights of permanent workers and entrepreneurs of the tourism industry. It appeals to the Multinational Corporations that they "should not exploit the dominant positions they *sometimes* occupy; they should avoid becoming the vehicles of cultural and social models artificially imposed on the host communities; *in exchange for their freedom to invest and trade which should be fully recognized,* they should involve themselves in local development, avoiding, by the excessive repatriation of their profits or their induced imports, a reduction of their contribution to the economies in which they are established".

The Code, which thus carefully details the rights of permanent workers, small entrepreneurs and MNCs, however, silent about the informal sector and informal sector workers, who are mostly women and children in the third world. This is a painful neglect when we consider that the informal sector jobs are, more often than not, taken up by workers displaced from their traditional occupations that disappear consequent on the aggressive incursion of the tourism industry.

Histories of many of the third world tourism destinations are littered with the stories of displacement and inadequate rehabilitation of marginalized communities. The Code of Ethics offers no perspective on this important question. The failure of the Code of Ethics to address satisfactorily the issues and concerns raised by the civil society appears to be ignored in the contemporary discussions on the topic. The mistaken emphasis is often on the 'implementation issues'. The inherent limitations, tensions and contradictions of the text are invariably overlooked. The Code in its present form is essentially a document that serves the interests of the industry while ignoring the rights of the marginalized and the oppressed. It attempts to legitimize the economic exploitation perpetuated by market-oriented policies of liberalization and globalization. In this context, I strongly feel that it is necessary to formulate an alternative Code of Ethics for Tourism, which would incorporate the ideals and aspirations upheld in the position paper of the civil society organizations.

Global Code of Ethics for Tourism

Tourism's contribution to mutual understanding and respect between peoples and societies

1. The understanding and promotion of the ethical values common to humanity, with an attitude of tolerance and respect for the diversity of religious, philosophical and moral beliefs, are both the foundation and the consequence of responsible tourism; stakeholders in tourism development and tourists themselves should observe the social and cultural traditions and practices of all peoples, including those of minorities and indigenous peoples and to recognize their worth;
2. Tourism activities should be conducted in harmony with the attributes and traditions of the host regions and countries and in respect for their laws, practices and customs;
3. The host communities, on the one hand, and local professionals, on the other, should acquaint themselves with and respect the tourists who visit them and find out about their lifestyles, tastes and expectations; the education and training imparted to professionals contribute to a hospitable welcome;

4. It is the task of the public authorities to provide protection for tourists and visitors and their belongings; they must pay particular attention to the safety of foreign tourists owing to the particular vulnerability they may have; they should facilitate the introduction of specific means of information, prevention, security, insurance and assistance consistent with their needs; any attacks, assaults, kidnappings or threats against tourists or workers in the tourism industry, as well as the wilful destruction of tourism facilities or of elements of cultural or natural heritage should be severely condemned and punished in accordance with their respective national laws;
5. When travelling, tourists and visitors should not commit any criminal act or any act considered criminal by the laws of the country visited and abstain from any conduct felt to be offensive or injurious by the local populations, or likely to damage the local environment; they should refrain from all trafficking in illicit drugs, arms, antiques, protected species and products and substances that are dangerous or prohibited by national regulations;
6. Tourists and visitors have the responsibility to acquaint themselves, even before their departure, with the characteristics of the countries they are preparing to visit; they must be aware of the health and security risks inherent in any travel outside their usual environment and behave in such a way as to minimize those risks.

Tourism as a Vehicle for Individual and Collective Fulfilment

Tourism, the activity most frequently associated with rest and relaxation, sport and access to culture and nature, should be planned and practised as a privileged means of individual and collective fulfilment; when practised with a sufficiently open mind, it is an irreplaceable factor of self-education, mutual tolerance and for learning about the legitimate differences between peoples and cultures and their diversity. Tourism activities should respect the equality of men and women; they should promote human rights and, more particularly, the individual rights of the most vulnerable groups, notably children, the elderly, the handicapped, ethnic minorities and indigenous peoples.

The exploitation of human beings in any form, particularly sexual, especially when applied to children, conflicts with the fundamental aims of tourism and is the negation of tourism; as such, in accordance with international law, it should be energetically combatted with the cooperation of all the States concerned and penalized without concession by the national legislation of both the countries visited and the countries of the perpetrators of these acts, even when they are carried out abroad.

Travel for purposes of religion, health, education and cultural or linguistic exchanges are particularly beneficial forms of tourism, which deserve encouragement.

The introduction into curricula of education about the value of tourist exchanges, their economic, social and cultural benefits, and also their risks, should be encouraged.

Tourism, A Factor of Sustainable Development

All the stakeholders in tourism development should safeguard the natural environment with a view to achieving sound, continuous and sustainable economic growth geared to satisfying equitably the needs and aspirations of present and future generations.

All forms of tourism development that are conducive to saving rare and precious resources, in particular water and energy, as well as avoiding so far as possible waste production, should be given priority and encouraged by national, regional and local public authorities.

The staggering in time and space of tourist and visitor flows, particularly those resulting from paid leave and school holidays, and a more even distribution of holidays should be sought so as to reduce the pressure of tourism activity on the environment and enhance its beneficial impact on the tourism industry and the local economy.

Tourism infrastructure should be designed and tourism activities programmed in such a way as to protect the natural heritage composed of ecosystems and biodiversity and to preserve endangered species of wildlife; the stakeholders in tourism development, and especially professionals, should agree to the imposition of limitations or constraints on their activities when these are exercised in particularly sensitive areas: desert, polar or high mountain regions, coastal areas, tropical forests or wetlands, propitious to the creation of nature reserves or protected areas. Nature tourism and ecotourism are recognized as being particularly conducive to enriching and enhancing the standing of tourism, provided they respect the natural heritage and local populations and are in keeping with the carrying capacity of the sites.

Tourism, A User of the Cultural Heritage of Mankind and Contributor to its Enhancement

1. Tourism resources belong to the common heritage of mankind; the communities in whose territories they are situated have particular rights and obligations to them;
2. Tourism policies and activities should be conducted with respect for the artistic, archaeological and cultural heritage, which they should protect and pass on to future generations; particular care should be devoted to preserving and upgrading monuments, shrines and museums as well as archaeological and historic sites which must be widely open to tourist visits; encouragement should be given to public access to privately-owned cultural property and monuments, with respect for the rights of their owners, as well as to religious buildings, without prejudice to normal needs of worship;
3. Financial resources derived from visits to cultural sites and monuments should, at least in part, be used for the upkeep, safeguard, development and embellishment of this heritage;
4. Tourism activity should be planned in such a way as to allow traditional cultural products, crafts and folklore to survive and flourish, rather than causing them to degenerate and become standardized;

Tourism, A Beneficial Activity for Host Countries and Communities

1. Local populations should be associated with tourism activities and share equitably in the economic, social and cultural benefits they generate, and particularly in the creation of direct and indirect jobs resulting from them;

2. Tourism policies should be applied in such a way as to help to raise the standard of living of the populations of the regions visited and meet their needs; the planning and architectural approach tc and operation of tourism resorts and accommodation should aim to integrate them, to the extent possible, in the local economic and social fabric; where skills are equal, priority should be given to local manpower;
3. Special attention should be paid to the specific problems of coastal areas and island territories and to vulnerable rural or mountain regions, for which tourism often represents a rare opportunity for development in the face of the decline of traditional economic activities;
4. Tourism professionals, particularly investors, governed by the regulations laid down by the public authorities, should carry out studies of the impact of their development projects on the environment and natural surroundings; they should also deliver, with the greatest transparency and objectivity, information on their future programmes and their foreseeable repercussions and foster dialogue on their contents with the populations concerned;

Obligations of Stakeholders in Tourism Development

1. Tourism professionals have an obligation to provide tourists with objective and honest information on their places of destination and on the conditions of travel, hospitality and stays; they should ensure that the contractual clauses proposed to their customers are readily understandable as to the nature, price and quality of the services they commit themselves to providing and the financial compensation payable by them in the event of a unilateral breach of contract on their part;
2. Tourism professionals, insofar as it depends on them, should show concern, in co-operation with the public authorities, for the security and safety, accident prevention, health protection and food safety of those who seek their services; likewise, they should ensure the existence of suitable systems of insurance and assistance; they should

accept the reporting obligations prescribed by national regulations and pay fair compensation in the event of failure to observe their contractual obligations

3. Tourism professionals, so far as this depends on them, should contribute to the cultural and spiritual fulfilment of tourists and allow them, during their travels, to practise their religions;
4. The public authorities of the generating States and the host countries, in cooperation with the professionals concerned and their associations, should ensure that the necessary mechanisms are in place for the repatriation of tourists in the event of the bankruptcy of the enterprise that organized their travel;
5. Governments have the right – and the duty-especially in a crisis, to inform their nationals of the difficult circumstances, or even the dangers they may encounter during their travels abroad; it is their responsibility however to issue such information without prejudicing in an unjustified or exaggerated manner the tourism industry of the host countries and the interests of their own operators; the contents of travel advisories should therefore be discussed beforehand with the authorities of the host countries and the professionals concerned; recommendations formulated should be strictly proportionate to the gravity of the situations encountered and confined to the geographical areas where the insecurity has arisen; such advisories should be qualified or cancelled as soon as a return to normality permits;
6. The press, and particularly the specialized travel press and the other media, including modern means of electronic communication, should issue honest and balanced information on events and situations that could influence the flow of tourists; they should also provide accurate and reliable information to the consumers of tourism services; the new communication and electronic commerce technologies should also be developed and used for this purpose; as is the case for the media, they should not in any way promote sex tourism;

Right to Tourism

1. The prospect of direct and personal access to the discovery and enjoyment of the planet's resources constitutes a right equally open to all the world's inhabitants; the increasingly extensive participation in national and international tourism should be regarded as one of the best possible expressions of the sustained growth of free time, and obstacles should not be placed in its way;
2. The universal right to tourism must be regarded as the corollary of the right to rest and leisure, including reasonable limitation of working hours and periodic holidays with pay, guaranteed by Article 24 of the Universal Declaration of Human Rights and Article 7.d of the International Covenant on Economic, Social and Cultural Rights;
3. Social tourism, and in particular associative tourism, which facilitates widespread access to leisure, travel and holidays, should be developed with the support of the public authorities;
4. Family, youth, student and senior tourism and tourism for people with disabilities, should be encouraged and facilitated;

Liberty of Tourist Movements

1. Tourists and visitors should benefit, in compliance with international law and national legislation, from the liberty to move within their countries and from one State to another, in accordance with Article 13 of the Universal Declaration of Human Rights; they should have access to places of transit and stay and to tourism and cultural sites without being subject to excessive formalities or discrimination;
2. Tourists and visitors should have access to all available forms of communication, internal or external; they should benefit from prompt and easy access to local administrative, legal and health services; they should be free to contact the consular representatives of their countries of origin in compliance with the diplomatic conventions in force;

3. Tourists and visitors should benefit from the same rights as the citizens of the country visited concerning the confidentiality of the personal data and information concerning them, especially when these are stored electronically;
4. Administrative procedures relating to border crossings whether they fall within the competence of States or result from international agreements, such as visas or health and customs formalities, should be adapted, so far as possible, so as to facilitate to the maximum freedom of travel and widespread access to international tourism; agreements between groups of countries to harmonize and simplify these procedures should be encouraged; specific taxes and levies penalizing the tourism industry and undermining its competitiveness should be gradually phased out or corrected;
5. So far as the economic situation of the countries from which they come permits, travellers should have access to allowances of convertible currencies needed for their travels;

Rights of the Workers and Entrepreneurs in the Tourism Industry

1. The fundamental rights of salaried and self-employed workers in the tourism industry and related activities, should be guaranteed under the supervision of the national and local administrations, both of their States of origin and of the host countries with particular care, given the specific constraints linked in particular to the seasonality of their activity, the global dimension of their industry and the flexibility often required of them by the nature of their work;
2. Salaried and self-employed workers in the tourism industry and related activities have the right and the duty to acquire appropriate initial and continuous training; they should be given adequate social protection; job insecurity should be limited so far as possible; and a specific status, with particular regard to their social welfare, should be offered to seasonal workers in the sector;

3. Any natural or legal person, provided he, she or it has the necessary abilities and skills, should be entitled to develop a professional activity in the field of tourism under existing national laws; entrepreneurs and investors-especially in the area of small and medium-sized enterprises-should be entitled to free access to the tourism sector with a minimum of legal or administrative restrictions;
4. Exchanges of experience offered to executives and workers, whether salaried or not, from different countries, contributes to foster the development of the world tourism industry; these movements should be facilitated so far as possible in compliance with the applicable national laws and international conventions;
5. As an irreplaceable factor of solidarity in the development and dynamic growth of international exchanges, multinational enterprises of the tourism industry should not exploit the dominant positions they sometimes occupy; they should avoid becoming the vehicles of cultural and social models artificially imposed on the host communities; in exchange for their freedom to invest and trade which should be fully recognized, they should involve themselves in local development, avoiding, by the excessive repatriation of their profits or their induced imports, a reduction of their contribution to the economies in which they are established;
6. Partnership and the establishment of balanced relations between enterprises of generating and receiving countries contribute to the sustainable development of tourism and an equitable distribution of the benefits of its growth;

Implementation of the Principles of the Global Code of Ethics for Tourism

1. The public and private stakeholders in tourism development should cooperate in the implementation of these principles and monitor their effective application;
2. The stakeholders in tourism development should recognize the role of international institutions, among which the World Tourism Organization ranks first, and non-

governmental organizations with competence in the field of tourism promotion and development, the protection of human rights, the environment or health, with due respect for the general principles of international law;

3. The same stakeholders should demonstrate their intention to refer any disputes concerning the application or interpretation of the Global Code of Ethics for Tourism for conciliation to an impartial third body known as the World Committee on Tourism Ethics.

Tourism Codes of Conduct

Codes of Conduct for Tour Operators

Guidelines for tour operators working in environmentally-sensitive areas:

Make Tourism and Conservation Compatible

* Develop a positive relationship with organizations and people that play a role in conservation, particularly in the areas that you will visit with your clients.
* Encourage your clients to become members of conservation organizations.
* Encourage governments and businesses to support projects such as new nature reserves through writing letters or personal contacts.
* Contribute time and money to conservation organizations and projects.
* Plan tourism activities so that they do not conflict with conservation efforts. Obtain permission before visiting nature reserves or other areas where access is restricted. When visiting these areas, be sure that your activities comply with the rules of the park or reserve.
* Know the laws and regulations that apply to the import and export of products made from wildlife, and make sure that your clients understand and follow these laws. Encourage your clients to buy products made by local people, so long as these products are not made from endangered species and their sale does not violate the law.

* Develop an environmental plan for your daily operations. If you are an operator employing more than 20 people, have a written environmental plan that states your company's commitment to conservation, to using resources in a sustainable way and to the principles itemized in these Codes of Conduct. Include specific procedures that your company uses in its daily operations to prevent and minimize detrimental environmental impacts. Make the plan available to your clients.
* Use post-trip evaluations to confirm that your tour was environmentally sound. Feedback from clients is a good way to find out if your tour met their expectations. In your post-trip evaluations, ask your clients whether or not they felt the tour avoided unnecessary negative environmental impacts, and if the tour operator demonstrated consideration of the natural and cultural environment. Written post-trip evaluation forms are preferable, although oral evaluations are acceptable, especially for smaller operations.

Support the Preservation of Wilderness and Biodiversity

* Promote the maintenance of large, undeveloped areas. The undeveloped regions of the Arctic, for example, have a unique value, and are one of the primary reasons why tourists come to the Arctic. This unique value is undermined by roads, pipelines and other kinds of unsightly large-scale development that fragments the environment.
* Support wildlife conservation programs and projects. Make your clients aware of these efforts and ensure that they do not hunt or fish protected or threatened species, enter sensitive wildlife habitats, or buy products made from protected species.

Use Natural Resources in a Sustainable Way

* Where laws permit hunting and fishing, follow all rules and take only what you can use. Ensure that your clients obey the laws and regulations and do not contribute to the over-depletion of local wildlife stocks. Cooperate with community and indigenous hunters' associations.

* Make sure that your clients use only appropriate and well-maintained hunting equipment that they know how to use correctly.
* When determining the number of clients that will visit an area, consider area specifics (wildlife, nesting birds, fragile vegetation, etc.) and any special vulnerability of the site. Inform other operators in the region of your plans in order to avoid over-visitation of a site.
* Use only established trails and existing campsites to avoid creating new ones.
* Avoid disturbing wildlife. Instruct your clients on local wildlife behaviour, and make sure that they view it from an appropriate distance.

Minimize Consumption, Waste and Pollution

* Your choice of products and the amount that you and your clients consume makes a difference.
* Whether you bring supplies with you or buy them, choose biodegradable or recyclable products with minimal packaging.
* Compress garbage and take it with you.
* Recycle where possible and encourage the communities that you visit to develop recycling programs if they do not have them already. If feasible, provide financial support to encourage the development of these programs, and show your commitment to the communities you and your clients visit.
* Limit energy use, including your use of heat and warm water. Keep records of your water and energy consumption, and recycling and waste-reduction efforts.
* The transportation you choose for your clients makes a difference. Opt for the means of transport that has the least environmental impact. Minimize the use of fossil fuels and try to use non-motorized transport whenever possible. Where motorized transportation is necessary, choose the technology that causes the least environmental damage and minimal noise (four-stroke instead of two-

stroke engines, for example). Do not use motorized transport such as snow mobiles and helicopters unnecessarily; these should only be used to get from one area to another or for seeing specific sites.

* Choose accommodations compatible with local traditions and that minimize negative environmental impacts. Choose lodging that has effective waste treatment systems, recycles and disposes of non-recyclable garbage appropriately.
* Support efforts to clean up waste and polluted areas by providing money, lobbying governments and businesses, contributing your time and that of your staff, and by encouraging your clients to support these efforts as well. Ensure that no trace of your visit remains behind.
* Follow responsible practices for camping and tours, including those that concern waste disposal.
* Retain all plastic for proper disposal, and compact all wood products, glass, and metal for a disposal facility. Ensure that any incinerators you use function properly.

Respect Local Cultures

* Coordinate with the communities that you visit to ensure that you are welcome, and that your visit is not disruptive.
* Arrange visits to communities well in advance, and avoid visits that are not pre-arranged.
* Reconfirm your visit, preferably 24 hours in advance, and be prepared to pay the community for costs associated with cancelled visits.
* Arrange what you and your clients will do during your visit with the community beforehand. Be sure you have permission to visit and to undertake the activities you have planned.
* Find out what size of group the community prefers for the planned activities.
* Keep away from sites where people are working, including hunting and fishing sites, unless you have specific agreements with locals.

* Be aware of the laws and regulations in the area or waters in which you are operating, and obtain the necessary permits.
* Respect the culture and customs of the people whose communities you visit, and make sure that your clients do so as well.
* Give all visitors a thorough cultural briefing before visiting local communities. Where possible, hire local lecturers to conduct these briefings. Include information on local customs and traditions and on appropriate behaviour for tourists in the area. Use local "Codes for Visitors" if available.
* Ask permission to photograph or videotape.
* Ensure that your clients respect religious grounds, churches, cemeteries and other sites with religious or cultural significance, and that they do not remove any artifacts.

Respect Historic and Scientific Sites

* Respect historic sites and markers, and make sure that your clients do not remove any artifacts. If access to historic or archaeological sites is restricted, obtain permission before visiting. Ensure that your clients behave respectfully, particularly if a site has religious significance.
* Respect the work of scientists. Do not enter scientific installations or work sites without making prior arrangements. Do not disturb scientists while they are working, and do not disturb their work sites.

Communities Should Benefit from Tourism

* Whenever possible, hire local staff and contract local businesses. Train and hire local people for your operations. Where local people lack the training you require, provide it. Use locally-owned businesses as subcontractors. Develop long-term partnerships with local operators, businesses and suppliers. A local connection most often means a better tourism experience.

* Operate in ways that benefit the communities you visit, particularly with respect to supplies. If feasible, buy supplies and services locally. Ask communities what supplies you should bring with you so that your visit and use of supplies does not cause hardship to local people. Encourage your clients to buy locally-made handicrafts and products.
* Where possible, choose accommodations owned, built and staffed by local people.

Educate Staff

* Hire a professional team.
* Hire only knowledgeable, environmentally and culturally aware staff, or train your existing staff in these areas. Provide training in how to avoid negative environmental impacts, in safety and in providing service. Evaluate the performance of your staff, at least annually.
* If you are a ship-based tour operator, hire lecturers and conservation-oriented naturalists who will not only talk about wildlife, environmental protection, history, geology and local cultures, but who can guide passengers ashore and who are familiar with safety and local conservation requirements.

Make Your Trip an Opportunity to Learn

* Provide your clients with information about the environment and conservation. Provide lectures and written materials about the environment, its special characteristics and its global significance. Include information about conservation in general, specific conservation efforts in the areas that you will visit, and specific ways — financial and otherwise — that your clients can support these conservation efforts.
* Provide your clients with specific information about the regions they will visit. Include information about climate, wildlife species and habitats, as well as appropriate behaviour for these areas.

Follow Safety Rules

* Provide local authorities with your itinerary. This is both for safety reasons and to be sure you are complying with local regulations.
* Brief all clients and staff on the dangers of wildlife encounters.
* Have at least one staff member who is responsible for co-coordinating safety and avoiding dangerous encounters with wildlife.

With international tourism forecast to reach 1.6 billion arrivals by 2020, members of the World Tourism Organization believe that the Global Code of Ethics for Tourism is needed to help minimize the negative impacts of tourism on the environment and on cultural heritage while maximizing the benefits for residents of tourism destinations.

The Global Code of Ethics for Tourism is intended to be a living document. Read it. Circulate it widely. Participate in its implementation. Only with your cooperation can we safeguard the future of the tourism industry and expand the sector's contribution to economic prosperity, peace and understanding among all the nations of the world.

Satsa Code of Conduct

All Members of the Southern Africa Tourism Services Association (hereinafter referred to as Members) shall comply with the Association's Code of Conduct as hereunder:

AIMS

* To ensure that the public receive the best possible service from Members.
* To maintain and enhance the reputation, standing and good name of the Association and its Membership.
* To encourage the continuous growth and development of the Tourism industry consistently with the above aims.

Principles

This code is designed to regulate any activities of Members between themselves and members of the public; between themselves and both non-members and member Principals; between themselves and their fellow Members and between themselves and other travel concerns.

This code recognises and embodies the relevant parts of all acts of Parliament and Government regulations which relate to the travel industry as well as the codes and regulations of recognised organizations or associations such as the Advertising Standards Authority, which shall regulate the standards and practices of Members in relation to advertising.

This code recognises the necessity for enforcement of its standards and practices and embodies measures and procedures by which Members can uphold observance of the Code under the authority of the National Executive Committee of the Association.

Conduct Between Members and The Public

Standard of Service

(i) Members shall maintain a high standard in serving the public and shall comply with all relevant statutory requirements.

(ii) Members shall make every effort to ensure that accurate information is provided to enable clients to exercise an informed judgment in making their choice of facilities.

Advertising

(i) No advertisement, document, website, email, statement or other publication, whether in writing or otherwise, shall contain anything which is likely to mislead the public.

Alterations to or Cancellation of Tours or Travel Arrangements by Members

(i) When alterations are made to travel arrangements for which bookings have already been accepted, Members shall inform their clients immediately they are advised of the situation by a Principal, or another travel concern and act as intermediaries between such Principals and their clients in any subsequent negotiations.

(ii) A member shall only cancel a tour or travel arrangements if final payment has not been made; and only after the balance of payment has been made if it is necessary to do as a result of hostilities, political unrest or other circumstances amounting to force majeure.

(iii) If a member has to cancel a tour or travel arrangements as the result of circumstances amounting to a force majeure, he shall inform agents and direct clients without delay and shall offer clients the choice of an alternative tour or travel arrangements, at least comparable in standard, if available, or alternatively a prompt and full refund of all money paid less reasonable expenses.

(iv) Should a material alterations become necessary to a tour or travel arrangement for which bookings have already been made, the Member concerned shall inform clients without delay and shall offer such clients the choice of either accepting the alteration, which must be of comparable standard, or of receiving a prompt and full refund of all money paid, less reasonable expenses when the alteration is due to circumstances amounting to force majeure.

Cancellation by Clients

(i) A Member shall clearly state in his booking conditions the amount of the cancellation fees which the client shall be liable to incur, as well as the terms and conditions under which the client shall be liable to incur such fees.

Complaints

(i) Complaints shall be dealt with promptly and efficiently and in the event of a dispute with a client, every effort shall be made to settle the matter amicably and as quickly as possible. Where complaints are of such a nature that reference to a Principal is necessary, a Member shall use his best endeavour, acting as intermediary, to bring about a satisfactory conclusion.

Transactions and Correspondence

(i) Transactions with clients shall be treated as confidential and correspondence shall be dealt with promptly.

* Members shall give a full service to the Principals

they represent and shall conform to all lawful and reasonable instructions issued to them as agents of such Principals.

* Member shall always carry out contractual obligations in an honourable manner and observe the Code of Good Business Practice.
* Members and their staff shall make themselves conversant with the tariffs, rules and regulations of the Principals with whom they have dealings and visa versa.
* Members should accept or release accommodation and other reserved services as quickly as possible and within the periods stipulated by the Principal.
* Members shall endeavour always to adhere to truthful statements and to good taste when called upon to express opinions of any other travel organisation.
* Members will always settle supplier's accounts promptly and within the period specified of payments becoming due.
* Whenever a complaint or grievance by a client involves any Principal, Members will give the Principal concerned every opportunity to make a full investigation before taking any action against the Principal or seeking to publicise the grievance.

Conduct Between Members and Fellow Members, Retail Travel Agents and other Travel Concerns

Members should endeavour to use qualified guides and other SATSA members as business partners whenever possible; Members shall deal fairly with one another and shall not damage the reputation of, nor disparage the business practices of or services offered by fellow members.

Members providing tourism transport services will not operate any services unless fully authorised to do so and unless licences for the conveyance of tourists, issued by the Operating Licence Board are held. Members will not use the services of transport operators who do not have the necessary licences to operate tourist services requiring the authority of the Operating Licence Board

Members shall not allow non-licensed companies or individuals to utilise their licences with the object of circumventing the Operating Licence Board regulations.

Infringement and Enforcement

* Any Member becoming aware of unethical practices on the part of fellow Members should advise the National Executive Committee of SATSA, providing full information and evidence of the alleged malpractices.
* In the event of an infringement of this Code of Conduct, all facts pertaining to the alleged infringement will be fully examined by the Association's National Executive Committee.
* The Member against whom an allegation has been made shall provide, at the request of the National Executive Committee, such further information or documentation as may be required within such period as may be specified.
* The National Executive Committee shall, before reaching any final conclusions, give the Member concerned the opportunity of making representations either personally or in writing in cases where disciplinary action if imposed can result in a reprimand and, or, fine or expulsion.
* The National Executive Committee's decision in regard to a reprimand, fine or expulsion shall be taken in terms of the Constitution and shall be binding on the Member concerned.

General

* Members shall familiarise themselves and their staff with the provisions of this Code of Conduct.
* Members shall observe not only the letter but also the spirit of the Code of Conduct and its ethics and ideals thus giving true significance to the aims and objectives of the Association.
* All advertising material and brochures produced by Members must indicate membership of the Association and carry the SATSA logo. Members must also display the

SATSA insignia in a prominent position in their business premises.

Australia's North West Tourism Code of Conduct and Ethics

Aims of the Code

* To ensure that all visitors to the North West receive the best possible service from all service providers within the tourism industry, whether members of a Visitor Centre or not.
* To maintain and enhance the reputation, standing and good name of Australia's North West Tourism, the North West Visitor Centres and their collective membership.
* To encourage initiative and enterprise in the belief that properly regulated competitive trading by and between service providers within the North West tourism industry will best serve the public interest and well being of the tourism industry.
* To ensure that the public interest shall predominate in all considerations of the standards of competitive trading between member service providers in the Australia's North West Tourism membership.
* To encourage the growth and development of Australia's North West tourism industry consistent with the preceding aims.

Code of Conduct and Ethics

Service Provider Relations with Trade and Consumers

* Service Providers will, unless circumstances render it impossible, inform their customers of all pertinent facts concerning tours, transportation, accommodation or other tourist services which they provide.
* Service Providers will be factual and accurate when called upon to provide information to the trade and to customers.
* Service Providers will keep their employees informed in an accurate and timely manner of any alterations to their services.

* Service Providers will endeavour to eliminate any practise which could be damaging to the trade or customers or to the dignity and integrity of the tourist industry in general, Australia's North West Tourism or any of the North West Visitor Centres.
* Service Providers shall ensure that their advertising contains no information, superlatives or photography that is either misleading or doubtful.
* Service Providers must advise their intending customers in writing, prior to the time initial payment is made for any booking, about cancellation policies and any service charges that may be imposed.
* Service Providers will ensure that employee dress standards are consistent with an acceptable level of professionalism within their particular section of the industry.
* Service Providers will at all times act in accordance with any rules and regulations applying to their particular industry.
* Service Providers will at all times act in accordance with current Trade Practices legislation, or in the spirit of such legislation where it does not formally apply to that Service Provider.

Service Provider Relation with other Service Providers

* Service Providers shall follow the best traditions of salesmanship and fair dealing by according fair, objective and impartial representation of other service providers they may from time to time represent on behalf of Australia's North West Tourism, or the North West Visitor Centres.
* Service providers should conduct their business so to try and avoid controversies with fellow providers. In the event of a controversy between service providers, such controversy shall be referred for mediation or arbitration, whichever appropriate, initially to the Executive Committee of Australia's North West Tourism.

* If an opinion is sought about a competitor, service providers shall render such opinion with professional integrity and courtesy.
* Service Providers are to encourage and promote membership of the North West Visitor Centres so that the entire tourism industry and the public benefit from the training, experience and high standards of all member service providers.

Conduct of Service Providers

* Service Providers will minimise operational and client environmental impacts by adopting sustainable practises, offering information, leading by example, and taking corrective action when and where necessary.
* Service Providers will endeavour to prevent both accidental and purposeful actions that cause damage to the environment such as crowding, harassment of wildlife, trampling, off road track / trail / road driving, walking and riding (except as authorised) and the improper disposal of waste.

Dealing with Complaints

* If a complaint is lodged in writing against a service provider by trade, consumer, and / or another service provider, the service provider concerned will take immediate steps to amicably deal with the complaint.
* Service Providers are required to comply with agreements reached through mediation.
* Written complaints will be dealt with in consultation with the North West Visitor Centres and referred to the Executive Committee of Australia's North West Tourism, if there is a need for further action.

Enforcement of Code of Conduct and Ethics

* If the Service Provider fails in one or more nominated ethical standards, they may be censured or suspended from membership of the North West Visitor Centres. The fact of member suspension will be advised to all tourism bodies associated with Australia's North West Tourism.

* Failure of a service provider to abide by the "Code of Conduct and Ethics" shall render an operator liable for disciplinary action by Australia's North West Tourism.

Asia Adventures Responsible Tourism

Travellers Code of Conduct

Responsible Tourism is a holistic approach to tourism and to be fully effective all participants involved in the tourism experience need to believe in and uphold its principles. Amongst others this includes; tour operators, accommodation providers, guides, restaurants, transport providers, local communities, travel agents; retail outlets, and you – the traveller! We always provide general advice on the countries being visited to all our guests in our predeparture 'Travel Pack'.

However, below we have listed some important pointers that will assist you in being a more 'Responsible Traveller'. The following advice, we hope, covers some of the more important issues to be aware of during your travels.

Environmental Considerations

- consider what you pack in your suitcase before leaving home. Waste disposal systems in many developing countries are ill equipped to deal with the increased pressures that tourism brings, and a few simple measures can make an enormous difference to the effect you have on your destination. Where possible remove the wrapping of packaged goods before you leave, e.g. unwrap soaps and take bottles / tubes out of boxes. Please take more harmful waste, such as batteries, back home with you where they may be disposed of or recycled more responsibly;
- consider bringing a refillable water bottle with you as these can often be refilled hygienically from large water containers in hotels and certain attractions, this limits the amount of plastic bottled water you would use;
- try to reduce other plastic use, for example when shopping use your own bag to carry purchases, and refrain from having straws with your drinks;

- on our tours we have a 'zero litter' policy – 'carry in, carry out', so please do not drop litter. As well as being unsightly bottles, cans, plastic, cigarette butts, etc. can be deadly to wild animals;
- remember that in many places water is a very precious commodity and should not be wasted, use a minimum both in your accommodation and whenever possible throughout your trip, e.g. turn off the tap when brushing your teeth, take a shower rather than a bath;
- where they exist comply with local environmental initiatives, for example if your accommodation provider has a policy for reusing sheets or towels try to support this as it helps to reduce water, detergent, and energy use;
- remember to turn off lights and electrical equipment in your room if you are not using them, e.g. turn your TV fully off rather than leaving it on stand-by, and turn off air-conditioning units when they are not needed or when you leave the room (air-conditioning is a large energy user, so try to use it sparingly);
- never buy products that exploit wildlife or aid the destruction of species or habitats, i.e. souvenirs made from endangered species such as: ivory; animal skins; teeth; coral; shellfish; tropical hardwoods etc. Doing so will only encourage the trade, and many of the products will have been sourced illegally. In addition if you do buy these products you might find yourself with problems when you reach customs control;
- we are an accredited 'Heritage Friendly Business – Gold Status', as such we are totally against the trade in ancient artefacts. Archaeological theft is illegal and a problem in Cambodia. Do not purchase any ancient artefacts, such as glass and stone beads, pottery, stone tools, and Asia Adventures Co. Ltd., PO Box 1266, Phnom Penh, Cambodia Company Registration No: Co. 9447/07P Tourism License No: 016-09 metal objects. Even if you purchase reproductions ensure you obtain a certificate stating that the object is a reproduction otherwise you may face problems when you reach customs control;

- in your free time consider getting around by environmentally friendly transport such as bicycles, electric bikes; cyclos, horse drawn carts etc;
- when visiting ancient sites please respect them as they are often active religious monuments and world heritage treasures. In addition refrain from touching any carvings and bas-reliefs as this damages the stone;
- if you will be travelling to remote areas, before leaving home purchase environmentally friendly detergents and shampoos for hand / hair washing, and clothes washing, and use as little as is practical. This will help to keep valuable fresh water supplies, rivers, streams and the sea free from pollution. In additional use a bucket or similar and wash well away from the water sources to prevent your dirty water polluting someone else's drinking water;
- in addition where toilet facilities exist, however unsavoury, they should be used. Where they do not, always bury your waste and make sure it is never near (at least 30m) from a water source;
- when visiting national parks / protected areas stay on set paths in order to preserve natural habitats and leave animals undisturbed. Keeping noise to a minimum also helps, and allows you to enjoy the sights and sounds of nature and have a better chance of spotting wildlife;
- although we insist that our guides maintain suitable distances from wildlife, allowing the animal a suitable escape route, there is always a temptation to get closer. For this reason we recommend that you don't encourage your guide or driver to get closer to the animals than is acceptable and to take the most powerful lens for your camera you can get;
- do not pick wild flowers, and never feed wild animals or attempt to touch them;
- if snorkelling, diving, or observing marine mammals such as turtles and dolphins, observe environmental guidelines. Never touch or break living coral, and never touch or feed any marine animal or fish.

Social Considerations

- we hope that those who choose to travel with Asia Adventures do so with a genuine desire to enhance their holiday by learning more about the people of the host community;
- before you travel try to learn about the local culture and traditions of the places you will be visiting. A little time spent researching the unique customs of the region can avoid embarrassment and offence. In addition arriving with some understanding about the background of the country you are visiting will help reduce 'culture shock' and you will get more out of your travels and your interactions with local people;
- it is quite easy in a small, simple community to appear an arrogant rich foreigner, so be aware of the feelings of other people, and avoid extravagant displays of wealth such as ostentatious jewellery and technological gadgetry, not only can this accentuate the gap between rich and poor but in rare cases it can be an incitement to robbery;
- being able to speak a few phrases in the local language is always appreciated, and locals are very supportive of your efforts-plus the experience can greatly enhance your visit. In your predeparture 'Travel Pack' you will find various simple phrases which we have found useful;
- dress appropriately, especially in places of worship or cultural significance. Asians generally dress conservatively, women tend not to wear revealing tops nor skirts or pants that show their knees and even men will usually prefer long pants to shorts (smart knee-length shorts are fine). 'Follow suit' and dress with a sense of decorum. As well as showing respect to local dress norms you may also find that you are afforded better all round reception from local people-first impressions count for a lot in Asia;
- in many regions of the world it is considered offensive to take someone's photograph without obtaining their permission beforehand. Please try not to be offended should they decline, even if you do not understand why. If people seem reluctant or look away then please do not take a picture;

foreign currency, credit cards and cheques and other negotiable instruments.

Knowledge of Act, Code and Other Legislation

An in bound tour operator must have a reasonable knowledge and understanding of the Act, this code, the Fair Trading Act 1989 and the Trade Practices Act 1974 (Cwlth) in so far as they relate to the carrying on of the business of an in bound tour operator.

Policy About Dispute Resolution Process

(1) An in bound tour operator must have a written policy for resolving disputes between the in bound tour operator and a tourist who uses a travel package arranged by the in bound tour operator about goods or services supplied to the tourist under the travel package.

(2) The in bound tour operator must ensure that the policy—

  (a) allows the tourist to participate in a timely and appropriate dispute resolution process that has regard to the tourist's status as a person who is only temporarily in Australia; and

  (b) states, in a prominent way, that—

    (i) the tourist may contact the commissioner if the tourist is concerned about the conduct of the in bound tour operator; and

    (ii) the dispute resolution process described in the policy does not stop a tourist from exercising the tourist's rights to other legal remedies.

(3) The in bound tour operator must inform each tourist who uses a travel package arranged by the in bound tour operator, before the tourist enters Queensland, about the in bound tour operator's policy, and, if the tourist asks, give the tourist a copy of the policy.

(4) The copy of the policy given to the tourist under subsection must be in the tourist's first language.

Honesty, Fairness and Professionalism

(1) An in bound tour operator must act honestly, fairly and professionally in carrying on the business of an in bound tour operator.

(2) Without limiting subsection, an in bound tour operator must treat tourists honestly and fairly.

Skill, Care and Diligence

An in bound tour operator must exercise reasonable skill, care and diligence in carrying on the business of an in bound tour operator.

High-pressure Tactics or Harassment

An in bound tour operator must not, in dealing with a person in relation to a travel package arranged by the in bound tour operator—

(a) use high-pressure tactics or harass the person; or

(b) encourage or engage another person to use high-pressure tactics or harass the person; or

(c) condone the use of high-pressure tactics or harassment of the person by any other person.

False or Misleading Representation

(1) An in bound tour operator must not, in dealing with a tourist using a travel package arranged by the in bound tour operator—

  (a) make a false or misleading representation to the tourist; or

  (b) encourage or engage another person to make a false or misleading representation to the tourist; or

  (c) condone the making of a false or misleading representation to the tourist by any person.

(2) Without limiting subsection, an in bound tour operator must not make, encourage or engage another person to make, or condone the making of, a false or misleading representation about any of the following relating to the travel package—

  (a) the mode and standard of transport used for transfers and sightseeing;

  (b) the existence or location of, or access to, a place or attraction;

(c) the time required or route used to go to a place or attraction;

(d) the standard, style or price of accommodation;

(e) the standard or price of food or beverages;

(f) guiding services;

(g) the price of entry to tourist attractions, tours, entertainment or other activities including, for example, whether the price is included in the travel package;

(h) restrictions that apply to the travel package, including, for example, restrictions about baggage, children, seat allocation or smoking;

(i) conditions about reservations, payment, refunds or cancellations;

(j) the management of tours included in the travel package.

(3) Also, without limiting subsection, an in bound tour operator must ensure—

(a) that a quotation given by the in bound tour operator for goods or a service included in a travel package discloses the total cost of the goods or service, including any taxes or other charges payable by a tourist; and

(b) that an advertisement or promotional material about goods or a service included in a travel package arranged by the in bound tour operator discloses any conditions or restrictions applying to the supply of the goods or service.

Maximum penalty for subsection—20 penalty units.

Tour Not to be Dominated by Shopping

(1) An in bound tour operator must not use undue influence or high-pressure tactics to have a tourist go shopping instead of doing all or a part of another activity the tourist may reasonably have expected to do as part of the tourist's travel package.

(2) An in bound tour operator must ensure that a travel

package arranged by the in bound tour operator for a tourist does not consist predominantly of shopping excursions unless—

(a) the in bound tour operator and tourist agree, before the travel package starts, that the package is to consist predominantly of shopping excursions; or

(b) the tourist consents, during the course of the travel package, to it consisting predominantly of shopping excursions.

In bound tour Operator Not to Charge for Free Goods or Service

An in bound tour operator must not charge a tourist for goods or a service that are available free of charge to the public.

Provision of Goods or Services Included in Travel Package

(1) An in bound tour operator must ensure that goods or a service included in a travel package arranged by the in bound tour operator are provided in accordance with any representation about the goods or service made in an itinerary, quotation or promotional material for the package.

(2) Despite subsection (1), if, because of circumstances reasonably beyond the in bound tour operator's control, goods or a service (the unavailable component) are unavailable when required to be provided under the package, the in bound tour operator must—

(a) provide, as far as reasonably practicable, goods or a service of a similar type, value and quality as the unavailable component; or

(b) if the in bound tour operator can not reasonably comply with paragraph (a), refund the cost of the unavailable component.

(3) However, if goods or a service of a similar type, value and quality are unavailable, an in bound tour operator may, with the informed consent of the tourist who purchased the travel package, substitute other goods or another service of similar value.

In bound Tour Operator's Responsibilities About Guiding Services

(1) An in bound tour operator must ensure, as far as reasonably practicable, that a tour guide, in providing guiding services arranged by the in bound tour operator—

(a) displays the tour guide's identification so it is clearly visible to other persons; and Maximum penalty—20 penalty units.

(b) does not stop a tourist—

(i) shopping in a retail outlet; or

(ii) gaining access to or buying goods or a service, including, for example, a travel service offered by an alternative supplier; and

(c) does not—

(i) obstruct a person lawfully advertising or giving information to a tourist about travel or other services; or

(ii) obstruct a tourist's access to an advertisement or information about travel or other services, including, for example, travel services offered by an alternative supplier; and

(d) does not confiscate or withhold a tourist's money, passport, personal documents or other property; and

(e) does not exert or use unfair pressure, undue influence or unfair tactics on a tourist; and

(f) does not make a false or misleading representation to a tourist, including, for example, a false or misleading representation about any of the following—

(i) the existence or location of, or access to, a place or attraction;

(ii) the time required or route used to go to a place or attraction;

(iii) the characteristics of an alternative supplier;

(iv) the quality or availability of products or services offered by an alternative supplier;

(v) a reason, including the existence of any lawful requirement, for confiscating or withholding a tourist's money, passport, personal documents or other property.

(a) is in English and the language used predominantly by the tourists for whom the tour guide is providing the guiding services; and

(b) includes—

(i) the tour guide's full name and business address; and

(ii) the in bound tour operator's name, and business name or trading name, if any; and

(iii) a recent colour photograph of the tour guide.

obstruct includes hinder and attempt to obstruct.

In bound Tour Operator's Responsibilities

An in bound tour operator must, as far as reasonably practicable, ensure that a person including, for example, a tour guide, employed or engaged by the in bound tour operator to provide goods or a service to a tourist—

(a) is entitled, under the laws of the Commonwealth or the State, to work, or provide the goods or service, in the State; and

(b) is aware of, and carries out, the person's obligations under the Work place Health and Safety Act 1995; and

(c) has a level of fluency in a language used by the tourist that is appropriate for providing the goods or service to the tourist; and

(d) if the person employed or engaged by the in bound tour operator is a tour guide—is, while the tour guide is working in Queensland, employed under the Tour Guides Award-State (the award) as in force from time to time, or on conditions not less favourable to the tour guide than the award.

Code of Conduct for Tourism South East Member's

Compliance with the Code of Conduct is a condition of membership with Tourism South East;

Guiding Principle

To set out the standards of practice which members taking part in the Board's marketing and other activities undertake to follow in their dealings with customers.

1. To deal fairly and reasonably with their customers at all times and to ensure their satisfaction with the goods or services purchased.
2. To manage the business in such a way as to provide the highest practicable standards of customer care, cleanliness, hygiene and maintenance.
3. To adhere with the assessed only policy by participating in the National Quality Assurance Scheme for the duration of membership. To only promote other providers who also participate in Quality Assurance.
4. To ensure that all staff should be clearly identifiable and be conversant with company policy and procedure.
5. To ensure that if customers are required to make a purchase prior to receiving the goods or services then adequate and clear information must be available before the decision to purchase is made.
6. To ensure that customers should be made aware of the opening/operating times of the business and whether there are any charges for admission, or additional payments for specific items, attractions, services or facilities.
7. To ensure that no information should knowingly be given to customers that is misleading. All advertisements, brochures and other promotional means should fairly and accurately describe the amenities, facilities and services offered. Any significant restrictions on entry, access or purchase should be clearly stated.
8. To give due consideration to the requirements of disabled people or those with special needs and make suitable provision where practicable.
9. To deal promptly and courteously with all enquiries, requests, correspondence and complaints from customers. In case of dissatisfaction customers are asked to advise a staff member at the time. All staff who deal directly with the public should be aware of company policy in these matters and be able to assist customers.
10. To comply with all applicable legislation. Members should also observe all requirements of Codes of Conduct, Charters, etc., that apply to their membership of business organisations, or participation in applicable schemes.

11. To ensure the provision of adequate public liability insurance or other equivalent arrangements.

In cases of non-observance of this Code of Conduct, Tourism South East reserves the right to withdraw a Member's eligibility to participate in any of the Board's activities

Explanation Code of Conduct

One of the most sensitive issues that the tourism industry faces refers to the commercial sexual exploitation of children. It mainly happens in developing countries, by tourists coming from developed countries. The travel and tourism industry make efforts towards preventing and reducing the commercial sexual exploitation of children by implementing the ECPAT Code of Conduct for the Protection of Children from Sexual Commercial Exploitation in Travel and Tourism.

The Code of Conduct offers the travel industry (beside tour operators, also airline companies, hotels, travel agents, etc.) guidelines to help reduce the prostitution of minors in a concrete and visible way. The aim of the Code of Conduct is to make travellers and travel staff more aware of sexual exploitation of children.

Suppliers of tourism services adopting the Code of Conduct commit themselves to implement the following six criteria:

* To establish an ethical policy regarding commercial sexual exploitation of children.
* To train the personnel in the country of origin and travel destinations.
* To introduce a clause in contracts with suppliers, stating a common repudiation of commercial sexual exploitation of children.
* To provide information to travellers by means of catalogues, brochures, in-flight films, ticket-slips, home pages, etc.
* To provide information to local "key persons" at the destinations.
* To report annually.

3

Modern Trends in Tourism

Hospitality Industry: Hotels Business Current and Future Trends

Hospitality has Long been Synonymous with the Hotel Industry

have wide scale implications on an otherwise diverse industry. What might be an opportunity for a traveller can be a matter of survival for hotels? It will not be an oversimplification to suggest that the emerging concepts in hotel industry reveal an atmosphere of stiff competition. Here is a look at a few major issues:

Is Green better?

Amid growing concern over environment friendly services, a majority of travellers now prefer Green and Eco lodgings. Recent surveys by trade associations such as Partnership Travel Industry Association and online retailers like Yahoo revealed that nearly seventy percent of the tourists are willing to pay extra when it comes to environmental friendly lodgings. These surveys further revealed that these guests will pay anywhere from nine to ten percent premium on the already advertised prices.

What can be stated as a welcome relief for the educated traveller might pose real challenges for the hotel business. To better understand the scenario, it should be noted that hotels are presently facing severe shortages in occupancy rates which are at their lowest since 1971. Such a crisis and lack of funds can definitely hamper any efforts to install appliances that comply with the LEEDS standards (Leadership in Energy & Environmental Design). Some experts agree that a trade off may lead hotels into removing free amenities that include little bottles of shampoos, jams and free basket of fruits; all of which are the hallmark of these eco lodgings.

Where are the Workers Gone?

The hotel industry gives employment at a very large proportion of part time workers, who after gaining substantial experience, leave for other lucrative jobs at restaurants and outdoors. Low wages in the hotel industry is one of the primary reasons for low retention rates.

Hotel industry Gurus are already thinking of ways to attract and retain qualified workers by increasing the pay scales and by reducing the long working hours. The top management is now devising constructive methods that will retain the existing workers by sponsoring education and creating attractive career paths.

Mega Hotels

The rising cost of construction and a struggling real estate has prompted hoteliers to deploy the prefabricated and cost effective solution in the construction of new hotels. In fact they are fighting back by producing highly efficient designs that utilize a greater proportion of space for revenue generating purpose. Future trends in the hotel construction will seek to maximize the use of building areas by constructing a multi purpose facility that will include Casinos, shopping outlets and Theatres. The stand alone hotel concept is likely to vanish as the new properties will be constructed as a mixed use development to provide guests with facilities such as Church, Hospitals and Theme Parks. Such a variety will ensure that guests remain at one spot which will help generate revenue for the entire hotel complex.

The Evolution of Savvy Traveller

The evolution of internet has given rise to a phenomenon where travellers are becoming ever more demanding. Industry professionals suggest that an increase in a trend, to review properties online, will make travellers less forgiving as they are able to post their travel experiences. Such an overemphasis on web may even lead to stiff competition and price reduction strategies where only large players may be able to survive.

To ward of such threats, the small business owner is now turning towards opening a boutique establishment as an alternate to 70,s style motels. Such niche properties are popping up everywhere by advertising a more personalized "home away from home" kind of experience. The introduction of such boutique properties has also given rise to the popular and widely accepted theme of modern hostels. These hostels are keen to provide a clean and safe environment for budget conscious travellers. Their goal is to wipe out the myths associated with cheap motels and dingy guesthouses.

Whatever may be the case, one thing is for sure that constant remodelling of the hotel industry has made it more functional and practical not only for the guests but also for the hotel owners.

Disaster Management Plan for the Hospitality Industry

The idea behind India's 9/11 was to do a Marriott at the Taj, i.e. like the Marriott was reduced to rubble in Islamabad, the same was expected to be done at the Taj... To reduce India's symbols of economic strength, even as the country struggles with a slowing economy... To hit hard the visible symbols of pride of the country, which the historic Taj was... To create an atmosphere of insecurity in the country: a visit to the grocer maybe as safe/dangerous as that to the Taj. Terrorism is a reality in India, today. The Indian tourism industry, considered to be amongst the world's top three performers (behind China)-defined as countries set to grow fastest over 2007 and the decade to come – will be negatively impacted as tourists prefer to visit safe destinations. However, history shows that there are other popular tourist destinations such as New York, London, Madrid and Bali that have also suffered from terrorist attacks. These places and their countries have recovered from the sudden downturn in image that had a correspondingly negative effect on the international tourism industry and the country's economics. There are lessons to be learnt from the experiences of others. While Spain used a 'business as usual' approach in recovering from its terrorist attacks, Tunisia used 'counter messages' inviting tourists to create peace. Essentially, in due course and with correct marketing the image can be changed to a favourable one. It is our belief that there would be a recovery in due course as every destination at some time of its existence faces a threat from either a natural disaster or one through malevolent human action, as was the case in Mumbai.

Perhaps the need of the hour is the formulation of a framework for disaster management for the hospitality industry. A previous disaster that visited the hotel industry was the 2004 Indian Ocean tsunami when coastal resorts/ hotels were wiped out or greatly damaged and most literature pertaining to disaster management in this industry deals with such scenarios. However, crises do not emerge just out of natural conditions. To start with, what is a crisis/disaster? Perhaps the best accepted definition is by Selbst who defines a crisis as 'any action or failure to act that interferes with an organisation's ongoing functions, the acceptable attainment of its objectives, its viability or survival, or that has a detrimental personal effect as perceived by the majority of its employees, clients or constituents.' In relation to tourism, Faulkner considers the principal distinction between what can be termed a 'crisis' and a 'disaster' to be the extent to which the situation is attributable to the organisation itself, or can be described as originating outside the organisation. Thus, a 'crisis' describes a situation 'where the root cause of an event is, to some extent, self-inflicted through such problems as inept management structures and practices or a failure to adapt to change', while a 'disaster' can be defined as 'where an enterprise... is confronted with sudden unpredictable catastrophic changes over which it has little control'. The incidents at the Taj and Oberoi certainly classify as disasters. And there is a need to learn from these disasters and not allow them to strike the death knell for the Indian hospitality industry.

There is a need to capture the experiences of the hotel staff and the measures they employed in guiding their guests through this dark hour. Hotel staff displayed tremendous courage and India's famed hospitality in the truest sense even at this hour. Scores of tales have emerged of unnamed workers hiding guests, feeding them, barricading doors, tending the vulnerable and issuing orders. A hotel worker, identified only as Mr. Rajan, put himself between one of the gunmen and a family, taking the bullets in his own abdomen. Another example is that of a general manager who was seen assisting guests out of the hotel within the initial hours of the attack, but unable to save his own family. The staff of the hotel has emerged as heroes, reaffirming our faith in humanity, which had been stripped by the terrorists' remorseless and indiscriminate firing. There are many lessons to be learnt through this tragedy and the brave contributions of those who have put their own safety at risk to save others should not go in vain.

Hotels-especially those vulnerable to such motivated violence as that witnessed at the Taj and Oberoi-should incorporate crisis management planning into their overall sustainable development and marketing/management strategies to protect and rebuild their image of safety/attractiveness, to reassure potential visitors of the safety of the area, to reestablish the area's functionality/attractiveness, and to aid local travel and tourism industry members in their economic recovery. These lessons should include the following:

Security would obviously be the most important element of this disaster management plan and guests at five-star hotels should expect to be checked along with their baggages. The way luggage is scanned through x-ray machines in airports, it should be also done in hotels. The screening should start at the very entrance where minimum damage can be done. Since this iconic bastion of hospitality has been stormed, hospitality too should sit up and be hospitable to guests who do not abuse their name and premises and threaten their very existence. The terrorists were met with ill-equipped and thus inadequate initial resistance when they stormed in. Hotels, thus, need to have their own effective security systems and intruder deterrents in place so that they can react immediately to the situation before essential time is lost in calling for help from external agencies. The security, especially, at the entry points and perimeters needs to be strengthened so that an easy walk in like at Mumbai is not replicated in future. Security should be supported by latest technology, for example a sensor like system by way of which the general manager would know that the security had been breached and immediate action may be initiated before being faced with terror at such close quarters. Since it was the National Security Guard (NSG) commandos who eventually evacuated the hotel, it maybe prudent to get them on board and learn from their experiences while formulating such guidelines.

Knowledge of hotel layout and who has this knowledge is critical as the recent crisis has shown. The NSG commandoes at the press conference clearly enunciated that the terrorists had a clear advantage as they knew the layout of the hotel well and were able to move about freely creating much destruction. On the other hand, the NSG were disadvantaged as they did not know the layout of the hotel and had to go room-to-room. In such crucial situations where knowledge is power, hotel blueprints should be available with the disaster management team so they can readily brief the security forces/rescuing agency. At the same time, care should be taken to secure them so that they do not fall into wrong hands. Moreover, like emergency fire exits, multiple contingency plans for exit of hotel guests in case of terrorist attacks should be in place. There may even be a need to take this reality into account when constructing new hotels.

A sophisticated communication system needs to be in place. Even though the cable network to the rooms where the terrorists were holed in was cut, they had access to updated information with mentors through satellite phones.

A superior communication system that could perhaps jam the links of the terrorists and give hotel staff the upper hand in their communication with guests and external coordinating agencies needs to be evolved. The hotel must at all times have access to the most recent communication system. While technology can be made available it is important to practice it in dummy situations for enhanced effectiveness.

A coordinated, team approach is required to be developed, given the range of private and public sector organisations directly and indirectly involved. While in the Mumbai case the hospitality sector was the target, terrorism may be faced by any sector. Thus, it is incumbent to have a well coordinated security cover with a specified person 'incharge' and more importantly 'responsible and thereby accountable'.

The government response and guidelines and the regulatory framework to provide the resources need to be put in place. A case in point is the obligation on the Telecom industry to provide the specified inputs to the security agencies. The security agency by itself has to have a person 'by name' made responsible to avoid having a typical fallout of passing the buck.

International security standards and guidelines that are well defined and internationally accepted should be evolved at this juncture by the international community. A case in point is the ISO 27001 and 27002, which are the international best practice information security management standards, defining and guiding Information Security Management System (ISMS) development. These will provide the necessary benchmarking for individual users to know the type of cover and the responsibilities that are defined and provided by that institution for its guests. Most importantly, training, to staff needs to be regularly imparted in dealing with such situations.

Modern Tourism and the Third World

Tourism fulfills a human need for rest and recreation. People normally set out to see other places and meet other people. Other people, meanwhile, extend their hospitality to their guests-a national trait worthy of praise.

But tourism also satisfies the thirst for profit. Big business, hungry for megabuck profits, resort to gross commercialism and imposes unsuitable development programs.

In the process, people get trampled upon, cultures erode and eco-systems deteriorate. Third World nations, main recipients of these 'development programs,' usually end up the losers.

Alternative Tourism, as a counter trend, seeks to right these abuses by challenging the profit structure and commercial premise of the tourism industry. Alternative Tourism works to redefine tourism back to its original spirit of exchange and solidarity among peoples.

A Billion Dollar Industry

Tourism has increased rapidly since the end of the Second World War as improved mass transportation provided people with cheaper and faster ways of getting to other places. It also enabled them to go to farther and farther destinations and meet more people.

From around 70 million people who spent a few billion dollars in 1960, the number of tourists rose to half a billion, spending some $324 billion, in 1993. With a yearly average increase of 7%, the number of international tourists is expected to reach 956 million by the end of 2000.

The tourism industry employs 74 million people and domestic and international tourism receipts account for 9.3% of GNP worldwide.

The hotel and airline industries control the bulk of the tourist business, as tourist spending goes mainly to the carrier and to accommodation. A good part of the earnings also goes to the tour and travel operators. These transnational companies, either affiliated with each other or subsidiaries of larger conglomerates, earn billions of dollars from the tourist money spent on holiday travel, rest and recreation, and even business and convention activities. Transport industry suppliers such as the shipbuilding and train industries also rake in a good profit. The construction industry, likewise, profits from hotel and resort building contracts.

Tourism in the Third World

Many Third World nations in the early 1970s embraced tourism as a quick recipe for development. Staggering from high unemployment rates and heavy indebtedness, many governments saw tourism as a source of foreign exchange to fund balance of payments deficits and service their foreign debts. Tourism also promised a viable source of investments for their backward economies and a source of quick livelihood and employment for their unskilled workers.

With encouragement from the United Nations (UN) and the IMF-World Bank, this tourism-development strategy paved the way for the entry of TNCs and other investments in hotel and resort development, foreign-funded government infrastructure and other tourism-related projects and tourism programs. Bilateral and multilateral loans poured in to finance these projects.

Too poor to resist and not given much choice, many Third World countries soon adapted the strategy. Bilateral and multilateral loans poured in to finance these projects. Various aid organizations like the UNDP, WTO, ESCAP, JICA and the ADB lent their 'expertise' in supporting and promoting tourism or tourism-related projects in Southeast Asia, South America, the Caribbean and the Pacific islands. People from industrialized countries were treated to cheap, exotic and unspoiled destinations in the Third World. In the process, the social, economic and cultural life of many third world countries were opened up to widescale tourism exploitation and their natural resources displayed for despoiling. Whatever initial financial relief Third World countries had was eventually lost in the form of repatriated profits or debt service money. Tourism's negative impact on the third world countries and their peoples is staggering. Self-sufficient economies get smothered, social relations break, cultures eroded and environments are laid waste. The list is long and well-documented: Self-sufficient agricultural economies giving way to tourism-reliant economies; women and children being forced into prostitution to service sex-tours and pedophiles; fishermen turning into waiters; and urban poor and indigenous communities domains giving way to golf courses and large hotels.

Alternative Tourism

Alternative tourism emerged from the Third World as a reaction to the negative effects tourism heaped on its countries.

Alternative tourism came in different names and various models. All tried to stop the onslaught and improve the situation. Backyard tourism, for instance, sought 'to preserve the original rural appeal' of the tourist destination. It also relied on the services of small local enterprises while rejecting the development of modern resorts.

Endemic tourism, on the other hand, used the 'special characteristics of individual communities which attracted tourists' and the 'great value of the cultural characteristics of communities' as tourism assets.

Increasing global concerns for the environment, meanwhile, produced ecotourism which tried to 'shy away from commercial destinations and focused on environmental themes.' Sustainable tourism is yet another new form of alternative tourism that is led by an 'empowered and gender-sensitive community' that 'protects and enhance ecological resources.'

The Philippine Experience

The Philippine experience remains a classic case of what tourism has done to a third world country. Tourism's impact on our society, culture, economy and environment already gives a perfect picture of what the Third World has gone through in its adoption of tourism-development.

Sex-tourists and pedophiles walking hand-in-hand with women and children is a common site in the red-light districts of Manila, Cebu and Davao. Golf courses, hotels and large shopping malls are continually displacing peasants in CALABARZON and urban dwellers in the poor districts of Metro Manila. Indigenous tribes like the Mangyans and Igorots are turned into tourist attractions. And who will forget the former US military bases in Subic and Pampanga. These monuments to tourism left thousands of Amerasians fatherless and hooked on drugs and prostitutes dying of AIDS while awaiting the promised return of his 'sailor boy.'

Early attempts at alternative tourism in the country dates back to the mid-1970s when residents of Puerto Galera in Mindoro built cottages for 'back pack' tourists searching for the ambience of nature and warm smiles of the local people. The residents also employed family members to serve drinks and wash the clothes of these tourists. These family-owned enterprises, soon to be known as backyard tourism, were at first modestly successful as they managed to do away with the expensive accommodations offered by hotels and the degrading work of serving foreign owners.

Foreign tour operators, however, learned to adjust to the negative image of tourism and soon began building their own cottages and not touching the natural ambience of the place. Soon backyard tourism became another adjunct of the mainstream tourism industry as foreigners took over management and ownership of the local cottages.

Other types of alternatives to tourism came out through the eighties and nineties still in reaction to the worsening negative effects of tourism. These models also tried to adjust to the failures and co-optation of the earlier models by working on broader concerns and action plans.

People's organizations, cause-oriented groups and NGOs began promoting their own type of 'exposure programs' to interested and 'concerned' foreigners. These groups offered an alternative tourism hinged on a much broader nationalist program that directly challenged the profit motive of tourism and worked for a 'real empowerment for the people as masters of their fate' and ready to reject imposed development models on them.

PGX and Alternative Tourism

The People's Global Exchange (PGX) is one of many NGOs that started alternative tourism programs in the mid-80s.

PGX has long been hosting foreigners active in the solidarity movement for the Philippines. Its Development-Education program served to deepen the circle of friends already familiar with Philippines realities and active in solidarity work by immersing them in the day-to-day lives and struggles of the different sectors.

Soon it was hosting 'walk-ins' and other visitors unfamiliar to Philippine realities, but who were otherwise interested to learn from an 'exposure' program and possibly do 'concrete things' upon return to their countries.

Working with a broad network of people's organizations and organized communities, PGX began promoting alternative tourism as a new program and concept for the unfamiliar but interested people from industrialized nations.

A 1992 PGX paper says alternative tourism is 'an educationally-oriented' and 'non-commercial' program. It also 'promotes a socially and ecologically responsible' tourism that is 'people-centered.' Most important, it 'creates a venue for initiating friendships and solidarity between peoples.'

Since the late 1980s, PGX has hosted more than a thousand visitors who came individually or in groups. It even managed to host boatloads of Japanese 'tourists' belonging to Peaceboat, a Japanese NGO also active in alternative tours, in 1991, 1992, 1997 and 1998. These exposurees numbered more than three-hundred per boat-load and were divided into groups of fifty or more people who then went to different communities.

With its partners, PGX offers a range of programs aimed at promoting sectoral issues as well as broader concerns. Sectoral issues range from peasant landlessness to poor working conditions in factories to demolitions of squatter families to evictions of tribal groups. Similarly, the accompanying struggle of said sectors are highlighted and their calls for solidarity extended to the visitors.

Broader concerns, notably ecological problems (poisoning of rivers and lakes), women issues (prostitution, wife battering), children (pedophiles, drugs) have gained increasing interest on the visitors' part.

Exposure programs usually last from seven-day mini-exposures to 2-year internships. Visitors come from different groups: students, academics, factory workers, homemakers and even children. These alternative programs seem to pay off as many exposurees, upon returning to their countries, have taken up Philippine issues and linked-up with Philippine support groups. Some have even influenced their families and friends to try the same exposure they have gone through. A few have formally joined and became active in solidarity groups.

Prospects

Concerned groups and individuals have taken many alternatives and paths in facing the issues of tourism. Some proved effective for some time but eventually failed. Others were co-opted by big business interests who have learned to adjust to changing perceptions of tourism. Others remained and, in their own way, continued trying to change the system by testing new models.

More than three decades of experience suggests that true alternative tourism is one that is not subject to the profit motives of big business interests. Alternative tourism also work for an empowered community that can and will reject development impositions on their lives.

New Directions in Tourism for Third World Development

Globalization-Tourism the New Imperialism

Aside from war, tourism is the single most destructive global force unleashed by man. Tour companies, for their image, often claim to adhere to a code of conduct, on the ground they rarely even bother to pay lip service.

Tourism is the fastest growing global industry. In 1996 tourism revenue amounted to $423 billion, the number of tourist arrivals clocked in at 592 million. By the year 2000, if not before, tourism is expected to be the world's largest industry.

1 in 4 Brits now travel abroad on a package holiday. This is an industry that has grown from nothing not long after the Second World War. The early operators were viewed in the same light as second hand car dealers, the way the travelling public is still treated little has changed. The growth in the package holiday business has destroyed much of the Mediterranean and the tour operators are now looking further afield for places to despoil.

Majorca, population 700,000, has 6 million tourists each year, 2 million of them Brits. It has brought in a lot of money and taken the local people on a journey to hell.

Tourism is having a massive global impact, not just on the global economy. Airports are seizing vast tracts of land. Residents living near airports are having their lives made a misery. Aircraft are rapidly becoming the number one global polluter, the effect is made all the more dramatic as the pollutants are emitted at high altitude where they have the maximum effect. Local cultures are being destroyed. In Tenerife local bars serve English beer and pander to English tourists, in Cyprus local Cypriot bars make way for karaoke nights and moronic English DJs. Hotels and tourist resorts need land and water. In Cyprus water is rationed to ensure a plentiful supply to hotel resorts. It is in the Third World that tourism is having the maximum impact.

Hotels, Tourist Resorts, the Supporting Infrastructure Needs Land

In Akamas, an area of outstanding natural beauty in the West of Cyprus, there is pressure to open it up for development and tourism.

In Malaysia, 29 local shops were destroyed to make way for a tourist development project.

Tourists like to be on prime coastal sites. These sites are often important fishery grounds, places where turtles come ashore to lay eggs.

Tourist Resorts Need Water

The villagers of Sinquerim (Goa) were denied piped water and have to rely on a well. Water is piped through the village to the nearby Taj Holiday Village and Fort Aguada complex.

Golf courses consume vast tracts of land. 350 new golf courses every year. The golf courses demand large volumes of water for irrigation; the pesticide, fertiliser, and herbicide run-off effects local water courses bringing damage to fisheries, polluting drinking water.

In Thailand the health of many local people has been damaged through eating fish poisoned by pesticide run-off from golf courses.

In Bali local people were forced from their land to make way for a golf course and hotel complex by shutting off the water that irrigated their fields.

Not everywhere are local people compliant. In Vietnam when Daewoo (one of the biggest exploiters in Vietnam) planned a £93 million golf course near Hanoi local villagers set up barricades and refused to budge. They were offered a paltry £125 per family to move.

Tourism is Destroying the Environment

Tenerife is rapidly becoming one big building site. The pleasant green Orotava valley in the north of Tenerife will soon have disappeared under concrete. Inter-island high speed ferries are killing whales and dolphins. In the south of Tenerife the sheer mass of whale watching trips is harassing whales and dolphins to death.

UK tour companies have codes of conduct on protecting the environment. These same tour companies are promoting whale watching trips, inter-island day trips that use high speed ferries.

Tourist feet trample across sacred religious sites, showing no respect to the indigenous cultures. Native people are often expected to perform sacred rituals on demand

In Peru, Yagua indians were forced from the remote Upper Amazon region to more accessible areas to enable tourists to see them perform their sacred rites. Viewing stations were built for the voyeurs.

In Hawaii many tourist complexes have been built on sites sacred to indigenous Hawaiians. Many burial grounds have been destroyed.

Tourism Directly and Indirectly Supports and Finances Human Rights Violations

Burma is one of the world's most repressive regimes. In scenes reminiscent of the Japanese occupation, forced labour is being used to prepare infrastructure and resort complexes. On one railway project alone, it has been estimated that 200-300 people have died through illness and exhaustion. On other similar projects the death rates are reported as averaging one a day. 30,000 forced labourers helped to construct the new airport at Bassein, when cholera broke out they received no medical care. Hundreds of thousands of people have been forced from their homes and lands to make way for tourist projects.

Like Burma, Turkey is another country with an appalling human rights record. Tourists who rarely venture beyond their air-conditioned hotel complexes fail to see the squalor or abuses. Hard currency earned from the tourists is used to buy military hardware to continue the repression against the Kurds and the illegal occupation of northern Cyprus.

Sexploitation is a growing sector of the tourist trade, with many tour companies offering special package tours to the best sex spots. Favoured destinations are Sri Lanka, the Philippines, Thailand, Brazil, with Eastern Europe rapidly developing its sex market-all perversions well catered for. Many children are forced to work as prostitutes in brothels. In Sri Lanka a survey showed that 86% of children had their first sexual experience with a foreign tourist, for the majority of the children they were aged between 12 and 13 years old at the time.

There is no such thing as a cheap holiday. The price is bought on the back of some one else's pain.

Tourism is often offered as a model to Third World countries as a means to earn hard foreign currency. Like many other models forced on the Third World, it tightens the shackles, for which only the West has the keys.

Third World countries are encouraged to build their tourist sector as a means of earning hard foreign currency. The reality is somewhat different. The holiday will be run by a foreign tour company, foreigners build, own and manage the tourist complexes, food and capital equipment is imported. What little is paid to local people will be marginally higher than the local wage rate thus ensuring the destruction of local industry. The few crumbs that trickle down to a handful of local people do not make up for the destruction of their environment and culture.

Zanzibar has a fragile eco-and social system dependent upon agriculture and fishing. Villagers are being evicted from their coastal villages and placed in compounds, their beautiful coral cottages left to rack and ruin. All inclusive tourist compounds surrounded by razor wire and protected by armed guards are built on the vacated land. Fish bought from local fisherman for the tourist compounds drives up the price reducing local people to a diet of boiled rice.

In Cuba dollar tourism is destroying the country its people and its culture. Two internal markets are developing-the dollar market and the pesos market. The real Cuba is discovered by visiting local people in their homes, not interacting with dollar prostitutes who work the tourist trade. Fidel Castro should hang his head in shame for turning his beautiful country into a dollar whore. Air transport is the fastest growing transport sector, with a consequential effect on global pollution. Air travel is the most energy intensive, polluting mode of travel.

Air transport has been growing at a rate of about 10% a year. Emissions from aircraft account for about 3% of global emissions, but because these emissions take place at high altitudes their significance and impact on climate change is considerably higher than the figure would suggest (aircraft have more than half the global warming potential of road traffic). Aircraft emissions are currently exempt from the Kyoto protocol under the climate convention. The aviation industry enjoys many tax concessions, including duty free fuel. Within the EU alone, the externalised costs are estimated at 4.6% of EU GDP, 16.4 billion euros/year.

Knock on effects include large infrastructure demands, noise, generation of road traffic etc.

Does Tourism Benefit the Third World?

Third World governments invariably justify the promotion of tourism as a driving force for economic development. *Anita Pleumarom* questions this claim and says that it is time to stop treating tourism as a holy cow to be protected and nurtured at all costs.

Tourism discourses are full of high-sounding rhetoric, liberally peppered with such terms as 'poverty reduction', 'sustainability', 'fair trade', 'participation', 'good governance', 'corporate social responsibility', and 'peace-building'. Moreover, concepts of 'new tourisms', such as community-based ecotourism, are projected as ways forward to reform mass tourism, which is increasingly dreaded because of its negative impacts.

But what about the reality behind the glossy rhetoric? What can be observed is, the more tourism leaders vow to protect ecosystems and natural resources in destinations, the more the environment gets thrown out of balance due to the continued frenzied construction of tourism facilities. The more we are told about tourism as a force for peace and understanding, the more the world is affected by the 'war on terrorism', and human-rights-abusing dictatorships like Burma use tourism to prop up their bad image.

The more decision-makers parade tourism policies for poverty elimination, the more the gap widens between the rich and the poor among and within nations, due to aggressive and unfair economic liberalisation. While people in rich countries drown in conspicuous consumption thereby destroying their own and others' life bases, communities in less and least developed countries only receive the crumbs from the wealth that capitalist growth produces.

A Global Business

Like other big industries, tourism is characterised by unhealthy mass concentrations of people, mass production, and mass activities. Today, it is common for people to criss-cross the globe to search for an exotic paradise, go shopping, attend a conference, play golf, cheer at a big sporting event, gamble in a casino, get thrilled in a theme park, relax in a spa resort or have medical or cosmetic surgery in a five-star hospital. En route, the travelling consumers can satisfy their needs and desires in the same fast food chains, supermarkets and designer brand shops like at home.

Tourism is a truly global business that turns everything on Earth-even the most sacred domains-into commodities. Most travellers would not want to wake up to the fact that they are just feeding a multi-billion-dollar industry and contributing to unsustainable patterns of consumption and production. And there is little awareness that as always, it is the poor who have to pay for the social and environmental costs of excessive tourism.

Governments emphasise tourism as a driving force for economic development. The latest World Tourism Barometer released by the United Nations World Tourism Organisation (UNWTO) indicates that international arrivals will amount to 880 to 900 million by the end of 2007, which points to a continuation of the sustained growth rate experienced over the past years. The Asia-Pacific region is the acknowledged motor behind the global tourism growth, with China and India representing the fastest-growing markets. According to the World Travel and Tourism Council (WTTC), travel and tourism presently employs approximately 231 million people and generates over 10.4% of the world's GDP.

Illusory Picture

However, the positive statistics offered by the WTTC and UNWTO project an illusory picture of the contribution of tourism particularly to the Third World.

These data often serve to justify expensive infrastructure developments that primarily benefit the top echelons in travel and tourism. Many of the projects are based on external borrowings, deepening the financial debt crisis for poor nations, and many of the supplies and equipment used in the development of these projects are imported and the personnel involved in construction engaged from abroad. Meanwhile, governments increasingly neglect the basic needs of local communities. Following the earthquake/tsunami disaster on Boxing Day 2004, for example, Thailand, Sri Lanka and India spent huge amounts of aid and taxpayers' money to help the tourism industry back on its feet, while fishing and agricultural communities were displaced; and until today, poor tsunami victims are lacking adequate housing, water supply, social services and opportunities to rebuild economic livelihoods.

'Leakages'

Tourism is a big money-spinner, but local residents do not get a fair share because most of the tourism revenue is siphoned away by urban-based and foreign investors. The tourism sector is notorious for causing financial 'leakage' (due to high import content, repatriation of profits by foreign-owned tourism companies, etc.), and unbalanced and inequitable distribution of income. According to current statistics compiled by the UN Conference on Trade and Development (UNCTAD), leakages in the tourism sector total up to 85% in some African least developed countries (LDCs), more than 80% in the Caribbean, 70% in Thailand and 40% in India.

Globalization has only worsened the economic conditions for poor countries. Tourism services negotiations under the World Trade Organisation (WTO)'s General Agreement on Trade in Services (GATS) as well as bilateral and regional free trade agreements (FTAs) have been used particularly by the US and European Union to increase pressure on governments of developing countries to abolish restrictions on foreign ownership and to allow a high degree of self-regulation by transnational corporations in the sector. As a result, tourism-related industries in developing countries are experiencing unprecedented mergers and acquisitions, squeezing local businesses that are ill-equipped to face the cut-throat competition favouring giant foreign firms.

New policies for tourism development as part of Special Economic Zones (SEZ) just add to the increasing inequality and asymmetry. The establishment of SEZs often involves the selling or leasing out of vast tracts of land to private developers and allows massive unregulated exploitation of natural and human resources for tourism purposes.

In recent years, however, tourism has as never before been highlighted as a dependent and high-risk industry. Frequent natural and man-made disasters, oil price hikes, exchange rate fluctuations and political turmoil have shown up the extreme vulnerability of the industry. Unexpected events such as the 11 September attacks in the US (2001), the Bali bombings (2002), the outbreaks of the SARS and avian flu epidemics (2003-04) and the tsunami disaster (2004) have all been the cause of major tourism slumps.

Ironically, the worsening climate crisis, to which the tourism industry itself has contributed significantly, is now ticking like a time bomb for the industry as many tourist attractions may be irreversibly destroyed by the impacts of climate change. Particularly threatened are low-lying coastal regions and small island developing states (SIDS). Many SIDS have developed tourism monocultures, with tourism receipts constituting up to 90% of services exports in the Bahamas, the Dominican Republic and the Maldives; in Antigua and Barbuda, tourism contributes directly and indirectly to over 75% of the GDP, according to the UNWTO.

While large tourism companies have responded quickly to impending emergencies by sponsoring high-tech disaster-warning systems and anti-terror security schemes, urgent mitigation and adaptation measures to enable poor communities to cope with any impending catastrophe are often delayed due to governments' lack of funding and other shortcomings.

Employment Effects

Tourism is seen as a boon in terms of employment for people in developing nations. But in fact, tourism-related jobs are uncertain, seasonal and part-time, with a high turnover of staff.

The loss of livelihoods through tourism-e.g., in agriculture and fisheries-has rarely been subjected to research. But the high out-migration of locals from tourist centres is a clear indication that tourism destroys more jobs than it creates.

Despite the tourism leaders' new affection for 'corporate social responsibility' (CSR), exploitation of tourism workers remains rampant. Worldwide, the industry is taking advantage of migrant workers who provide the cheapest labour, endure the harshest working conditions and are least likely to organise in trade unions.

Women in tourism are found to have the most dehumanising and the worst-paid jobs. Tourism has an infamous reputation of boosting the sex industry wherever it takes root. Efforts to make industry comply with the Code of Ethics promoted by the UNWTO have not helped to curb trafficking in women and girls for sex work in tourist destinations, which in many cases deprives the victims of their fundamental human rights and exposes them to health risks such as HIV/AIDS.

Industry self-regulation has proven an utterly inadequate tool in tourist centres, such as Pattaya in Thailand, Cancun in Mexico or Johannesburg in South Africa, where the sex, drugs and crime, gang violence, mafia-style politics and corruption are out of control.

The erosion of culture and traditional values is visible in all tourist destinations driven by over-commercialisation. Even many of the UN Educational, Scientific and Cultural Organisation (UNESCO)'s World Heritage sites are not properly protected from privatisation and 'Disneyfication'.

Tourism-including 'ecotourism'-also exploits indigenous and local communities and their cultures, turning them into mere exhibits for tourists' entertainment. The ugliest creations are 'human zoos' as set up by tour operators in the borderlands of Burma and Thailand to feature women from the Kayan ethnic group, also known as 'Long Neck' people because they wear rings that elongate their necks.

Many indigenous peoples' rights groups are therefore condemning tourism as a form of development aggression. Highlighting incidents of land rights violations and biopiracy, they have raised serious concerns about the rigorous approach of the 'ecotourism' industry that threatens indigenous peoples' sovereignty and aggravates conflicts and tensions in their communities in tourism-related processes at the UN (e.g., at the Commission on Sustainable Development, meetings of the Convention on Biological Diversity and the International Year of Ecotourism 2002).

Environmental Impacts

Tourism as 'sustainable development' is a myth as it continues to wreak havoc on land and marine ecosystems and biodiversity. Despite the industry's 'greenwash' attempts, fertile agricultural lands are still being cleared, forests cut down, mountains flattened, beaches dug up, and coral reefs destroyed to provide resources for more and more monstrous tourism complexes.

Moreover, tourism accelerates unhealthy urbanisation processes and contributes to traffic congestion, noise and air pollution and the dumping of waste and untreated sewage. The depletion and degradation of scarce water resources, particularly due to mushrooming golf courses and spa businesses, aggravates the water supply crisis in many communities. According to a UN study, the average tourist consumes as much water in 24 hours as a Third World villager requires to produce rice for 100 days.

High energy consumption in tourism facilities and greenhouse gas emissions linked to transportation, especially the explosive growth in air travel, contribute significantly to climate change.

Given all these serious impacts, tourism must no longer be treated like a holy cow that is protected and nurtured at all costs. Particularly in these times of looming social and environmental crises, governments and inter-governmental agencies like the UN should prioritise people's basic needs, particularly food security. Decision-makers should take a more responsible approach to tourism, by establishing strong legal and regulatory frameworks and ensuring the enforcement of these rules and regulations on the industry.

Corporate-driven voluntary initiatives, such as guidelines, codes of conduct and accreditation schemes, are not the key to effectively tackling tourism-related problems. What is needed instead is a people-centred approach to development that is aimed at reversing the negative impacts of globalization and restoring the values of justice, democracy and self-determination in development-an approach that allows local communities to reclaim land and resources that have been unfairly taken away, to rehabilitate the environment that greedy capitalists have ravaged and to revive traditions and cultures that have been distorted and exploited for profit-making purposes.

Internet Use in Tourism Industry

The Hospitality and Tourism industry was one of the earliest to go online. Since travel had few geographical boundaries, and, thanks to the widespread adoption of e-tickets, which airlines aggressively pushed, the airlines faced none of the logistical issues of online product retailers such as shipping and variable tax-collection schemes, the travel industry was uniquely suited for the Web. As the travel industry took off in the late 1970s and early 1980s, five major components came to comprise what this report will call the travel supply chain: Providers, Distributors, Travel Agents, Charge Card companies, and Travellers.

Providers-airlines, hotels and transportation companies; these entities invested in products (planes, properties, vehicles) and services for travellers.

Distributors-Computer Reservations Systems (CRSs); technology companies that consolidated supplier information, inventory and pricing data, and provided a way to electronically search, book and issue tickets and documents.

Travel Agents — Using CRSs, provided leisure and business travellers with one-stop shopping guidance and pricing and schedule advice to make reservations, issue tickets and provide ancillary services such as passport processing or currency conversion.

Charge Card companies-Played a role by making purchasing more convenient and secure for consumers, and by providing corporate buyers consolidated transaction data about their company's activities, which helped them with purchasing decisions and policy tracking.

Travellers — The end-user or customer, who may be leisure and/or corporate traveller, or a travel planner who books trips for an employee to take.

In addition, there are many matters involved in the selection and organisation of a holiday: gathering tour information, preparing the holiday package, confirming holiday information, actually having the holiday (including shopping for things and paying for them – not always easy in a foreign country), and sharing the holiday experience with other people during the holiday and once arriving back home.

Thus, it might be very difficult to manage all the people and matters precisely, and much of this potential complexity is about interaction through or using *information;* information management becomes an important consideration. One can deduce that information management will be important in the tourism industry, especially when one anticipates the consequences of the Internet – the most recent innovation in conveying information and sharing information between different parties.

We consider that it is necessary to combine the world of business and the world of technology in the tourism industry. In particular, information is interacting between tourism service providers and tourists.

The Online Travel Market

Use of the Internet by travellers to plan and book their trips continues to grow at a rapid rate. In the United States, according to the Travel Industry Association (TIA 2007), more than 75 million online travellers used the Internet in 2006 to get information on destinations or to check prices and schedules. From 1999 to 2006, online booking showed a remarkable double-digit growth for four consecutive years, with a spectacular 58% growth in 2001, followed by a 25% growth in 2002. While growth of the online traveller market has slowed, the number of online travellers who actually use the Internet to plan trips has remained relatively stable. A majority (67%) of online travellers say they consult the Internet to get information on destinations or to check prices or schedules.

Not surprisingly, nearly all online travel planners say that some of the trips planned on the Internet in the past year were for pleasure, vacation, or personal purposes. Three in ten say some of the trips planned on the Internet were for business or convention purposes. For online travel planning, online travel agency websites (such as Microsoft Expedia, Travelocity, or Priceline), search engine websites, and companyowned websites (airlines, hotels, etc.) are the most popular types of websites used. A majority of online travel planners also use destination websites.

Online travel planners do a variety of trip planning activities on the Internet. The most popular are searching for searching for airfares/schedules, maps or driving directions, and looking for places to stay.

While the growth in the number of Americans planning trips online has remained relatively stable, there has been strong growth in online travel booking. Indeed, four in ten (41%) online travellers are booking or making travel reservations online. This may include booking an airline ticket, hotel room, rental car or package tour online. Nearly all of those who make travel reservations online say they made reservations for pleasure, vacation, or personal purposes. About three in ten say they made reservations for business or convention purposes.

Among those who have booked travel online, the most popular item to purchase online is airline tickets. A majority of online travel bookers have reserved overnight lodging accommodations, and over one-third have made rental car reservations. The most popular types of websites used to book travel are online travel agency sites such as Microsoft Expedia, Travelocity or Priceline and company websites, such as airline, hotel, or rental car companies that sell directly to consumers. More than one-third of online travel bookers pay for or make their reservations

There is another important aspect and it is concerning the use of Internet While Travelling. Portable electronic communication devices such as cell phones, laptops, and personal digital assistants help people stay connected while away from home or office. In fact, large majorities of business travellers and pleasure travellers said that they brought cellular telephones with them on a trip taken in the past year. One in four business travellers brought a laptop computer with them on a trip, but only about one-tenth of pleasure travellers did so.

With the advent of wireless technology, portable devices are now being used to access the Internet for information, including travel information. Whether using a computer, cell phone, or PDA, four in ten business travellers say they have gone online while away from home. One in five pleasure travellers alsoclaim to have accessed the Internet while on a past-year pleasure trip.

Computer Reservation System (CRS) – Global Distribution System (GDS)

Deregulation meant that airlines that had previously operated under government-set fares which ensured they at least broke even now needed to improve operational efficiency to compete in a free market. While there were many aspects to this, one of the earliest changes was the development of the Airline Reservations System (ARS), its evolution into and proliferation of the Computer Reservations System (CRS), and then into Global Distribution System (GDS).

There are a few issuses about the use of CRS, like:

" *CRS are expensive for small and medium agencies to maintain and so Internet booking may be a more cost-effective medium;*

" *CRS do not always provide agents with improved business levels unless used to their full;*

" *The airlines have to pay fees to have a presence in CRS;*

" *There are new forms of technology that are overtaking CRS in some market segments (etravel agencies).*

The GDS took the place of CRS by the end of 1990s. The GDS operators collaborated with a variety of travel service providers such as airlines, cruise operators, hotels, railway companies and car rental companies, in addition to accepting special meal requests, managing seat allocation and performing backoffice accounting functions for travel agents.

There are about a dozen major GDSs worldwide. Amadeus had become the world leader after merging with SystemOne, achieving a 27 percent market share; Galileo and Sabre followed, each with 22 percent. After these came Worldspan, formed by Delta, Northwest and TWA, with a 10 percent share, and Abacus and Infini, the dominant CRSs in Asia, with a combined share of 9 percent.

The GDS technology developed with four functional components that, while integrated and interdependent, would later serve as points of differentiation when Internet providers entered the market and pulled apart the links of the supply chain. They were: inventory management and display; pricing-and fare-search engines; ticketing and document generators; and database reporting engines.

Use of the Internet by the Travel Agencies

Many travel agencies have developed an Internet presence by posting a website, with detailed travel information. Full travel booking sites are often complex, and require the assistance of outside travel technology solutions providers such as Travelocity. More and more tourists use the Internet websites to book and/or get useful informations.

These companies use travel service distribution companies who operate Global Distribution Systems (GDS), such as Sabre Holdings, Amadeus, Galileo and Worldspan, to provide up to the minute, detailed information on tens of thousands of flight, hotel, and car rental vacancies. Some online travel sites allow visitors to compare hotel and flight rates with multiple companies for free. They often allow visitors to sort the travel packages by amenities, price, and or proximity to a city or landmark.

Travel agents have applied dynamic packaging tools to provide fully bonded (full financial protection) travel at prices equal to or lower than a member of the public can book online. As such, the agencies' financial assets are protected in addition to professional travel agency advice. All travel sites that sell hotels online work together with numerous outside travel agents. Once the travel site sells a hotel, one of the supplying travel agents is contacted and will try to get a confirmation for this hotel. Once confirmed or not, the customer is contacted with the result. This means, that booking a hotel on a travel website will not get you an instant answer. Only some of the hotels on a travel website can be confirmed instantly (which is normally marked as such on each site). As different travel websites work with different suppliers together, each site has different hotels that it can confirm instantly. Some examples of such online travel websites that sell hotel rooms are Expedia, Orbitz and Trip Advisor.

There are also Internet travel agencies. These are Web sites that expand traditional agents' offerings. In addition to selling regular travel services such as air tickets and hotel rooms, they also offer travel tips, destination information and other services. Many large traditional agencies such as American Express and Liberty Travel have extended their shops to the virtual marketplace. Portal travel sites such as AOL and Yahoo! link customers looking for travel services to sites that may appear on their portals, but generally are powered by one of the big Internet travel agencies listed below. The last category for Internet travel agencies is bidding sites, such as Priceline. There, deep discount travel is available, but the travel provider's brand (usually an airline) is hidden until the purchase is complete.

The travel category lists those sites which are related to travel and the travel industry, including publications, travel agencies, transport services/people carriers, airports, destinations, resorts, travel and locality guides and accommodation.

The rise of online retail travel is taking place at a time whent the distribution function in tourism is changing in many ways. It is growing rapidly and will undoubtedly develop and change greatly in the future. It has provided an opportunity for non-tourism organisations such as Microsoft to enter the tourism market, and in doing so, to create competition for traditional high street travel agents.

Internet Marketing and the Norwegian Tourism Industry: A National Coordinated Marketing Effort on the Internet

The growth of the WWW on the Internet has created many opportunities as well as challenges for commercial businesses and industries. One of the challenges for a small-or medium-sized business is how to be found by the potential customer. This is underlined in a recent article about international marketing in *Sloan Management Review* (Quelch and Klein, 1996). The authors state that "the potential for 'information overload' is enormous". Even though the lack of rules on the net is critical to electronic commerce (Spar and Bussgang, 1996), this is not so critical for Internet as an information source. Stephan H. Haeckel, director of strategic studies at IBM's Advanced Business Institute writes (Deighton, 1996), "suddenly, and basically without warning, the Internet became a plausible and economical solution to a huge problem that has plagued business since 1960s: integrating increasingly heterogeneous IT systems between and within organizations.

The Web now offers providers and seekers of information around the globe easy access to one another that proprietary systems cannot match—but can easily benefit from".

It can be hypothesized that the net is of particular interest for the travel and tourism industry. In many countries the tourism industry has a high number of international visitors. Thus, the international travellers have a need for information. In tourism research, some scholars go even further and argue that "gathering, processing, and evaluating information can be seen as an integral part of the travel experience" (Snepenger and Snepenger, 1993. In Norway, the industry consists of many small-and medium-sized businesses.

Quite often, the tourists or consumers buy an experience, a holiday-product produced by a number of independent firms. Normally, this is also true when the consumer uses a travel agent or a tour operator. Moreover, independent travel has a substantial market share. In Europe, approximately 30% of summer travel abroad in 1996 belonged to the non-prebooking category, according to the *European Travel Monitor.* Thus, travellers have an obvious need for information, and businesses, on the other hand, have an information or marketing need. According to Pitt et al., " many marketing managers have (not) yet given careful consideration to the full potential of the WWW as a marketing tool, particularly with regard to its potential to move the prospective buyer from being a passive surfer to an interactive customer" (Pitt, Berthon, and Watson, 1996).

The purpose of this paper is (1) to present the NIN project and the Norwegian Tourism Guide, a Web site launched in January 1997, and (2) to discuss interactive marketing and interactivity as a basis for further development for the ongoing Norwegian project.

The Norwegian Tourism Guide

A national initiative for building a NIN (NIN, 95) in Norway was established in 1994. A number of application areas were chosen, the tourism industry being one of them.

The goal of the project was to introduce and extend the use of computer networks within the tourism industry, particularly for connecting the numerous small-and medium-sized businesses around the country.

The Internet was chosen as the main network, but the project is also following the development of other international network projects, such as the EU project TIM (Maartman-Moe et al., 1994), which are using point-to-point connections through Integrated Services Digital Network (ISDN) or Asynchronous Transfer Mode (ATM) networks (TIM, 1994).

The focus of the project is twofold: using the Net as a tool for cooperation and communication within the industry, and using the Net as a marketing and sales tool. We have started with the last focus and are now building a national framework on the WWW for marketing and selling Norwegian tourism products.

The project is run by NR, the Norwegian Computing Centre, on behalf of NORTRA, the Norwegian Tourist Board. The main activities in this phase were to develop demonstrators and define concepts and strategies.

During the preproject phase, we based the concept on three elements (Aanonsen, 1996): the organizational model for cooperation within the industry, the model for financing the system, and the technical solution. We chose distributed models for all three of the elements, to encourage participation of tourism businesses at all levels all over the country. During the implementation phase, user requirements became a significant part of the concept, and we included this as the fourth basic element of the solution.

National Cooperation and Strategic Alliances

To implement the solutions based on the elements we identified in the preproject phase, we made three main strategic decisions: to distribute responsibility for information to the regional level, to base the technical solution on regional Destination Information Systems (DIS), and to establish an alliance with a national ISP. The reasons for these decisions and our experiences from implementing them during the first phase is discussed in Aanonsen, 1997-1; how these related to relevant marketing and organizational theories in discussed in Tjostheim, 1997.

The basic element of the organizational model is cooperation between tourist boards around the country. The Norwegian tourism business is organized as a hierarchy with NORTRA on top, then five regional tourist boards covering most of the country, a number of local tourist boards or "destination companies" on the next level, and suppliers at the bottom.

Each regional tourist board is responsible for information from the region and for organizing further distribution of responsibility. The goal is to create a network where the responsibility is as close to the information source as possible.

NORTRA and the regional tourist boards are cooperating in a number of ways to promote Norway as a tourist destination on the international market.

An agreement between NORTRA and these partners is already established in such areas as brochure production and participation in fairs and campaigns. The cooperation on the Internet follows the same model, and the existing agreement will be extended to include this.

The regional tourist boards play a central role in the model for cooperation in this project. The responsibility for information about each region is distributed to these partners. The tourist boards produce presentations of their regions and provide general practical information. They also supply basic information about the suppliers in their region, which may include links to presentations from each business.

The regional tourist boards are also responsible for organizing the participation of local tourist boards and destinations within their region. These partners will be responsible for producing local presentations, including practical information about their destination. These partners may also take responsibility for the basic information about local suppliers and for linking their presentations to the framework.

The Partners in the Network

The project has also established cooperation with two main technical partners—an ISP and a provider of DIS (Sheldon, 1993). The national ISP contributes technical and marketing expertise for using the application on the Net.

Initially, the national ISP intended to contribute economically to the project since tourism was also part of their strategy for establishing new business on the Net. This intention changed for different reasons during the first phase of the project, and the tourism industry is taking over the costs, ownership, and responsibility for the solution.

At the regional and local level, the industry may chose any partner as ISP. The other main technical partner is the provider of DIS. They are providing a system the tourist board can use for a number of their tasks, such as producing brochures and providing information to local tourist offices.

The DIS also has extended routines for maintaining the quality of the information. Our main reasons for including this partner in the concept are to enable reuse of information and integrate Internet marketing in the set of tasks performed by a tourism organization. Our goal is both to increase the efficiency at the tourist boards and assure the quality of the information.

The Financial Model

The main element of the financial model is splitting costs and income between the different participants. The national tourist board is responsible for the central parts of the system, for the content at the national level, and for marketing the Web site. Their income will be from regional tourist boards and national providers of tourism products linked to the application. Regional and local tourist boards will finance the regional part of the solution and get the income from providers within their regions.

The Technical Solution

The main motivation for choosing this technical model is to enable reuse of information from regional and local tourist boards. These partners collect and distribute large amounts of information through their brochure production and daily work at the tourism offices. To make this information available on the Web, a technical solution based on their DIS was chosen. This information is combined with Web pages that profile destinations and products. The system consists of a Web application with a structure of national and regional front pages, a set of menus and icons, maps, and search functions accessing a national database. The information in this database is collected from the regional databases, which are part of DIS.

The Technical Model

The content of the Web site is based on information from brochures produced by the national and regional tourist boards. The design, layout, and structure is created for the Web and includes links, search functions, and "clickable" maps. The destination presentations are mainly created from the editorial parts of the brochures, which are designed to attract the tourist. They contain presentations of main attractions, activities, history, culture, nature, and geography. Useful practical information for travellers will also be part of a destination presentation. Presentations of products and providers will contain general information, "yellow pages" with basic information about each provider, the provider's own presentation, and direct access to main regional and national providers.

The information for the "yellow pages" is stored in the regional databases. This is in many ways the core of the system. The regional tourist boards maintain these databases for a number of purposes. By using them for Internet marketing, the tourist boards are able to reuse information efficiently. Local providers will also be able to present information about their products through these databases.

The regional tourist boards offers them differentiated presentations as either simple one-line entries, standardized one-, two-or three-page presentations, or links to their own Web presentation, by including their uniform resource locators (URLs) in the database.

User Requirements

The tourist can find different types of information through this Web application. The information is divided into presentations of destinations and presentations of products and providers. The user can navigate through the information in different ways, either by geography, by product type, or through the profiling material (Aanonsen, 1997-2).

These two types of presentations are also connected directly. The connection makes it possible for the users to find all products in one destination and to navigate from a presentation of a product to the presentation of the destination where the product is situated.

Modernisation of Hotel Industry

The hospitality and leisure sector is highly diverse and fragmented, consisting of organisations in gaming, attractions, golf, hotels, spa resorts, restaurants, pubs and clubs, health and fitness and holiday parks to name but a few.

Growth in Revenues – but also Costs

Over the last few years, growth in consumer spending has strengthened, providing a boost for the hospitality and leisure sector. In parallel to this growth, there has been a sharp increase in both utility and workforce costs, with increases in the minimum wage that have impacted profit margins with this growth in revenue.

The UK may well see its opt-out from the European Union working time directive phased out over the next few years, which could have a negative impact on the sector. Plans to overhaul immigration rules to attract more highly skilled workers from abroad may also add to an increasing wage bill.

Corporation tax changes will have differing affects on the industry, with hoteliers experiencing reductions in building allowances until 2011 when they will then be removed altogether. Smaller hospitality and leisure businesses face increases in the small business corporate tax rates.

The hospitality and leisure sector is extremely sensitive to consumer demand and as such is extremely susceptible to environmental, economic and market trends.

Interest rate rises in 2007 are expected to dampen consumer spending growth in 2008, and expected further strong growth in the euro zone over a more subdued growth in the US suggests that the number of overseas visitors is likely to slow, further impacting the sector.

Consolidation in Wet-led

With the implementation of the smoking ban in public areas, lack of outdoor space with current pub properties and restrictions on drink promotions, the outlook for growth in hospitality and leisure industries that are 'wet-led' is looking more subdued. As a result, this may lead to a period of consolidation in this sector, although restaurants may well improve due to the smoking ban.

Internet Booking Affects Growth

Growth in direct internet booking is putting further pressure on firms in the travel and hospitality sector, with travellers searching for better deals and booking later, resulting in shorter cash flow prediction analysis. Innovative firms, such as larger hotel operators, are increasing their use of in-house Internet booking systems and customer loyalty systems to help maximise revenue.

Changes in Health and Fitness

Government focus on tackling health issues will ultimately benefit the health and fitness sector. However, it is important that services offered are correctly aligned to demographic trends, older population requirements, spending capability and busy lifestyles. It is therefore important that the correct financial and operational metric information is available to maximise revenues and attract the correct customers.

Uncertainty in Gambling

Uncertainty around the government plans and revisions to the Gambling Act, allied to increased duty levied on casinos, will act as a deterrent to potential investors, which will dampen growth potential in this sector. This will be further exaggerated by the smoking ban referred to above.

Going for Growth

Whilst it is clear that the sector is and will continue to experience challenging times, there will be increased investment in the industry due to the successful Olympic 2012 bid, albeit predominately focused within the London region.

The winners in the highly diverse and fragmented hospitality industry will be those organisations that turn these challenges into opportunities, delivering against profit and growth targets, managing employee skills effectively and ensuring they have the right information available to them to increase the performance of their operations.

Online Travel: A Modern Trend of Tourism

eTourism is a subset of Travel technology with a particular focus on the tourism industry.

In June 2003, the United Nations Conference on Trade and Development, UNCTAD, established a Task Force on Sustainable Tourism for Development that proposes the use of the concept of e-tourism as part of a strategy to build sustainable and locally rooted tourism industries. The e-Tourism Initiative aims to promote ICT-driven growth through a participative strategy that includes networking and competitive collaboration for the tourism sector of developing countries.

4

Popularisation of Sustainable Tourism

Introduction: Recent and Future Trends in World Tourism

Tourism can be considered one of the most remarkable socioeconomic phenomena of the twentieth century.

From an activity "enjoyed by only a small group of relatively well-off people" during the first half of the last century, it gradually became a mass phenomenon during the post-World War II period, particularly from the 1970s onwards. It now reaches an increasingly larger number of people throughout the world and can be considered a vital dimension of global integration.

Although domestic tourism currently accounts for approximately 80% of all tourist activity (UN, 1999a), many countries tend to give priority to international tourism because, while the former basically involves a regional redistribution of national income, the latter has now become the world's largest source of foreign exchange receipts. According to the latest figures compiled by the World Tourism Organization (WTO), foreign exchange earnings from international tourism reached a peak of US$ 476 billion in 2000, which was larger than the export value of petroleum products, motor vehicles, telecommunications equipment or any other single category of product or service (WTO, 2001a).

While tourism provides considerable economic benefits for many countries, regions and communities, its rapid expansion can also be responsible for adverse environmental, as well as socio-cultural, impact. Natural resource depletion and environmental degradation associated with tourism activities pose severe problems to many tourism-rich regions. The fact that most tourists chose to maintain their relatively high patterns of consumption (and waste generation) when they reach their destinations can be a particularly serious problem for developing countries and regions without the appropriate means for protecting their natural resources and local ecosystems from the pressures of mass tourism.

The two main areas of environmental impact of tourism are: pressure on natural resources and damage to ecosystems. Furthermore, it is now widely recognized not only that uncontrolled tourism expansion is likely to lead to environmental degradation, but also that environmental degradation, in turn, poses a serious threat to tourism activities.

Pressure on natural resources In addition to pressure on the availability and prices of resources consumed by local residents—such as energy, food and basic raw materials—the main natural resources at risk from tourism development are land, freshwater and marine resources. Without careful land-use planning, for instance, rapid tourism development can intensify competition for land resources with other uses and lead to rising land prices and increased pressure to build on agricultural land. Moreover, intensive tourism development can threaten natural landscapes, notably through deforestation, loss of wetlands and soil erosion. Tourism development in coastal areas—including hotel, airport and road construction—is often a matter for increasing concern worldwide as it can lead to sand mining, beach erosion and other forms of land degradation.

Freshwater availability for competing agricultural, industrial, household and other uses is rapidly becoming one of the most critical natural resource issues in many countries and regions. Rapid expansion of the tourism industry, which tends to be extremely water-intensive, can exacerbate this problem by placing considerable pressure on scarce water supply in many destinations.

Water scarcity can pose a serious limitation to future tourism development in many low-lying coastal areas and small islands that have limited supplies of surface water, and whose groundwater may be contaminated by saltwater intrusion. Over-consumption by many tourist facilities—notably large hotel resorts and golf courses— can limit current supplies available to farmers and local populations in water-scarce regions and thus lead to serious shortages and price rises. In addition, pollution of available freshwater sources, some of which may be associated with tourism-related activities, can exacerbate local shortages.

Rapid expansion of coastal and ocean tourism activities, such as snorkelling, scuba diving and sport fishing, can threaten fisheries and other marine resources. Disturbance to marine aquatic life can also be caused by the intensive use of thrill craft, such as jet skis, frequent boat tours and boat anchors. Anchor damage is now regarded as one of the most serious threats to coral reefs in the Caribbean Sea, in view of the growing number of both small boats and large cruise ships sailing in the region. Severe damage to coral reefs and other marine resources may, in turn, not only discourage further tourism and threaten the future of local tourist industries, but also damage local fisheries.

Damage to Ecosystems

Besides the consumption of large amounts of natural resources, the tourism industry also generates considerable waste and pollution. Disposal of liquid and solid waste generated by the tourism industry has become a particular problem for many developing countries and regions that lack the capacity to treat these waste materials.

Disposal of such untreated waste has, in turn, contributed to reducing the availability of natural resources, such as freshwater.

Apart from the contamination of freshwater from pollution by untreated sewage, tourist activities can also lead to land contamination from solid waste and the contamination of marine waters and coastal areas from pollution generated by hotels and marinas, as well as cruise ships. It is estimated that cruise ships in the Caribbean Sea alone produced more than 70,000 tonnes of liquid and solid waste a year during the mid-1990s (UN, 1999a). The fast growth of the cruise sector in this and other regions around the world has exacerbated this problem in recent years. In fact, it is sometimes argued that the rapid expansion of cruise tourism calls for "the enforcement of an environmental protection 'level playing field' across the world's oceans and between the world's maritime tourism destinations" (Johnson, 2002). In addition, relatively high levels of energy consumption in hotels—including energy for air-conditioning, heating and cooking—as well as fuel used by tourism-related transportation can also contribute significantly to local air pollution in many host countries and regions. Local air and noise pollution, as well as urban congestion linked to intensive tourism development, can sometimes even discourage tourists from visiting some destinations.

Uncontrolled tourism activities can also cause severe disruption of wildlife habitats and increased pressure on endangered species. Disruption of wildlife behaviour is often caused, for example, by tourist vehicles in Africa's national parks that approach wild cats and thus distract them from hunting and breeding; tour boat operators in the Caribbean Sea that feed sharks to ensure that they remain in tourist areas; and whalewatching boat crews around the world that pursue whales and dolphins and even encourage petting, which tends to alter the animals' feeding and behaviour.

Similarly, tourism can lead to the indiscriminate clearance of native vegetation for the development of new facilities, increased demand for fuelwood and even forest fires. Ecologically fragile areas, such as rain forests, wetlands and mangroves, are also threatened by intensive or irresponsible tourist activity. Moreover, as will be discussed below, it is increasingly recognized that, the rapid expansion of nature tourism (or 'ecotourism') may also pose a threat to ecologically fragile areas, including many natural world heritage sites, if not properly managed and monitored.

The delicate ecosystems of most small islands, together with their increasing reliance on tourism as a main tool of socioeconomic development, means that this environmental impact can be particularly damaging since the success of the tourism sector in these islands often depends on the quality of their natural environment (UN, 1999b). In addition, pollution of coastal waters—in particular by sewage, solid waste, sediments and untreated chemicals—often leads to the deterioration of coastal ecosystems, notably coral reefs, and thus harms their value for tourism.

The equally fragile ecosystems of mountain regions are also threatened by increasing popular tourist activities such as skiing, snowboarding and trekking.

One of the most serious environmental problems in mountainous developing countries without appropriate energy supply is deforestation arising from increasing consumption of fuelwood by the tourism industry. This often results not only in the destruction of local habitats and ecosystems, but also in accelerating processes of erosion and landslides. Other major problems arising from tourist activities in mountain regions include disruption of animal migration by road and tourist facilities, sewage pollution of rivers, excessive water withdrawals from streams to supply resorts and the accumulation of solid waste on trails.

Environmental threats to Tourism

In many mountain regions, small islands, coastal areas and other ecologically fragile places visited by tourists, there is an increasing concern that the negative impact of tourism on the natural environment can ultimately hurt the tourism industry itself. In other words, the negative impact of intensive tourism activities on the environmental quality of beaches, mountains, rivers, forests and other ecosystems also compromise the viability of the tourism industry in these places.

There is now plenty of evidence of the 'life-cycle' of a tourist destination, that is, the evolution from its discovery, to development and eventual decline because of over-exploitation and subsequent deterioration its key attractions. In many developing and developed countries alike, tourism destinations are becoming overdeveloped up to the point where the damage caused by environmental degradation—and the eventual loss of revenues arising from a collapse in tourism arrivals—becomes irreversible.

Examples of such exploitation of 'non-renewable tourism resources' range from a small fishing village in India's Kerala state—which saw its tourist sector collapse after two decades of fast growth, because inadequate disposal of solid waste—to several places in the industrialized world, such as Italy's Adriatic coast and Germany's Black Forest. It can also be argued that environmental pollution and urban sprawl tend to undermine further tourist development in major urban destinations in developing countries, such as Bangkok, Cairo and Mexico City.

In addition, tourism in many destinations could be particularly threatened by external environmental shocks, notably the potential threat of global warming and sea-level rise. Significant rises in sea level could cause serious problems to tourism activities, particularly in low-lying coastal areas and small islands. Global warming is also expected to increase climate variability and to provoke changes in the frequency and intensity of extreme climate events—such as tropical windstorms and associated storm surges and coastal flooding—that may threaten tourism activities at certain destinations.

Sustainable Tourism Development

Countries and regions where the economy is driven by the tourism industry have become increasingly concerned with the environmental, as well as the socio-cultural problems associated with unsustainable tourism.

As a result, there is now increasing agreement on the need to promote sustainable tourism development to minimize its environmental impact and to maximize socioeconomic overall benefits at tourist destinations.

The concept of sustainable tourism, as developed by the World Tourism Organization (WTO) in the context of the United Nations sustainable development process, refers to tourist activities "leading to management of all resources in such a way that economic, social and aesthetic needs can be fulfilled while maintaining cultural integrity, essential ecological processes, biological diversity and life support systems".

It is increasingly realized that promoting greater community participation in tourism development not only provides stronger incentives to conserve natural capital, but can also lead to a more equitable sharing of benefits and thus greater opportunities for poverty alleviation.

But while ecotourism and PPT both aim to increase community participation in general, PPT also goes beyond this goal in that it includes specific mechanisms to enhance the participation of and opportunities for the poorer segments of society. Three key components of the PPT approach are:

(a) improved access to the economic benefits of tourism by expanding employment and business opportunities for the poor and providing adequate training to enable them to maximize these opportunities;

(b) measures to deal with the social and environmental impact of tourism development, particularly the above-mentioned forms of social exploitation, as well as excessive pressure on natural resources, pollution generation and damage to ecosystems; and

(c) policy reform, by enhancing participation of the poor in planning, development and management of tourism activities pertinent to them, removing some of the barriers for greater participation by the poor, and encouraging partnerships between government agencies or the private sector and poor people in developing new tourism goods and services.

Some of these PPT concepts are beginning to be implemented in several developing countries, such as Ecuador, Namibia, Nepal and Uganda. In Namibia, for example, the implementation of a PPT approach to the development and management of the country's community-based tourism segment appears to have made a significant contribution towards poverty reduction.

Several studies have shown that financial returns from community-based natural resource management and tourism ventures in Namibia usually exceed their investments and are thus a viable option for generating sustainable economic returns, while promoting environmental conservation and cultural traditions in rural areas. There is now evidence of a successful introduction of the PPT approach by the Namibia Community-based Tourism Association

(Nacobta), a non-profit organization that supports poor local communities—including small entrepreneurs with inadequate skills or access to financial resources—in their efforts to develop tourism enterprises in the country.

Nacobta supports its members at both micro and macro levels, mainly through the provision of grants, loans, training, capacity building in the areas of institutional development and marketing training, as well as in negotiations with relevant government agencies and the mainstream tourist industry. Nacobta is explicitly propoor not only because it represents the poorest segment of the country's tourism industry, but also because most of its members live on communal land areas, where themajority of the inhabitants have an average per capita income of less than US$1 a day and depend on subsistence agriculture. One of the main objectives of Nacobta is "to raise the income and employment levels of these areas through tourism, in order to improve the living standards of people in communal areas".

The pro-poor tourism approach of Nacobta is thus different from conventional tourism because members of local communities both own and manage the tourism enterprises, whose economic benefits flow directly into community funds or as formal sector wages, temporary remuneration to casual labourers and income to informal sector traders. There is also evidence that the financial returns from most community-based tourism enterprises supported by Nacobta "has changed their communities from being poor or very poor to being better off".

The Impact of Tourism on Tribals

Tourism can be a very destructive force. Over years it can lead to the development of certain coastal areas and other sites, to become dedicated almost entirely to the business of tourism. Once the tourist demand changes and heads elsewhere, all that is left is an area full of hotels, bars and over used parks, that are basically degraded and not attractive for more tourists. One good example of this is the East Coast of Spain, which became very popular with tourists during the 1970s, but during the 1980s Spain fell out of favour. Everyone considered that particular coastline to be very degraded and so the crowds headed to Turkey instead.

This pattern is not just confined to coastal areas. Tribal and minority peoples in developing countries are also targeted by tourism and that has complicated effects on how such people see themselves or how they are treated in the development process. Perhaps one good example of this is the Masai in Kenya who happen to live near the large safari parks believe that the influence of tourism on the Masai has not been positive or at least that the Masai have not benefited from tourism as much as they could have. Often they are presented to foreign tourists as part of the safari package and "model" Masai villages have great numbers of tourists visiting to observe their lifestyle. Anthropologists would use the term "staged authenticity" for the idea that because one has travelled long distance, it is important to go and see something that is different, exciting, exotic and remote. Many places such as Peru, Thailand and India practice this. It doesn't necessarily follow that the people who partake in these exercises are necessarily having a bad impact upon the tribal communities. However, sometimes it hinders the integration of these people within wider society and it can also increase barriers between minority and majority groups who live in the country as a whole.

In Thailand, most tribes-people are found in the north and migrated over 100 years ago from the southern part of China into Laos, Myanmar (Burma), Vietnam and Thailand. Many argue that they have preserved their way of life. The impact tourism has had on this is controversial. There are six major tribes, the Karen, Hmong, Yao or Mien, Lisu, Lahu, Lawa and Akha. They have maintained their distinctive cultures and tourists do visit these hilly areas to catch a glimpse of their way of life. There are several smaller tribes including the Paduang, or the "Long Necks."

The term 'long-neck' stems from the practice of women adorning their necks with brass coils. This tribe has proved to be a major tourist attraction ever since they began fleeing Burma, more than a decade ago. By tradition, girls begin to wear coils before puberty, and these are augmented until they weigh as much as 11 pounds. The coils force the chin upward while pressing down the collar bones and ribs, elongating the neck.

Some critics argue that the custom has become distorted and exploited by tourism as busloads are encouraged to come and view the women, with their elongated necks.

Has tourism led to any breaches of human rights or the displacement of local communities?

This is one of the great controversies of tourism. There are many examples of national parks being formed by removing people to parks elsewhere. For example, to create the Lake Rara national park in Nepal, they had to move some 400 villagers, the Chhetri people, somewhere else. This is a big debate simply because on the one hand ecologists would like to believe that the park should be left to the native animals and plants. On the other hand, anthropologists and sociologists would like to see the people and the landscape together—indeed the landscape wouldn't exist if the people were not there already. Clearly, the problem is how far tourism can be used as a way to put into practise policies for moving people, which wouldn't be allowed under normal circumstances.

There are many examples of national parks, which have people involved: the question is how many people and also what sort of people? The Tambopata reserve in Ecuador is famous for its integration of the indigenous people who inhabit the forests. Tourists come to look at the forest area and observe local practices. Sometimes, the problem is that once a national park is created, there are new incentives for people to move into the area, cut down the trees, cultivate agriculture and then claim special status for being there. One of the real problems in creating a national park is deciding who is going to be included and who is not.

The Impacts of Different Kinds of Tourism from Backpackers to Package Tourism

There are many types of tourism and we should differentiate between them. When tourism simply consists of backpackers moving into a place, living in local houses and then moving on, it doesn't generally have much of an environmental or social impact. However, the other extreme where large hotels and theme parks are developed obviously has huge impacts upon the local environment, employment opportunities and the very nature of development within the region. It is important to differentiate between the two. Although a lot of people believe that once you start having backpacker tourism, over time, gradually it will change and become more like mass tourism, especially once a market has been established.

Many villages in developing countries around the world receive great numbers of tourists visiting to observe their lifestyle. Anthropologists would use the term "staged authenticity" for the idea that because one has travelled a long distance, it is important to go and see something that is different, exciting, exotic and remote. Many places such as Peru, Thailand and India practice this. It doesn't necessarily follow that the people who partake in these exercises are necessarily having a bad impact upon the tribal communities. However, sometimes it hinders the integration of these people within wider society and it can also increase barriers between minority and majority groups who live in the country as a whole. This tour notice board shows a "native" with a bone through the nose. It shows the mainstream view of hill tribes as primitive, using a colonial image of a black man with a bone.

It is up to the local authorities and governments to regulate these activities. Some may actively promote such cultural tourism. Others may wish to stringently police tourist behaviour in the presence of these communities.

Have governments and NGO's noted the negative impact mass tourism has had in some areas and what is being done about it?

Virtually all NGO's have noted the potential negative impact of tourism. The WWF is very keen to regulate the use of safari areas and concerned about the potential damage to wildlife resulting from tourism. Many governments, however, take a very different line. The government of Bhutan in the Himalayas, for example, is unusual because it has imposed a very high tourist tax upon tourists going into Bhutan—it can be something like $100-200 a day. This is a radical effort to try and reduce tourist numbers but also increase the revenue coming from tourism—a very successful strategy. Nepal on the other hand, just next door, doesn't take that strategy. It has gone for the "high numbers of tourists" approach. This might cause overloading of certain cities and trekking routes. Other countries such as Kenya and Peru are also very keen on increasing the number of tourists into the country.

How can sustainable tourism practices be made widely attractive and implemented? How much regulation of tourism is there already?

I think it is important to define sustainable tourism precisely. Many people talk about sustainable tourism, when they are actually thinking about ecotourism. Ecotourism is tourism which focuses upon remote ecological and attractive areas such as rainforests or reefs. It can also look at remote people such as the Masai. Many people believe that this can be an ecologically friendly form of tourism but there is a considerable body of research to suggest that this is not the case and that it can actually wreak a lot of damage on fragile eco-systems or increase the pressure upon remote people such as the Masai. It is much more important, I think, to talk about sustainable tourism which deals with all sorts of tourism from the mass tourism on the beaches of Spain, to the cultural tourism of Stratford upon Avon, as well as travelling to exotic rainforests and reefs. It is important to somehow try and increase awareness of the potential damages of tourism in particular localities. The trouble is that it is very difficult to achieve and one of the key problems in achieving sustainable tourism is that there is no such thing as "the" tourism industry. Tourism exists because of the juxtaposition of many different industries such as airlines, tour operators, hotels, tour guides and ice-cream sellers, all operating together at the same time. It is very difficult to come up with policy measures to try and integrate all these different people working in the same direction at the same time.

How do different countries respond to the need for sustainable tourism? Are developing countries more effective regulators than the developed world?

Generally speaking, developing countries have a harder time regulating tourism than the wealthier countries of Europe and North America. This is basically because these countries are much more used to dealing with tourism. They have a much greater local capacity for implementing policy, making decisions and regulating laws whereas in many developing countries it is very difficult to do anything once you are outside the capital city.

That said, there are some interesting initiatives going on. Bhutan is a good example of one country that has decided not to encourage large amounts of tourism. Within other countries there are other measures for managing tourism. One approach, for example, is land use zoning, which basically means you might send one kind of tourist to an area where they might do drinking, beaches, theme parks, and another sort of tourist such as bird watchers or cultural tourists somewhere else, and never mix the two.

This can increase the great ability to profit from both sides of the market as long as what happens at each place is carefully controlled. It is interesting to note that many developing countries are trying to overcome the ability for tourists to pick and choose between places by trying to market each location as distinctively special. During the 1970s, countries would only market places on the basis of sun, sea and sand, which was great, but so many places in the world offer those things.

However, if you try and present an image of a country as having not only sun, sea and sand but also offering a specific type of wildlife or culture then this can increase a regular flow of tourists who really want to visit that particular country. For example, have you ever seen an advert for Malaysia which doesn't have a picture of an orangutan in it? This is just one technique with which Malaysia can say, "Look we're different, come here".

The World Tourism and Travel Council has set up a number of schemes to try and regulate international tourism. This is a body that has been set up by many large tourism companies to try and regulate tourism and increase communication between different parties and to try and improve the level of tourism throughout the world.

In many ways it does a very good job but many developing countries also criticise the WTTC for not doing enough. The WTTC set up an organisation called Green Globe, which was an attempt to try and increase the environmental performance of tourism companies. However, it has also given a lot of awards to hotels in different countries, which have been criticised widely by local NGO's and activists for overlooking the rights of local people. The actual rules by which environmental performance is governed is extremely controversial.

Advertising exactly what environmental performance is remains a major problem, not just in tourism but in all areas of environmental policy. It is difficult to demonstrate that many people make claims about environmental performance, which are highly controversial. It's a sad fact that many high value tourist resorts advertise themselves as environmentally efficient and friendly just because they might use things like low wattage light bulbs or recycle a lot of waste within the hotel, but in fact they may not want to employ local people to work in the place and there might be all sorts of implications for land prices and access to scarce water supplies or fuel supplies which may impact negatively on other people in the area. There has to be a much more holistic approach to integrating tourist development with local communities and local environments.

What can companies and the private sector do to help? Is there self-regulation?

There are a lot of examples of self-regulation and many of these are quite successful within their own areas. For example, the sustainable hotels initiative is a generally successful programme to try and increase the adoption of environmental practices within hotels. This is the case mainly in developed countries, England in particular and some of these practices might include not washing towels every day because it wastes electricity; or using low wattage electricity bulbs or recycling soap containers.

These of course are not to be dismissed—they are important measures. However, they are somewhat reductionist. They are very easy to see within a hotel but they do not get involved with any issues outside the hotel.

One particularly controversial example is that many NGOS would like hotels to advertise that their customers should not get involved with local prostitution. But the hotels claim this is not their concern and do not want to be seen preaching to customers. Both sides have very good reasons for stating their own position. Knowing where to draw the line between how far a hotel can act and what it really shouldn't be involved with is a very difficult decision.

Travel Ethic for Responsible Travel

As the new millennium unfolds, we are becoming increasingly aware of the finite, interconnected and precious nature of our planet home. Likewise, tourism is becoming an increasingly popular expression of this awareness. With advances in transportation and information technology, ever more remote areas of the earth are coming within reach of the traveller. In fact, tourism is now the world's largest industry, with nature tourism the fastest growing segment. In response to this increasing appreciation of nature experiences, a new travel ethic has arisen which is now called ecotourism. The Nature Conservancy has joined the World Conservation Union (IUCN) in adopting the following definition of ecotourism:

> *"Environmentally responsible travel to natural areas, in order to enjoy and appreciate nature (and accompanying cultural features, both past and present) that promote conservation, have a low visitor impact and provide for beneficially active socioeconomic involvement of local peoples."*

Travelarks is a strong proponent of responsible travel ethics and here are a few pointers that will go a long way in ensuring

- Consumption of alcoholic beverage and smoking is prohibited
- Participants should try and be one with the group and add value to the ambiance
- Try not to venture alone without informing the concerned authority
- Please be responsible and take care of your own belongings and also remind others if they fail to do so
- Please do not litter-Leave nothing behind other than your foot prints (boot prints should we say!)
- Please do not harm the ecological balance
- Do not contribute unwanted decibels to the environment
- Respect the local culture and tradition
- Travelarks would not fetter you with undue restrictions, but when required please abide by them
- Remember that you are special in your own way and add a lot of value to the group in a unique way-please bring the best of your spirits.

OECD Tourism Trends & Policies 2010

The tourism sector, a vital driver of job-creation and growth, is under pressure. Facing an increasingly competitive landscape, tourism in many OECD countries has started to lag, in both growth rate and productivity. This book defines the major trends and challenges facing tourism in the next decade – from globalization to environmental issues.

To address these challenges, the book then provides specific policy guidance and recommendations for making tourism more competitive and environmentally sustainable. Tourism data from 42 countries are presented and analysed including all OECD countries, and fast-growing tourism centres such as Brazil, Chile, China and India.

OECD countries continue to play a predominant role in international tourism, representing about 60% of the global tourism market. They also benefit from a domestic tourism which is in many economies more important that international tourism.

During the last 20 years, the growth rate of international tourism arrivals in OECD countries, whilst 1.6% below the worldwide rate, has averaged 2.8% per year, well ahead of the GDP growth rate of 2.4% for the zone, with OECD countries accounting for about 60% of the global tourism market. In the OECD area, tourism GDP accounts for up to 11% of GDP and even more in terms of employment.

Many of the 12 non-member economies (Brazil, Chile, China, Egypt, Estonia, India, Indonesia, Israel, Romania, the Russian Federation, Slovenia and South Africa) included in this report have a tourism economy representing significant shares of GDP and of total employment. They are also among the fastest growing countries as international tourism destinations.

2010 Commonwealth Games

The 2010 Commonwealth Games are the nineteenth edition of the Commonwealth Games, and the ninth to be held under that name. The Games are scheduled to be held in Delhi, India between 3 October and 14 October 2010. The games will be the largest multi-sport event conducted to date in Delhi and India generally, which has previously hosted the Asian Games in 1951 and 1982. The opening ceremony is scheduled to take place at the Jawaharlal Nehru Stadium in Delhi. It will also be the first time the Commonwealth Games will be held in India and the second time the event has been held in Asia (after 1998 in Kuala Lumpur, Malaysia).

In addition to the Commonwealth Games, the city of Pune, Maharashtra hosted the 3rd Commonwealth Youth Games between October 12 and 18, 2008. The Youth Games offered nine sports: athletics, badminton, boxing, shooting, swimming, table tennis, tennis, weightlifting and wrestling.

Organisation

Organising Committee

The organisation was beset by delays: in January 2005, the Indian Olympic Association vice-chairman Raja Randhir Singh expressed concern that Delhi was not up to speed in forming and organising its games committee and, following a 2009 Indian Government report showing two thirds of venues were behind schedule, Commonwealth Games Federation president Mike Fennell stated that the slow progress of preparations represented a serious risk to the event.

Singh called for a revamp of the games' organizing committees: Jarnail Singh, a former Secretary of the Government of India, was appointed as the Chief Executive Officer and Indian Olympic Association president Suresh Kalmadi was appointed as head of the committee. In spite of delays, commentators stated that they are confident that India will successfully host the games and do so on time.

Costs

The total budget estimated for hosting the Games is US$ 1.6 billion and this amount excludes non-sports-related infrastructure development in the city like airports, roads and other structures.

This will likely make the 2010 Commonwealth Games the most expensive Commonwealth Games ever, being larger than the previous games in Melbourne 2006 (approx. US$ 1.1 billion).

Transport

In response to concerns over the large number of trains that pass by the Delhi metropolitan region daily, construction of road under-bridges and over-bridges along railway lines has been started. To expand road infrastructure, flyovers, cloverleaf flyovers, and bridges have been planned to improve links for the Games and city in general.

Road-widening projects have begun with an emphasis being placed on expanding national highways. To improve traffic flow on existing roads, plans are underway to make both the inner and outer Ring roads signal free.

To support its commitment to mass transport, nine corridors have been identified and are being constructed as High Capacity Bus Systems. Six of these corridors are expected to be operational in 2010.

Additionally, The Delhi Metro will be expanded to accommodate more people and boost the use of public transport during the 2010 games. At 420 km long, it will be one of the world's longest networks and it will extend to Gurgaon and the Noida area. For this exponential increase of the network, Delhi Metro will deploy 14 tunnel boring machines, an unprecedented number in an Asian country.

Indira Gandhi International Airport is being modernized, expanded, and upgraded. Costing nearly US$ 1.94 billion, Terminal 3 will improve airport passenger capacity to more than 37 million passengers a year by 2010. A new runway is being constructed, allowing for over 75 flights an hour and – at over 4400 metres long– it will be one of Asia's longest. The entire airport will be connected to the city via a six-lane highway and the Delhi Metro.

Venues

Existing and new stadia in Delhi will be used to house the sports during the Games:

- Jawaharlal Nehru Stadium, Delhi – Weightlifting
- Dhyan Chand National Stadium – Hockey
- Indira Gandhi Arena – Archery, cycling, gymnastics, wrestling
- Delhi University sports complex – Rugby sevens
- Thyagaraj Stadium – Netball
- Siri Fort Sports Complex – Badminton, Squash
- Dr. Karni Singh Shooting Range – Shooting
- Talkatora Stadium – Boxing
- SPM Swimming Pool Complex – Aquatics
- RK Khanna Tennis Complex – Tennis
- Yamuna Sports Complex – Table tennis.

The opening and closing ceremonies, athletics, lawn bowls, and weightlifting will take place at the Jawaharlal Nehru Stadium, Delhi, which will have a capacity of 75,000 spectators after renovation for the games.

Archery, cycling, gymnastics, and wrestling will take place at the Indira Gandhi Arena, the largest indoor sports arena in India and the second-largest in Asia, which seats 25,000 people. Located at the Indraprastha Estate in the eastern region of New Delhi, the arena will be connected to other venues via dedicated bus lanes and mass transportation. The arena will be renovated for the Games. There are 26 new stadiums which will be utilized for the Commonwealth Games. Some older ones will be upgraded and some new will be constructed.

Green Games

The organisers signed a Memorandum of Understanding (MoU) with the United Nations Environment Programme to show the intention to host a "sustainable games" and to take the environment into consideration when constructing and renovating venues.

Thyagaraj Stadium is intended to be a key example of environmentally-considered construction.

In opposition to this intention, a number of environmental controversies arose and the adverse ecological impact of various aspects of the games have been protested by city residents. City residents filed a public interest petition to the Supreme Court of India against the felling of 'heritage' trees in the Siri Forest area to make way for Games facilities.

The court appointed architect Charles Correa to assess the impact and he severely criticized the designs on ecological grounds. In spite of this, in April 2009 the Supreme Court allowed the construction on the grounds that "much time had been lost" and "the damage already caused to the environment could not be undone".

The Commonwealth Games village, located on the flood plains of the Yamuna, has also been the subject of controversies about the flouting of ecological norms.

After a prolonged legal battle between city residents and the state, construction was permitted to continue on the basis of an order of the Supreme Court of India in July 2009, which held that the government had satisfied the requirements of "due process of the law" by issuing public notice of its intention to begin construction work in September 1999 (a date four years prior to the acceptance of Delhi's bid for the games).

Marketing

The games mascot is an anthropomorphic tiger called Shera; a name derived from the Hindi word Sher – meaning tiger.

Other Preparation

In preparation for an influx of English-speaking tourists for the Games, the Delhi government is implementing a program to teach English, and the necessary skills for serving tourists, to key workers – such as cab drivers, security workers, waiters, porters, and service staff. In the two years prior to the Games 2,000 drivers were taught English. The program aims to teach 1,000 people English per month in the hope of reaching all key workers by March 2010. In addition to Delhi, the Indian Government plans to expand the program to teach people in local tourist destinations in other parts of India.

To prepare for the energy-usage spike during the Games and to end chronic power cuts in Delhi, the government is undertaking a large power-production initiative to increase power production to 7,000 MW (from the current 4,500 MW). To achieve this goal, the government plans to streamline the power distribution process, direct additional energy to Delhi, and construct new power plants. In fact, the government has promised that by the end of 2010, Delhi will have a surplus of power.

In addition to physical preparation, India and Delhi will offer free accommodation for all athletes at the Games Village, as well as free transport and other benefits, such as a free trip to the famed Taj Mahal and a reserved lane for participants on selected highways.

The Games Village will house over 8,000 athletes and officials for the Games. Indian states will train state police forces to handle tourist-related issues and deploy them prior to the Games.

A massive construction and "beautification" project has resulted in the demolition of hundreds of homes and the displacement of city dwellers – at least 100,000 of New Delhi's 160,000 homeless people have removed from shelters, some of which have been demolished. Bamboo screens have been erected around city slums to separate visitors from the sights of the slums, a practice which human rights campaigners have deemed dishonest and immoral.

The Delhi High Court is set to implement a series of "mobile courts" to be dispatched throughout Delhi to relocate migrant beggars from Delhi streets.

The mobile courts would consider each beggar on a case-by-case basis to determine whether the beggar should be sent back to his/her state of residence, or be permitted to remain in government-shelters.

Queen's Baton Relay

The Queen's Baton relay began when the baton, which contains Queen Elizabeth II's message to the athletes, left Buckingham Palace on 29 October 2009. The baton will arrive at the 2010 Games opening ceremony on 3 October 2010, after visiting the other 70 nations of the Commonwealth and travelling throughout India, reaching millions of people to join in the celebrations for the Games.

The baton was designed by Michael Foley, a graduate of the National Institute of Design. It is a triangular section of aluminium twisted into a helix shape and then coated with coloured soils collected from all regions of India.

The coloured soils are a first for the styling of a Queen's Baton. A jewel-encrusted box was used to house the Queen's message, which was laser-engraved onto a miniature 18 carat gold leaf – representative of the ancient Indian 'patras.

The Queen's baton is ergonomically contoured for ease of use. It is 664 millimetres high, 34 millimetres wide at the base, and 86 millimetres wide at the top and weighs 1,900 grams.

The Queen's baton has a number of technological features including:

- The ability to capture images and sound
- Global positioning system (GPS) technology so the baton's location can be tracked
- Embedded light emitting diodes (LEDs) which will change into the colours of a country's flag whilst in that country
- A text messaging capability so that people can send messages of congratulations and encouragement to the Baton bearers throughout relay.

Sports

The triathlon appears likely to be excluded from these games as there is no suitable location for the swimming stage. The organisers have also proposed removing basketball, but want to include archery, tennis, and billiards and snooker for men. Cricket, although in strong demand, may not make a come-back as the Board of Control for Cricket in India were not keen on a Twenty20 tournament, but the organisers did not want a one day tournament.

Participating Nations

There are currently 71 nations planning to field teams at the 2010 Commonwealth Games. As Fiji is suspended from the Commonwealth, it has been banned from participating in the Games. Rwanda may field a team for the games since becoming a Commonwealth member in 2009. Controversies

Labour Violations

Campaigners in India have accused the organisers of enormous and systematic violations of labour laws at construction sites. Although official numbers have not been released, it is estimated that over 415,000 contract daily wage workers are working on Games projects. Unskilled workers are paid 85 to 100 Indian rupees (INR) per day while skilled workers are paid 120 to 130 INR per day for eight hours of work. Workers also state that they are paid 134 to 150 INR for 12 hours of work (eight hours plus four hours of overtime). Both these wages contravene the stipulated Delhi state minimum wage of INR 152 (approx. US$3) for eight hours of work.

These represent violations of the Minimum Wages Act, 1948; Interstate Migrant Workmen (Regulation of Employment and Condition of Services) Act 1979, and the constitutionally enshrined fundamental rights per the 1982 Supreme Court of India judgement on Asiad workers. The public have been banned from the camps where workers live and work – a situation which human rights campaigners say prevents the garnering of information regarding labour conditions and number of workers.

There have been documented instances of the presence of young children at hazardous construction sites, due to a lack of child care facilities for women workers living and working in the labour camp style work sites. Furthermore, workers on the site of the main Commonwealth stadium have reportedly been issued with hard hats, yet most work in open-toed sandals and live in cramped tin tenements in which illnesses are rife. The High Court of Delhi is presently hearing a public interest petition relating to employers not paying employees for overtime and it has appointed a four-member committee to submit a report on the alleged violations of workers rights.

During the construction of the Games Village, there was controversy over financial mismanagement, profiteering by the Delhi Development Authority and private Real Estate Companies, and inhumane working conditions.

5

Hospitality Trends of Geographical Phenomenon

Tourism is an inherently geographical phenomenon. Tourism's concepts are embedded in the physical and cultural attributes of a visited place and the movement of people from the realm of the known to the realm of the unfamiliar or exotic. Each destination is important, as it holds some physical or cultural attribute that is distinctive to that place and thus the tourist seeks out this distinctiveness on the Earth's surface. Tourism also holds particular spatial characteristics that lure tourists, such as different climates, physical landscapes, cultural landscapes, and often ethnic variation. These spatial characteristics are an important quality to a specific region's tourism industry.

Geographers have approached tourism studies using spatial-analytical methods that helped to identify historical connections to contemporary patterns. This approach enabled scholars to forecast possible changes to the physical and cultural landscapes of a particular place resulting from tourists flows and activities.

The geographical scope and economic size of modern tourism encompasses a wide range of disciplines. Thus, the body of literature covering tourism related topics is enormous. In this chapter we will review some of the early literature that is important in understanding the ways in which tourism research has taken place. We will also discuss tourism as a modern industry in three separate but equally important and over lapping categories, world tourism, in Central America, and tourism in Honduras. We will also discuss my research methodologies in the field and the geographical perspectives we used as we conducted my fieldwork on one very small island.

Review of the Literature

Geographers became interested in tourism as a subject of research in the 1930s. *Ralph Brown (1935:471)*, in an article in the Geographical Review, offered "an invitation to geographers" writing "From the geographical point of view the study of tourism offers inviting possibilities for the development of new and ingenious techniques for research, for discovery of facts of value in their social implications in what is virtually a virgin field." However, as *Campbell (1966)* noted, this so called invitation, was accepted by only a few geographers and therefore techniques for collection, analysis, interpretation, and cartographic representation of tourism data lagged. After World War II, however, those who began conducting tourism studies did so under the guise of economic geography, and looked at the regional and destination economic impacts of tourism as well as travel routes. American geographers such as *Cooper (1947)* were involved in discussions concerning seasonality and travel motivations which became a major precursor to works conducted in the 1980s and 1990s. By the 1950s, although many scholars felt tourism studies had not yet received the proper attention by geographers, *McMurray (1954)* included tourism studies in a chapter in an overview text on the state of geography in the United States.

American geographers were not the only scholars conducting tourism research during these initial decades. In Britain and Canada, Gilbert and Wolfe, also delved into tourism studies. *Gilbert (1939, 1949)* published articles concerning British seaside resorts while *Wolfe (1951)* conducted research on "cottaging" in Ontario. Wolf's studies created a base for later works on second home development. After Gilbert's initial work little other research was conducted in the United Kingdom until the 1960s. During the 1960s geographical research on tourism accelerated and continued to grow rapidly over the next decade. Several influential reviews were produced in the 1960s such as, *Murphy (1963), Winsberg (1966), Wolfe (1967)*, and *Mitchell (1969a and b)*. These authors focused on the geography of the tourism industry which led to works conducted by regional geographers such as *Guthrie (1961), Christaller (1963)* and *Piperoglou*

(1966). However, as *Williams and Zelinsky (1970:549)* noted, "virtually all the scholarship in the domain of tourism has been confined to intra-national description and analysis...In view of its great and increasing economic import, the probable significance of tourism in diffusing information and attitudes, and its even greater future potential for modifying patterns of migration, balance of payments, land use, and general socio-economic structure with the introduction of third-generation jet transport and other innovations in travel, it is startling to discover how little attention the circulation of tourists has been accorded by geographers, demographers, and other social scientists."

The concerns of Williams and Zelinsky are at the forefront of tourism geography today, as well as the growing concern of the increases in leisure time world wide. *Mercer (1970)* suggested a discussion of the increase in leisure time in the affluent countries of the world in the 1970s and commented that, "leisure still remains a sadly neglected area of study in geography." Whether a dearth still exists today in this aspect in geographical studies is open for discussion, however, few can argue that it is important in determining source regions for tourist.

Several influential publications appeared during the 1970s and 1980s that indicated tourism studies in geography were increasing. Geographers such as *Cosgrove and Jackson (1972), Lavery (1971), McCannell (1973), Robinson (1976), Coppock (1977), Butler (1980), Pearce (1981, 1987a), Mathieson and Wall (1982), Patmore (1983), Pigram (1983)*, and *Smith (1983)* published articles and texts concerning the new field. However, as *Mitchell (1979:235)* noted in the introduction to a special issue of Annals of Tourism Research, "the geography of tourism is limited by a dearth of published research in geographical journals." Likewise, *Pearce (1979, 1995)* commented that the geography of tourism was not coherent and lacked a conceptual and theoretical base. Perhaps he was unaware that *Butler (1980; 1991)* had modelled cycles of evolution of destinations in the 1980s and has published on this topic into the 1990s.

While the study of the geography of tourism remains on the periphery of geography in general, this subject does not occur in, "isolation from wider trends in geography and academic discourse nor of the society of which we are a part". A large degree of the research conducted by geographers has used techniques inherent in spatial analysis and applied geography (ibid). *Hall and Page (1999)* suggested that the three most influential works on the geography of tourism written in the last two decades approached their research from a spatial perspective with a small emphasis on the role of behavioural research. However in the 1990s geographers such as *Shaw and Williams (1994)* took a more critical approach to tourism studies and showed the importance of other factors such as the political economy, production, consumption, commodification and globalization in the ever shifting character of tourism. This perspective shift is important, because tourism studies connect with many other aspects of geography. Tourism as its own phenomenon engages topics beyond what can be seen and experienced in the natural environment of a particular place. As *Matley (1976:5)* observed, "There is scarcely an aspect of tourism which does not have some geographical implications and there are few branches of geography which do not have some contribution to make to the study of the phenomenon of tourism."

Tourism as a World Phenomenon

Tourism is the world's largest industry and continues to grow. Total gross expenditures for travel and tourism were $3.2 trillion in 1993 or, approximately six percent of the global GNP *(WTTC 1993)*. By 2005 the number of tourism related jobs is expected to exceed 350 million *(ibid)*. In the 1990s more than 200 million people were directly or indirectly employed in the global tourism industry and 20,000 jobs are created for every 1 million dollars of revenue generated. Tourism accounts for more than 11 percent of all consumer spending world wide *(ibid)*. In the 1990s, in the United States, tourism produced 13.4 percent of the nation's GNP, generated $50 billion in tax revenue and employed 11 million people.

According to the World Tourism Organization (WTO) international tourist arrivals grew from 93 million in 1963 to 284 million in 1981 *(WTO 1997)*. By 1990 arrivals had reached 456 million and are expected to double by 2010 *(WTO 1997)*. However, after the recent international terrorist events these expectations are not likely to be met. It appears that the stage is set for the continued growth of tourism in the developed world in the quaternary sector of the economy. Many developing nations are also moving towards a more service-based economy as governments begin to comprehend the potential economic magnitude of the industry. In recent years the most rapid growth of the tourism industry has been in the developing world. In these countries tourism makes up a substantial portion of their gross national and gross domestic products as well as a major portion of their foreign earnings. Many scholars feel these countries show the greatest prospects for continued growth. However, tourism is not a panacea for the economic crises of the developing world although it has become an economic fact in today's society.

Tourism in Central America

Central America's reputation for political unrest and inadequate transportation and infrastructure has caused an uneven growth in tourism since the 1960s. However, in 1965 the Central American Bank for Economic Integration, in conjunction with the U.S. Agency for International Development's regional office for Central America, commissioned Porter International Company to examine the possibilities of the development and promotion of tourism in the region. According to Ritchie and his associates,

> *"The objective was that the conclusions and recommendations reached could serve as a basis for a Master Plan of Tourism, which would permit the promotion, financing, and execution of specific investment projects for the development of a tourism industry in Central America."*

For each country specific locations were designated as having qualities favorable for tourism. These qualities included important historical-cultural sites, such as Esquipulas in Guatemala, and areas where the physical geography was conducive to tourists, such as the Bay Islands of Honduras. David Weaver (1994), some three decades later, discussed characteristics of tourism development that followed the recommendations of Ritchie and his associates. Weaver suggested that tourism development in Central America was based on physical and cultural geographical factors. The insular region, according to *Weaver (1994)*, attracts tourists because of its appealing climate, extensive beaches, developed resorts, and its close proximity to the tourism markets of the United States. In this region the traditional "3s" (sand, sea and sunshine) type of tourism takes place. The mainland region of Central America relies on the extensive culture-history of the Maya and other pre-Colombian tribes and the more recent colonial additions for its tourism draw. However, this region also has the "3s" attraction along with more highly diverse natural areas and ecosystems *(ibid).*

The number of tourist visiting Central America from 1960 to 1970 grew from 124,000 to 744,000 *(WTO 1993, 1994, 1996, 1997).* This growth followed the international trend during this period. Annual tourist arrivals between 1970 and 1975 in this region rose from 744,000 to nearly 1.7 million *(WTO 1993).* This increase surpassed the global rate of growth, which was documented at 134 percent, as well as the rate of the growth to the Americas (118%) and to Mexico (143%) *(WTO 1993).* The next decade (1975-1985), however, did not follow this trend. Total tourist arrivals to the region dropped from 1.7 million to 1.1 million annually. The decline was associated with the highly publicized escalating violence throughout the isthmus. Guatemala, Nicaragua, and El Salvador, the countries with the most widespread public violence, lost the most tourists.

However, Costa Rica, the country with the most stable reputation, was also affected to a lesser extent by the regional drop. Honduras' international tourist arrivals during this time were slightly lower than the other countries in the region and remained relatively constant. Panama, the hub for air and sea travel in the region, according the West and *Augelli (1989),* had always enjoyed a steady flow of tourists. During the regional lull in tourism Panama's arrivals increased. Susan *Stonich (2000)* associates this increase with the inclusion of U.S. military personal and their families in the national statistics.

Since the 1980s the governments of the Central America countries have been in the process of strengthening their economies through new avenues of development. Stonich suggested that these avenues are designed to "integrate their economies, diversify exports, promote foreign investment, and increase foreign exchange earnings". One of the most important of these tactics has been the promotion of international tourism. However, because these countries are still considered developing relying on tourism as a means to fix their economics remains problematic. Tourism is cyclical in nature and in many developing countries disasters have ensued as tourism becomes a leading economic component. Much like the product cycle of economic theory, the product cycle of tourism development of a given area or the development of a specific type of tourism must pass through specific stages *(ibid)*.

The first stage of development, like that of a new product, begins as a relatively unknown place with just a trickle of visitors over a given period *(ibid)*. As it becomes better known its popularity grows until it reaches its popularity peak. Once this happens, visitation to this site will reach a saturation point and them it will begin its decline. Destination can take steps to overcome the likelihood of decline as suggested by Robert *Butler (1991)* that will reinvent the site and continue to attract tourists. However, further complicating the tourism product cycle is the capricious nature of the tourist. It has been suggested that tourists often favour the in-style, most publicly advertised places, and move on to new sites once the fad has dissipated. Unless the site can reinvent itself the likelihood of decline is probable.

Among other drawbacks discussed widely, and one of the most important for this discussion, is the possibility of economic leakage. Economic leakages occur most often in developing countries because unfettered foreign development and investment are allowed in hopes of gaining significant revenues from tourism growth. Leakages arise as a result of large ownership percentages held by foreigners or corporations and thus much of the revenue generated leaves the host country and returns to the country of investment origination. External labour brought into a host country by foreign investors can exacerbate leakage problems. John *Beekhuis (1981)* calculated that Central America's leakage rates ranged from 30 percent to 50 percent while in Cancún, Mexico estimates were as high as 90 percent. In 1994 Erlit *Cater (1994)* suggested that 90 percent of the coastal development in Belize was foreign owned thus leakage rates were much higher.

Under the leadership of Mexico, in 1988, the presidents of El Salvador, Belize, Guatemala, and Honduras began one of the region's earliest attempts at promoting regional tourism with the creation of El Mundo Maya. Relying upon the financial assistance of groups in the United States and Europe the five presidents signed a joint tourism promotion pact. The group's first goal was to secure financial and technical assistance from the European Community to expand both the public and private tourism sectors in the five countries *(ibid)*.

The goal of the project, as stated by Mexico's Minister of Tourism was to, "showcase the history and culture of the entire region as one entity without borders. Cancún would become the "doorway" for the world to the project *(ibid)*. In 1991 the European Community loaned the group $1 million and the project began. In each country three types of tourism were endorsed: cultural/historical tourism, coastal tourism, and ecotourism or adventure tourism. Fourteen tourism circuits were established, each containing one of the three types of tourism *(ibid)*.

Examples of three of the circuits established in Honduras were the Copán ruins (cultural/historical tourism), Roatán Island (coastal beach tourism) and la Mosquitia/Río Plátano Biosphere Reserve (eco/adventure tourism). The inclusion of Roatán and la Mosquitia are ironic because these two sites have never been inhabited by the Maya, although it is likely that Maya might have visited these places. However, these areas have become popular tourist attractions for Honduras and have been featured in several articles promoting Honduran tourism.

Other projects were planned, along with the initial circuits, which included infrastructural improvements (airports, roads and marinas), increased hotel construction and international marketing. In El Salvador and Chiapas, Mexico archeological projects were initiated and upon completion were to be included in El Mundo Maya *(ibid)*. More than two million international tourists visited Central America annually during the 1990s exceeding the arrivals from the previous decades *(WTTC 2001)*. The promotion of Central America as a single tourism region has become a trend in the 1990s. The joint initiative first began with the creation of El Mundo Maya and then in 1996 the Central American presidents signed the Declaration of Montelimar II. The declaration designated the tourism industry as the principal growth strategy for the isthmus and it emphasized the necessity for cooperative efforts among all the Central American countries in making the region a single tourism destination. The promotion of these initiatives has been supported financially by several international donors such as the

World Bank, the International Development Bank, the United Nations, and USAID.

In 1996 tourism contributed approximately $1.6 billion to Central America's foreign exchange earnings and more than 2.6 million tourists visited the region that year *(WTO 1997)*. 2001 estimates have suggested tourist arrivals reached 4 million and created $3 billion in foreign exchange earnings making tourism a viable component in the Central American economy *(WTO 2001)*.

Tourism in Honduras

The Honduran government began actively promoting tourism as a national development strategy in the late 1960s. Emphasis was placed on the development of three separate physical and cultural geographical areas: the Mayan archeological site of Copán, the beaches and colonial history of the North Coast, and the coral reefs of the Bay Islands *(ibid)*. La Mosquitia and the Río Plátano Biosphere Reserve were added as ecotourism became a popular world trend in the 1990s.

The government of Honduras, in the 1980s, established a set of laws creating special "tourism zones." These zones helped attract foreign investments by providing liberal tax and import incentives. However, Article 107 of the Honduran Constitution prohibited foreign ownership of land 40 km from the Caribbean Sea and Gulf of Fonseca or the international borders of Nicaragua, El Salvador, and Guatemala. Recognizing this barrier, the Honduran National Congress, in 1990, passed Decree Law 90/90 to allow foreign property purchases in designated tourism zones, established by the Ministry of Tourism, in order to build permanent or vacation homes.

Areas along the North Coast and the Bay Island were among the most popular for investment. Continued acceleration of these "neoliberal" economic policies occurred during the 1990s specifically with the creation of Tourism Free Zones in 1993. Tourism investors were given the same benefits as the private Export Processing Zones including; 100% foreign ownership of property, federal and municipal tax exemptions, tax free imports for any materials needed to further the industry (including boats, planes, and worn equipment).

During the first five months of 1995 the tourism industry in Honduras generated US $90 million which was a 62% increase from all of 1994. The Bay Islands accounted for almost one-fourth of this total *(ibid)*. According to Maria Callejas de *Durón (1995)*, Senior Commercial Officer for Honduras, in 1995 tourism ranked fifth in the revenue generation for the country and had not reached its full potential. Aside from the tourist attractions offered by the continuous "summer-like weather," *Durón (1995)* felt that the country still lacked additional attractions in the areas where the flow of foreign visitors was greatest. However, with the institution of the Tourism Free Zone Law, ecotourism programs, and the national demand for additional tourism projects, she felt tourism had the potential to become the country's leading industry.

By 1997 tourism ranked third in foreign exchange earnings (US $ 143 million) behind coffee (US $330 million) and bananas.

Following the Tourism Free Zone Laws, in 1999 the Law of Tourism Incentives was passed. The National Congress stated their intentions with this new law; it was to continue to:

> *"facilitate the development of the nation's tourism sector by providing fiscal incentives that will encourage greater participation by private investors, both local and foreign, in the development of tourism products, thereby stimulating the creation of jobs, promoting investment, and increasing the nation's intake of currency and tax revenue".*

The incentives granted under this law included: a ten year exoneration from income tax payments, exoneration from payment of taxes and tariffs on the import of goods and services including printed advertising materials, and exoneration from the payment of taxes, fees or any other kind of financial obligation on cultural presentations and shows. Tourism was also considered by the Honduran government to be an economic activity that would be closely linked to the cultural and social development of the Honduran people. Projects devoted to rescuing cultural heritage and conserving natural landscapes were given an added exoneration from the payment of municipal property taxes *(ibid)*. According to the Ministry of Tourism, all activities carried out under the stipulations of this law were to comply with the sustainable development of the entire nation *(ibid)*. Tourism was to have only minimal impacts on the cultural and natural resources of Honduras but being of maximum benefits to the Honduran people *(ibid)*. In 2001 tourism brought an estimated US $300 million to the economy of Honduras making it the third greatest financial generator of income for the country. According to the Honduran Institute of Tourism (2000) within an estimated four years tourism will be the number one source of dollars for Honduras. After Hurricane Mitch the tourism sector had 92% of its infrastructure intact and 90% of the country's natural and cultural attractions were unaffected. This well surpassed the countries leading dollar producer, agriculture, which suffered sever setbacks. These figures illustrate the overwhelming resilience of the industry and its potential for the future.

Specific Aims of the Study and Methodology

The purpose of this research is to document the development of tourism on the island of Utila, Honduras and the affects this new industry is having on the social, economic, and environmental aspects of the island. Traditionally, Bay Islanders have been culturally and economically oriented to the sea. Livelihoods once depended on agriculture and fishing and, more recently, merchant sailing. Documenting the shift from the merchant sailing economy to a tourism economy on Utila will be a major focus. In addition, because nearly two-thirds of Utila is mangrove swamp and tourism development is expanding into this area, ecological alterations will be documented.

Being the smallest of the three major Bay Islands, Utila has historically drawn a different type of tourist. Those not interested in big resorts and lavish facilities, looking for a fairly "cheap" way to see Central America and the Caribbean, find their way to this island. It would seem that this type of tourist has determined the character of tourism facilities on Utila. In the literature, a similar type of tourist population has been documented, gives an example of this type of tourist in a small fishing village in Brazil, and discusses the affects these tourists have on the economics, society, and cultural. As a subsidiary to the core of my research documenting a similar type of tourist and their effects on the island will also be addressed. Understanding how this new tourist economy has affected and potentially will affect the island's landscape also enters the research question. In addition to the international "backpacker" phenomena associated with tourism on Utila, the component of mainland Hondurans is growing. Documentation of this growth will also be discussed.

During the summer of 1999, as an undergraduate student, I visited Utila for the first time. During this trip this project began to take shape. Although we were in the country to observe the reconstruction efforts of the Honduran people after Hurricane Mitch, the week spent on Utila lead to the realization that the Bay Islands functioned much differently than the rest of Honduras. It was evident that tourism was the primary income producer for the island. However, the type of tourist visiting Utila was quite different than on the other two major islands and led me to expand this thesis to include a chapter on this character.

Over a three month period from May until August 2001, I lived and worked on the island. During this time I came to know many of the islanders and tourists and through these personal interactions gathered much of the information for this paper. There is a definite and distinct link between the islanders and their environment that is played out in social and economic interactions. Understanding this link and the ways in which the islanders manipulate these interactions to fit personal needs and gains is an important part of this research. Global factors, apparent during my visit on the island, continue to play a role in the economic and social lives of the islanders. Therefore, it was necessary to blend the theories of cultural ecology and political ecology in an attempt to make sense of the social, economic, and natural environmental state of the island.

Location and Size of the Bay Islands

The Bay Islands comprise one of the fifteen departamentos in the Republic of Honduras. Situated in an arc 29 to 60 kilometres off the north coast, the Bay Islands consist of three major islands, five minor islands and sixty-five cays. The largest and most predominant of these islands, in terms of land and population, are Roatán, Guanaja, and Utila is the smallest of the major islands, approximately eleven kilometres long and five kilometres wide. East Harbour is the only agglomerated settlement, however, twelve populated cays are located off the southwestern end of the island. The total land area of the Bay Islands is approximated at 238 square kilometres *(ibid)*. Roatán, the central island accounts for over one-half of the islands total.

Topography

The islands are the above water appearance of the Bonacca Ridge, which forms the northern edge of the continental shelf in the Caribbean. The ridge is a non-continuous underwater extension of the Sierra de Omoa. This mainland mountain range, located near the southern escarpment of the Bartlett Trough, disappears into the Caribbean Sea near Puerto Cortés *(Banks and Richards 1969)*.

On Utila this geological base is capped with coralline limestone. Thus, nearly two-thirds of the island is hardly more than a swampy basin, perfect for catching rainwater and in some places this limestone has eroded to sea level. Utila is also composed of volcanic materials that make up another important part of the island's topography. Pumpkin Hill, located near the eastern end of the island is the remnant of an ancient volcano that creating the ragged terrain in this area. This limestone and volcanic base has much to do with the western sloping perspective of Utila. And the creation of a cultural lingo associated with directions on the island. If one travels from the western end of Utila towards East Harbour, one is said to be going "up town"; to the west is "down." Moving eastward from Utila the elevations of the islands generally increase, with the eastern island of Guanaja having the tallest peak at approximately 415 meters. In addition to the increase in elevation as one moves eastward, so to does the terrain grow steeper, the vegetation and wildlife become more diverse, and the amount of fresh water resources increases.

The number of streams differs greatly on each of the three major islands. This also affects drainage patterns on the islands. Roatán has a number of run-off routes. These routes, however, do not retain water for any length of time after rain because of the steep slopes. Standing water on the island can only be found near the shoreline where the land generally becomes flat (ibid). This water is not good for human consumption because tidal variations and long-shore drift make it brackish *(ibid)*. Guanaja has the steepest slopes and on the northeast portion of the island, two major streams carry fresh water year-round. Utila differs from the other two major islands because it is flatter and has not developed any significant gulling. Rain seeps downward into limestone caverns and into the centrally located mangrove swamps. One small stream, located in the southeast of the island, seems to play only a minor role in the drainage process. Natural deposition of sediment on Guanaja and Roatán can be found where the hills near the shoreline and the slopes become gentler. Utila's dominating swampy area also accumulates upslope sediment.

Climate

Honduras has three major climate types. The Bay Islands, like the adjacent mainland coast, have a humid tropical climate. In the tropics rainfall, not temperature, determines seasonality. Two-thirds of the islands' rainfall normally occurs between October and January. Changing wind direction associated with North American cold fronts is a major cause of this winter rainfall. As is expected in the tropics, temperature variation is relatively slight. Average mean monthly temperature ranges normally do not exceed four degrees Celsius. However, a climatic phenomenon that occurs along the east coast of Central America from the Yucatán to Colombia, called veranillo, brings a short early midsummer rainfall increase and a slight drop in the July temperatures.

The Bay Islands are located in the belt of the trade-winds. Winds normally blow from the east, roughly parallel to the north coast of Honduras. Velocities range from thirty-two to forty kilometres per hour *(Cry 1965)*. In August, as noted by islanders, calm periods of up to five days occur. During the winter months, North American cold fronts cause winds to shift and come from the north and west. This creates the extended rainfall characteristic of the region. Like elevation on Utila, wind direction is also important in local lingo. Winds normally blow from east to west and therefore, walking into east winds (up-wind) correlates with up slope and going "up town."

Because Utilians are oriented to the sea ocean currents are an important part of local life. In this region, currents normally have an easterly flow along the southern portions and between the islands. Which makes westerly travel slower. However, during the winter months, there is a weakening of this easterly current because of the reversal of the current that flows north of the islands.

During the last century nearly 20 hurricanes have affected the Bay Islands. How the Bay Islands are situated in the Bay of Honduras, their distances from the mountains on the mainland of Central America, and the general northwestwardly paths of these storms, are all factors that reduce storm strengths. Davidson suggested that although the Bay of Honduras has seen developments of large storm systems only every ten years do these storms mature into hurricanes. The most destructive hurricanes that affect the islands, such as Hurricane Francelia in 1969 and Hurricane Mitch in 1998, develop in the open ocean and then strike the islands uncharacteristically from the north.

Marine Environment

In the Bay of Honduras reef systems are of two types: barrier and fringing. A barrier reef is a coral wall separated from the land by a lagoon. A fringing reef however, begins adjacent to the shore, often with only small breaks that might allow small boat passage. Many people make the mistake and assume that the barrier reef system off the coast of Belize is connected to that of the Bay Islands. This is an incorrect notion passed along primarily in tourism literature. Not only does the Bartlett Trough separate the two distinct systems, the Bay Islands reef is a fringing reef.

On the northern sides of Roatán and Guanaja the reef encloses much of the islands. Only small breaks allow for passage into tidal inlets associated with stream mouths *(ibid)*. Guanaja's reef begins about one mile offshore in places, farther than on the other two islands. Utila's northern reef exposes itself as iron shore that extends from the central portion of the island almost continuously around the eastern tip *(ibid)*. Utila's north side reef is characterized by "steep escarpments and spur and groove formations" *(ibid)*. In the middle of the north side is a small break in the coral that has become the entrance to a canal that extends across the island into Oyster Bay Lagoon.

Utila's eastern side, much like the north side, is covered by fossilized coral and low cliffs referred to as iron shore *(Harborne et al 1999)*. This side of the island has long and shallow fore reefs and large sandy areas *(ibid)*. Additionally, the eastern end of the island faces a deep trench that separates Utila and Roatán and is one of the few places in the world where whale sharks can be seen *(ibid)*.

The southern side of Utila, facing the Honduran mainland, is the more developed portion of the island. The southern reef is dominated by a sloping fore reef that is the widest of the reef zones *(Harborne et al 1999)*. Also characteristic of the southern reef are some spur and groove formations *(ibid)*. The back reef consists of exposed bedrock and sand and covers a smaller area and is much less diverse in coral types and topographic features *(ibid)*. East Harbour, located on southeastern Utila, is protected by an uplift of the southern reef. Roatán's south side reef is similar and runs almost the entire length of the island *(Jacobson 1992)*. Guanaja also has an expansive southern reef where the two cays of Bannaca Town are located.

The western end of Utila is dominated by fringing reefs. The southwestern reef supports Utila's twelve cays. Also found in this area are patch reefs and expansive sea grass habitants that surround the cays. Inside the reefs Utila also has a number of bays, bights, and harbours that interrupt the shoreline. These include, Spotted Bay, Carey Bay, Turtle Harbour, Rock Harbour, Jack's Bight, Swan Bay, Big Bight, East Harbour, and Little Bight, which provide anchorage for shallow vessels.

East Harbour, however, is the only place on Utila where large watercrafts such as shrimpers, sail boats, and cargo and passenger ships can safely moor. These factors were probably taken into consideration when the original founders settled in East Harbour. Perhaps because of the reefs the Bay Islands are known for their diverse tropical fish and other marine populations. These fish include porgies, old wife, black fin, wahoo, red snapper, dogteeth snapper, hogfish, and the whale shark. Conch, crawfish, and four species of turtles can also be found around the islands. These marine species have been historically important to the economy of the islands and recently many have become of interest to sport fishermen. The islanders have long depended on the sea to sustain them. The reef provides a place for the abundant fish population to feed and survive. It also provides the islanders with protection from the dynamic ocean. More importantly, in recent years, the reefs have been the major draw for the developing tourism industry.

Flora and Fauna

Island vegetation has been altered drastically since first recorded by Christopher Columbus on his fourth voyage to the New World in 1502. Although Columbus and his crew did not provide detailed descriptions, they did mention the presence of pine trees on Guanaja and named the island "isla de pinos". Although pines are still present, they have undoubtedly been depleted since this first account because of human needs, for ship building and house construction, and environmental destruction, especially from fires and hurricanes. Today, as noted by the Bay Island Conservation Association, the main vegetation types include pine savannas on the higher ridges of Roatán and Guanaja and tropical dry forests, mangroves, and beach plant communities on the three major islands. In 1975 Lord noted, on Utila, that most food plants and animals were imported beginning in the 1830s. These include mango, papaya, breadfruit, plantain, banana, citrus (grapefruit, lime and orange), canop, mamey, mamea, almond, guava, tomato, melon, cassava, cocoyam, and star apple *(ibid)*. Most of these plants are still present on the islands and still very much part of local diet. Lord named the groups that contributed to the cultivation of these plants as the Cayman Islanders, some mainland Hondurans, and the American fruit companies.

Utila is nearly two-thirds swampland leaving only one-third of the island available for settlement and farming activities. Therefore, perhaps the most important and abundant plants on the island are mangroves. Utila has three species of mangrove; white mangrove (Laguncularia racemosa), red mangrove (Rhizophora mangle), and black mangrove (Avicennia germinaus). These plants have adapted to saline coastal environments in the tropics and subtropics *(West 1998)*. They can live in a wide variety of water types, from fresh to salt, but tend to do best in brackish water (salinities from 10 to 20 parts per thousand) *(ibid)*. Mangrove are associated with tidal zones where they form a cover that ranges from shrubs to taller trees *(ibid)*. On Utila these plants can be found in both brackish (to the interior) and along ocean-fronts protected by the fringing reef. The mangrove is important for natural land building on the island. They also act as nurseries and spawning grounds for many species of open ocean marine life *(ibid)*. Additionally, growths associated with interior swamp and marsh areas are an important feeding ground for various species of crabs and snails. Thus large accumulations of these species can be found here and attract other fauna such as turtles and iguanas which have been traditionally important to the Utilian diet and economy. In recent years, associated with the growing tourism economy, large portions of Utila's mangrove have been destroyed.

The Bay Islands also have an abundant wildlife population that has been suggested as an additional resource for the further diversification of the island's tourism industry. In a conservation plan prepared by Tropical Research and Development, Inc. the authors identified potential trials for hiking, bird-watching, and horseback riding that would allow alternatives to scuba diving which is the current draw for the islands *(ibid)*. One of the biggest limiting factors to human use of Utila is its size and topography. Although agriculture has become less important to Utilian life the lack of available arable land has forced the islanders to turn to the sea for survival. Recently, as tourism has become an important part of the economy on the islands, the surrounding ocean has been the strongest draw for international tourists.

Utila's Cultural History

The cultural landscape is fashioned from the natural landscape by a cultural group. Culture is the agent, the natural area is the medium, the cultural landscape the result. The Bay Islands, including Utila, have a distinctive and diverse cultural heritage. The mélange of ethnicities stemming from its settlement history has created the diverse population seen today. As noted by William Davidson in his 1974 publication of these past and present populations, seven distinct groups have inhabited the islands. Before European contact, Paya Indians probably occupied the islands. After Contact, Spaniards, buccaneers, Garífuna, English, English-descended Antilleans, African-descended Antilleans, and North Americans have settled for varying time periods on the islands.

Utila was inhabited by only six of these groups because the Garífuna only settled on Roatán. In recent years, however, other ethnic groups have found their way to the island, specifically European tourists and Mainland Hondurans. As mentioned in the introduction, in the 1960s Honduras became interested in the sustainable development of its tourist industry. Since this time the ethnic make up of Utila has changed. This chapter will discuss the historical and modern populations that settled on the island.

Pre-Columbian Inhabitants

Just prior to Spanish Contact the north coast of Honduras, including the Bay Islands, appeared to be sparsely inhabited by aboriginal tribes. In Central America the pre-Colombian populations are designated as "high" and "low" cultural groups. Geographical boundaries that separate these groups have some relationship to the islands. The high cultural groups included the Maya and Aztec. These people lived primarily in the southern Central Plateau of Mexico and the Yucatán, and the highlands and Pacific lowlands of Central America *(ibid)*.

They could be distinguished from other populations in the area because they lived in agglomerated settlements comparable to modern cities, their agriculture could support the large numbers of people in the settlements and was much more advanced than the low cultural groups, and their economy was controlled by social organizations and theocratic states. The presence of large temples and ceremonial centres were also characteristic of these "high cultures" *(ibid)*. In contrast, the "low cultures" of Middle America inhabited the West Indies, much of the Central American lowlands, and northern Mexico.

These groups included the Chichimecas of northern Mexico, the Caribs of the West Indies, and the many tribes of the Central American lowlands such as the Paya and Jicaque. Characteristics of these groups included, smaller much less organized, dispersed settlements, simpler agricultural techniques, tubers as the primary food source, and lack of large ceremonial centres. It should be noted that these two groups did have contact with each other. Aztec and Mayan traders probably travelled throughout much of the isthmus and to many of the islands off the coast.

The Paya have been suggested as the first inhabitants of the Bay Islands. The boundaries for this group on the mainland were established as being from Trujillo to Cape Gracias a Dios. William Strong and William Davidson, among others, seem to believe that this aboriginal group extended its boundaries to include the Bay Islands. Others have suggested that islanders were Maya, Lenca, and Jicaque. For this paper, we will support Davidson and Strong's notion that the aboriginal population was Paya. Evidence presented alludes to similarities between the mainland Paya populations and sites found on the Bay Islands. These island sites have been classified in three categories with the addition of a fourth focusing on burials. The first of these three are residential sites. Archeologists pinpoint residential sites when the presence of kitchen ware and shards are prevalent. Sites containing these items have been found on Roatán, Utila, and Guanaja of the larger islands and Helene of the smaller islands in this region.

The largest of these main sites is found at "80 Acre" on Utila and encompasses forty acres of land *(ibid)*. Locations are generally forty to sixty feet above sea level, on sloping land, a few hundred yards from the beach *(ibid)*. Davidson suggested that these aboriginal populations located their villages at these specific elevations and distance from the shore to escape mosquitoes and sand flies *(ibid)*. In addition, it seems reasonable to assume that these people relied heavily on the ocean therefore making site location close to the water important.

Ceremonial sites, being the second in this list of site classifications, are located near the large residential areas of Utila and Guanaja. These sites, however, are in no way comparable to the sites associated with the Maya and Aztec of mainland Mesoamerica. No large ceremonial structures, such as temples, have been located on any of the Bay Islands. However, there are identifiable artifacts associated with this type of site, such as large stone monoliths, earth mounds, stone mounds, and stone causeways. Utila had one a site located on Stewart's Hill. This site is supposedly the origination point of an aboriginal paved road system on the island *(ibid)*.

The third site classification deals with the deposition of offerings. These offertory sites, lacking the monuments found in ceremonial locations, have objects that have been placed in nature and elicit help from a higher power. Artifacts ranging from shell ornaments to clay figurines can be found in association with these sites. The largest in the Bay Islands are on the island of Roatán and the smaller island of Barbaret. Nearly every occurrence of these sites where located on tops of hills. Although a separate category, burial sites on the islands seem to be located close to and hypothetically in conjunction with offertory sites. However, on islands such as Utila, burials were located on sandy beaches There is no archeological evidence that offertory sites were located on Utila.

Eight known burial sites exist on the Bay Islands. They have been located in three different physical settings; beach, hilltop, and refuse heaps. Utila has three of these eight sites and all of them were located on the beach *(ibid)*. Characteristics of these beach sites include slate slab coverings, multiple burials, skulls placed in large urns, with bones and other goods nearby *(ibid)*.

The Paya Indians apparently lived in only a few settlements with one residential area on the major islands. Artifacts and residential patterns resemble those of their mainland Paya neighbours, making it possible to hypothesize that the groups were related. Trade seemed to be occurring between these groups as well as with other aboriginal groups from the mainland, showing that the Bay Islanders were not living in cultural seclusion. It seems the Paya were the first of many ethnic populations to call the islands home.

Christopher Columbus and the Encomenderos

Christopher Columbus made contact with the aboriginal populations on the Bay Islands on his fourth voyage in 1502. Hence, Utila and the rest of the Bay Islands became a part of history on July 30, 1502, when Columbus and his crew anchored off the north shore of Guanaja. Columbus documented the island's appearance and subsequently called it Isla de Pinos, for the large pine stands located there. For nearly 136 years the Spanish crown held virtually uncontested rule over the Bay Islands

The Paya populations on the Bay Islands were inevitably subjected to slaving raids. Queen Isabella of Spain, however, commanded her conquistadores to make slaves of only those aboriginal populations who were unwilling to become Christians or those designated as "cannibals". Even though the populations of the Bay Islands were noted as being relatively peaceful it served the purposes of the conquistadores based in Cuba to inform the Queen that the Bay Islanders were hostile, cannibalistic, and opposed to Christianity.

In 1516, Queen Isabella allowed Diego Velasquez to remove the aboriginal populations on the Bay Islands to be used on plantations in Cuba where populations had already been exterminated. Allegedly only two raids took place in the Bay Islands and according to Sauer, it was during the second in 1525 that the name Utila appeared for the first time. Although some islanders survived slaving seeds had been planted for future Spanish settlement.

The Roman Catholic Church had little influence on the Bay Islands unlike other places in Latin America. A seemingly more important landscape and cultural change occurred with the institution of the encomienda initiated in Honduras in 153. This system called for Spanish occupation of the islands where the encomenderos would Christianize the Indians. Utila obtained only one. The encomienda brought the islanders into constant contact with the Spanish encomenderos, thus changing the lifestyles of the natives.

Buccaneering, Early English Inhabitants, and the Garífuna

As the Spanish made their presence known in the New World other European explorers began to see the potential of the Caribbean and Central America as a whole. Yet another cultural group saw the opportunity to carve its name in the ethnic history of the Bay Islands. By 1536 the French had appeared in the western Caribbean and the Dutch soon after in 1594. The English, however, were the most successful in disrupting the Spanish shipping routes and appeared sometime in the 1560s. The English, French, and Dutch realized that the Bay Islands were in a strategic position to loot Spanish vessels. The islands had fresh water and protected natural harbours that the freebooters valued.

Although the pirate settlements had no lasting impressions on the natural landscape, they did create myths that still exist among islanders. Myths of sunken treasures draw amateur relic hunters and tourists to the islands today. Town names found on Roatán (Coxen Hole) and business names on Utila (Captain Morgan's Dive Shop and the Bucket of Blood Bar) are also reminders of the pirate presence from earlier days. Ironically, Utila was not one of the popular hideouts for the pirates and has not been mentioned in the literature as having any involvement with these scallywags.

By 1639, however, the harassment caused by the pirates towards the Spanish became intolerable. Buccaneers had completely disrupted the role the Bay Islands were playing in Spanish shipping. Consequently, the Spanish Crown ordered the Indians removed so they could no longer provide for the pirates. The Spanish hoped that the removal of the natives would deter the pirates from hiding on the islands.

However, the opposite occurred, and instead of leaving the Bay of Honduras, the British intensified their efforts to settle the islands. By the late 1600s however, buccaneering reached its zenith in the Bay of Honduras and Spanish shipping had been significantly disrupted. The English became the most successful in this pirating trade and eventually had the longest lasting impact on the Bay Islands. Among the most famous English pirates who took refuge on the islands were Morgan, Jackson, Coxen, Sharpe and Low. These names are still present on the islands as last names, settlement names, and business names.

The Bay of Honduras was in constant turmoil because of the many conflicts the Spanish were having with other European nations. Between 1638 and 1782 Spanish colonists constantly were hassled at the hands of the English. The Spanish and the British, for the next 150 years, struggled for control over the Bay Islands. This struggle left lasting impressions on the islands. In the late 1630s, the first English colonists attempted to establish permanent settlements on the Islands, specifically on Roatán. A Puritan-based company, Providence Company, laid the foundations for this settlement and assigned a North American colonial, William Claiborne, to Roatán. The English renamed the island Rich Island after Lord Henry Rich, Earl of Holland. However the specific settlement location has never been determined. Apparently engaged in agricultural, these colonists set the stage for another ethnic transition.

The first military occupations of the Bay Islands by the English began in 1742 and lasted seven years. It was the intentions of the British to take control of the entire Atlantic Coast. Fortifications were constructed on the Island of Roatán and at the mouth of the Río Negro (up the coast east of Trujillo). The forts built on Roatán were to provided a base to provoke rebellion on the mainland, so that the English could keep control of the logwood trade and that their cutters from Belize and Mosquitia had a place to go when the Spanish became aggressive. On numerous occasions Spanish colonists tried unsuccessfully to remove the English. In 1744 negotiations began to rid Roatán of its unwelcome English guests. However, it was not until late 1749 that the English finally evacuated the island in accordance with the Peace of Aix-la-Chapelle signed by Britain and Spain in 1748.

A second English occupation of the Bay Islands began thirty years later. During the period between these separate occupations little change was documented on the islands. In 1779, in an attempt to reach Lake Nicaragua, the English used the existing Fort George on Roatán as a military base. In 1782 the English were finally disposed of at the Battle of Port Royal Roatán. Fort George was burned, and the Spanish forces captured the remaining inhabitants of the island. Once again the Bay Islands were left to nature. Neither the English nor the Spanish formed permanent colonial settlements that have survived until the present.

In 1797 the Bay Islands received its first permanent settlers. Again Roatán was the site for this settlement. These permanent settlers were the Garífuna (Black Caribs). A colonial tribe, the Garífuna, evolved over 300 years ago on the island of St. Vincent in the Lesser Antilles. In the seventeenth century an English slave vessel shipwrecked off the island, and the African born slaves escaped. Carib Indians already inhabited the island, and the cultures began to mix.

This new ethnic group proved to be intolerable for the English settlers, and in 1797, over 2,000 Black Caribs were removed from the island and exiled to the Bay of Honduras. They were first abandoned on the uninhabited island of Roatán. The Spanish feared this was an attempt by the English to reestablish control and therefore moved the Garífuna to Trujillo. However, some managed to stay on the island and formed the settlement now known as Punta Gorda. In 1980, there were fifty-four villages along the Caribbean coast extending from northern Nicaragua to southern Belize.

The British and the Spanish continued to have sporadic conflicts until September 15, 1821 when the Central American Federation proclaimed its independence from Spain. Of the two European countries colonizing in this region during this time, Spain was the weaker, thus allowing Britain unhindered expansion along the Caribbean Coast from what is now Belize to Mosquitia.

Utila, led a rather quiet existence during the colonial conflicts of the seventeenth and eighteenth centuries. However, early in the nineteenth century, Utila began attracting "people who were basically farmers interested in good, free land that they could cultivate for subsistence crops". It has been suggested that the quiet existence of the island, was one of the attractions that lead these new settlers to relocate on Utila's Cays, and by the 1830s nearly a dozen people migrate.

Antillean Populations

In the nineteenth century the modern landscape of the Bay Islands began. Black Caribs, a few Spanish soldiers, two Americans, and two French families made permanent residences on the islands. Honduras, including the Bay Islands, became a sovereign state and the official position of the English was to adhere to this sovereignty. However, the Bay Islands were still seen as strategic for the domination of the Bay of Honduras. The Cayman Islanders became important in the British quest for the Bay Islands.

Established as British colonies, the Cayman Islands had developed an agrarian economy. With this reliance on agriculture slave labour was necessary. By 1830 the Angelo-Antillean settlers of the Cayman's were outnumbered 5 to 1 by its slave populations. The British Crown, in this same decade, began its abolition of slavery. The English on the Cayman Islands, fearing the break down of their society, decided to relocate. They resettled in Belize and the Bay Islands. Suc-Suc Cay, Utila, and Coxen Hole, Roatán where the first settlements made by these people. Lord documents the first family of Cayman Islanders to settle on Utila in his 1975 work as follows,

> *"Joseph Cooper, his wife and nine children— two boys and seven girls— came to Utila from the Caymans by way of Belize. He was apparently one of the many land hungry British subjects of peasant or working class extraction that found the British isles too constricting. The Cooper family and an American named Samuel Warren who had been born in Massachusetts and served with Perry in the Battle of Lake Erie formed the nucleus*

> *of Utila's future populations. Warren and another American surnamed Joshua (who early dropped out of the historical picture) were already cultivating small plantations in the cays. Cooper also settled there to avoid the clouds of mosquitoes and sandflies that infested the bush-covered main island."*

A few years later, other families such as the Thompsons, Morgans, Boddens, Diamonds (or Dimon), Howells, and Gabourels had settled on Utila's Cays.

Subsequently, within a few years of the white landholding Cayman Islanders immigrating to Utila, many of the former Cayman slaves also moved to the Bay Islands. Likewise, settlers from the United States, British Honduras, Germany and Sweden took up residence on Utila. As 1858 came to a close so did the British colonial era on the Bay Islands. The islands legally became a part of greater Honduras. Many of the islanders left when this change took place but their culture has lasted until today.

Twentieth Century Utila

As Utila rounded the corner of the nineteenth century and entered into a new millennium, the ethnic and cultural melting pot that the island had become with the Anglo and Afro Cayman populations, Americans and Europeans, particular social stratifications were becoming evident. In 1975 when Lord was conducting his research on the remittance system on Utila he also paid particular attention to this developing phenomenon. He pointed out two key factors in understanding the social organizations that had arisen on the island. The first was that there were, and still are, three locally recognized strata based on ethnicity and the second dealt more with gradations of prestige, that were present in these strata, based on income and lifestyle.

Social Stratification

In Utilian society, social distinctions are not simply a matter of socioeconomic differences between societal sectors. Rather, these strata lie in skin pigmentations that have created ethnic prejudices and stereotyping that are basic to the ordering of Utilians social existence. Lord compared these strata to the caste system of India, where a person is born into a certain caste and carries this distinction for life *(ibid)*. However, marriage into the highest strata is allowed, but those who married in are still second class to those who were born into that class. Utila's social hierarchy, according to *Lord (1975)*, developed in much the same way focusing on three colour based classes.

At the top of the social hierarchy are the "whites" of Utila. This position is based primarily on skin colour and with it comes social prestige, important local leadership roles, wealth, and occupation of prime real estate. Most of this segment of society came from the British West Indies colonies and made up the original founders of the modern settlement on Utila and its related cays. In 1975 nearly three-fifths of Utila's population was considered part of this class *(ibid)*.

The second tier of the social stratification system noted by Lord was made up of those Utilians with Afro-Antillean ancestry. In 1975, this group was collectively called "coloured" *(ibid)*. However, during my research on the island I did not hear this term used, rather the general term "black" was used to refer to this group, perhaps reflecting modern contacts with the United States. In 1975, as Lord documented, the "white" Utilians did not feel that the "black" Utilians were "mentally or morally inferior," however, he did note that, "there was a qualitative difference between themselves and coloureds that would forever separate the two groups even though they lived side by side". This attitude or these first two ethnic strata still exist on Utila maybe problematic, however there still is a geographic component related to these ethnic groups.

The third stratum, the more recent migrants from the mainland, is still very much present on the island. Since the mid 1960s Spanish Hondurans have become another part of the cultural mélange present on the Utila. Although native-born islanders see themselves as having no relation to these "Spaniards," this group is nevertheless carving its niche.

This group makes up the third rung of the social ladder on Utila. The term "Spaniard" denotes both an ethnic group and a derogatory epithet on the island. In the 1970s Spaniards were, "individuals of Spanish heritage (usually from mainland Honduras) who bear Spanish surnames, speak little or no English, and are common labourers recently arrived on Utila". This group is generally poorer than native Utilians, thus they live in the worst housing on the island and subsequently exist in some of the most extreme conditions. Locals see them as, "immoral...uncouth and uncivilized". Often times the term "Indian" is used interchangeably with Spaniard, not to denote differing physical characteristics but to further emphasize their perceived "uncivilized" behaviour *(ibid).*

In 1975 Lord noted little interaction between the Spaniard and other Utilians. However, in recent years many young Utilian men have married mainland women. One such marriage occurred during the summer of 2001. Additionally, Lord did extensive research focused on marriages since 1881, and noted that only two "white"/"black" marriages had been documented *(ibid).* He further remarked that the white men were not Utilians and had come with the merchant fleets because there seemed to be a standing consensus among islanders that "blacks" and "whites" did not marry. Similarly, the recent "black"/"white" marriages on the island had young black Utilian men marrying young white European women. As tourism continues to grow, these isolated incidences might be expected to become more common.

Geographical Boundaries

The social stratifications of Utila also manifest themselves geographically. Lord noted this phenomenon in 1975 and it was still present in 2001. There were six ethnically derived barrios or neighbourhoods in East Harbour and one on the combined two populated cays (Pigeon and Suc-Suc). Today, East Harbour has three more. Barrios on Utila were initially established for identification in official documents such as birth and death certificates and maps. However, islanders began using them as geographical identifications for what kind of Utilian one was, based on the strata discussed above.

In 1975 the barrios in order by size were, Punta Calienta, (the Point), Aldea de los Cayitos (the Cays), Cola de Mico (Monkey's Tail), La Loma (the Hill), Main Street, Sandy Bay and Holland. In the preliminary figures for the 2000 Honduran Census, the barrios listed in order of size were; Sandy Bay, La Punta (The Point), Cola Mico (Monkey Tail), Los Cayos (the Cays), El Centro (Main Street or the Centre of Town), Mamey Lane, La Loma (the Hill), Lozano,

Camponado, and Holland. The number of houses in a given barrio determines size.

However, as *Lord (1975)* noted, size was not the important factor for these neighbourhoods. Instead the ethnic composition became the dominant factor when islanders would discuss the barrios. In 1975, Sandy Bay was almost exclusively "black," as it is today. A section of Cola de Mico was also "black." Main Street was completely "white" with the exception of one Spanish household *(ibid)*. The Point was made up of transplanted Cayans (a term used to distinguish those who live on the Cays from those who live on Utila) with a few scattered Spaniards and "blacks" *(ibid)*. The Cays consisted of only "whites" as did La Loma because this was the first area settled when the original Cayman Islanders moved from the Cays to the main island of Utila. Lord also noted other landscape features that came into play in areas of mixed ethnicity such as Cola de Mico. In this neighbourhood the Bucket of Blood Bar (which is still in operation) was a reference point in the landscape. Those that lived below the bar were either white or upper class "blacks," in contrast to those that lived above the bar who were manly lower class "blacks". Today many of these same general ethnic distinctions exist on Utila, with the inclusion of one predominantly Spanish neighbourhood, Camponado.

However, because of the general increase in population and the new economic dependence on tourism, the 1990s the predominantly "white" and "black" areas of Utila became more diverse. For example, the Cays are no longer totally "white" but have a few Spanish and "black" families. Additionally, economics do not seem to play a major role in the original neighbourhoods, rather families seem to stay in place generation upon generation with little heed to their economic situations. The biggest changes that are taking place in relation to neighbourhoods have little to do with the islanders and more to do with developers who have followed the tourism industry.

Utila, and the other Bay Islands, have established themselves as a cultural hearth culminating into a distinct landscape apparent to modern visitors. From the Paya to the various European invaders an imposition of cultural identities has influenced this development. It seems that the geographic location of the islands made them more vulnerable to these landscape changes.

Economic History of Utila as a Precursor to Tourism

Utila has a diverse economic history. The islands' pre-Columbian inhabitants relied primarily on subsistence agriculture and, more importantly, were oriented to the sea. This seaward orientation also can be linked to all post-Columbian settlers of the island. This chapter will discuss the economic history of Utila as it relates to the different cultural groups that inhabited the island. These economic escapades can also be related to landscape change on the island. The unique cultural traits associated with Utilian culture that Lord documents in his work in 1975 will be linked to the new tourism economy of the island. Tourism follows in the traditions of the other economic systems as being yet another catalyst for economic, social, and landscape change.

Underlying every culture are interfaces among economy, society, and polity. These relationships shape and direct these cultures into their respective livelihoods. *Lord (1975)* documented Utila's preadaptive traits that stimulated the island into a remittance system. He noted such things as, "the traditional importance of the nuclear family as the production and consumption unit, and a heritage of maritime activity in shipping and fishing" on the island.

Other important features included orientations of individualism, commercialism, and non-cooperation *(ibid)*. He also suggested that because of the nature of a remittance system (i.e. men being absent from the island for months at a time) the men enjoyed a level of indulgence and relaxing of laws and social norms when they return from sea. Therefore, an atmosphere of "rest and recreation" developed on the island as the men participate in "heavy partying and drinking". These pre-adaptive traits formed an easy transition from an economy based in agriculture to one dependent on maritime service *(ibid)*. These traits also helped in the development of the tourism industry on Utila today.

Pre-Columbian Economy

Only scant archeological evidence exists of the indigenous island cultures. However, documentation is available on the locations of settlement sites and the initial contact Columbus had with the indigenous people and their lands. The "80-Acre" site on Utila provides evidence that Indians lived and worked on the island. According to Columbus's notes on Bay Islands' vegetation and what is present today, early islanders probably hunted, cultivated local vegetation, and fished. In addition, his brother Bartholomew, who went ashore on the island of Guanaja, briefly described the local peoples and their "white grain from which they made a fine bread and the most perfect beer".

From the account of Columbus with the indigenous trader it is probable that islanders had contact with their mainland neighbours as well as with the other inhabited islands. According to Diaz del Castillo, while Cortés was visiting Trujillo, twenty years later fish and turkeys were brought to him that were found in abundance on the islands.

The archeological records and reports from the Spanish conquistadors suggest that the original Bay Islanders did not live in cultural seclusion. Instead, they traded with the mainland tribes close to Trujillo and possibly farther. These first inhabitants mastered the fine art of beer making as well as bread and possibly metallurgy. After Spanish Contact, for the next 136 years, the Bay Islanders were subjected to, and treated like, many other Caribbean populations. Following the initial slave raids religious "crusades" sought labourers to transport to plantations on Cuba and the Central American mainland. For the next 400 years the Bay Islands went through many economic transitions.

Encomiendas and Buccaneering

The Bay Islanders, unlike many other unfortunate indigenous Caribbean populations, survived initial contact with the Spanish only to be forced into servitude most likely on the Spanish encomiendas. The original economic components of the aboriginal Bay Islands, such as fishing, farming and trading, were not abandoned. These activities, especially farming, were probably expanded to fit the inclinations of the new Spanish colonial systems. Spanish needs not related to food production, such as craft production, were also begun.

Many of the initial reports concerning the physical geography of the islands characterized them as being fertile. The Spanish, who were based in Trujillo less than twenty-five years after contact, viewed the islands as a potential source for food. In addition, European livestock such as chickens and hogs were introduced to the islands, further diversifying the economy. This increase in diversity and eventual productivity gave the islanders prominence as the lone agricultural supporters of the port of Trujillo.

Some suggest that this increase in production was related to the introduction of encomienda system. This economic institution was initiated in Honduras in 1536 by Pedro de Alvarado and was documented in Trujillo in 1539. Early encomiendas were associated with significant landscape and cultural change on the islands as well as elsewhere in the New World. This system regulated all aspects of the indigenous persons' life from dwelling size and land standardization to religion and language.

Another change that took place because of this economic system dealt with the ways in which the islands were used and seen by the Spanish. Before the institution of the encomienda, the Bay Islands were treated as a single unit and the islanders were closely tied to each other in terms of production of goods and services to the mainland. However, this system broke the cohesion between the islands, and Utila was no longer attached to Trujillo. Instead, probably because of its geographical location, Utila was first attached to Puerto Caballos and then to Munguiche, coastal towns located farther to the west. At this time, Trujillo and Puerto Caballos were the major ports in this region and by 1582 the Bay Islands were producing sufficient foodstuffs to support the Spanish ports and ships returning to the Spanish homeland.

While the Spanish were successfully exploiting their new territories other European countries began to understand the value of the New World possessions. Spain's rivals thought that the best way to reap quick benefits would be to intercept Spanish ships of New World goods as they left their Central American ports. In 1643 the Bay Islands became a strategic point of interception because of their location in the Bay of Honduras.

As the Spanish encomienda system was thriving, the freebooters from France, Netherlands and mainly England found refuge in the islands. Because of the pirating activities, which began in the 1600s, the Spanish eventually called for the complete removal of the Bay Islands' population as well as any significant economic activity on the islands. For Utila, it was nearly one hundred years before any real economic activity resurfaced.

Agricultural Phase and the Cayman Islanders

Unlike the other nearby islands, Utila had a relatively quiet existence during the Spanish and Buccaneering period. Although *Lord (1975)* found evidence of an encomienda present on the island there was not much in the way of pirate activity because of the island's physical geography.

Utila had fewer places for the pirates to hide and it was much more difficult for them to penetrate the surrounding reef. It has been suggested that, as England considered the abolition of slavery, plantation owners of the Caymen Islands began to look elsewhere to settle. Utila and its cays were an inviting possibility. The early 1830s brought a new culture and subsequently a new economic agenda to the island.

The Cayman Islanders were one of the first groups to settle permanently on the Bay Islands. The first wave of islanders chose the Utila Cays as their final destination. It has been documented that nearly a dozen people migrated here. These farmers were looking for a place to go that had free land so they could cultivate subsistence crops. Because these new residents were of British origin they began to create ties, mostly commercial in nature, with the closest British outpost in British Honduras (Belize). However, Utila was fairly autonomous during its first years after permanent settlement. Not until 1849 did the Bay Islands petition the Crown to be included in the British Empire. Their first attempts were directed unsuccessfully towards Belize but three years later the islanders were successful. The political compact did little to improve Utila's economy. Development began only in 1868 when the small island gained a relationship with the United States, one that lasts until the present. About 1854 the islanders began to cultivate coconuts and bananas, among other things, to sell to a few ports around the Bay of Honduras. This growing trade relationship spurred the original Cayman settlers to relocate to Utila (now East Harbour) where land was more plentiful for plantation agriculture. This new Utilian economy based on export farm production coincided with the United States agricultural import interests, especially fruit that took Utila's economy to a new level.

According to *Lord (1975)*, economic expansion occurred in 1868 when two schooners from Portland, Maine arrived on Utila to buy bananas and coconuts for sale in New Orleans. Limes, bananas, coconuts, and other tropical fruits were also exported to New York, Tampa, and Boston. As shown in table as late as 1881 Utila was shipping goods to the United States. However by the end of the nineteenth century, the much larger United States fruit companies such as Standard Fruit and United Fruit overwhelmed the small operations from Utila.

Table 1: Utilian Goods exported to New Orleans, 1881

Coconut	Banana	Plantain	Mango	Lime	Pineapple
950	1880 bunches	5000	5 lbs	1 lb	16 dozen

The initial fruit operation on Utila was much different than that which developed later. The system that was prominent in the mid 1800s relied on "pickups". The Bay Islands were just one of many tropical ports that these companies visited to support their business. However these "pickups" were time consuming and gave the companies little control over the quality of product they received. Therefore, by the early 1900s the precursors of the United Fruit in Tela and Standard Fruit in La Ceiba had clearly made themselves the new fruit ports and the "pickup" ports, like Utila and the rest of the Bay Islands, had become obsolete. In 1872, Utila's economy suffered another blow when the Bay Islands became a department of Honduras. Although the islands continued to govern themselves, Honduras wanted to enforce the Wyke-Cruz Treaty. In doing this, the Honduran government was essentially curtailing the islands' relationship with the United States. Rose commented on the situation as follows:

> *"...the (ensuing) change of laws gave a crippling blow, for some time, to the industries in the islands and to the hopes of the people. There was general discontent chiefly on account of the high import duties imposed under the new laws. And this discontent was perhaps excusable, because the people had always been accustomed to very low tariffs."*

The islanders honored the stipulations of the treaty to a certain extent, but many believed that they could continue living under English common law. This was a mistake on their part, and in 1902 the islands were visited by the H.M.S. Psyche, a vessel sent to inform the Bay Islanders that they were no longer British citizens. The islands did not prosper from the fruit business that was booming on the mainland, instead, the islanders, for the next 40 years, struggled to reverse the slump they had entered into at the turn of the century.

On Utila islanders were forced to begin making concessions, both socially and economically, while trying to regain their former lifestyles *(Rose 1904)*. American imported luxury items, which the islanders had become accustomed to purchasing, were no longer economically possible. Specialized plantation crops that were sold during the "pickup" period were diversified to fit the available markets. From 1929 to 1939, these agricultural markets declined; wage labour was scarce because little craft specialization had taken place on the island, and the shipping industry was defunct *(ibid)*. Thus, in 1929 the "Coconut Oil" years began on Utila *(ibid)*. Coconuts were one of the crops that had become more important after the brief fruit trade business ended and became the island's primary income producer. The process of making coconut oil was time consuming, labour intensive, and rather arduous *(ibid)*. The population of Utila became very resourceful during this time of economic depression and certain social and cultural traits began to form. In fact, the beginning of the next decade was a turning point for Utilian society.

In the words of *Lord (1975:36)*, "the decade of the 1940s marked a dramatic turning point in Utila's history, and two events in particular at the beginning of this period coloured the socio-cultural systems in Utila today." More importantly, for the purposes of this work, this new economic system and the cultural adaptations which developed out of it have been influential in the development of the tourism industry that dominates the island's economy today.

The Remittance Period

Although the coconut industry on Utila did see a veritable boom period and islanders began aspiring to travel and become educated in the United States, reality struck as the price of coconut dropped to only 5 US cents each in the 1950s. Yet another economic slump ensued on the island. However, large scale merchant shipping had reached the Bay of Honduras by the 1940s, and the versatile islanders, who were already competent and experienced sailors, took advantage of the opportunity. The heritage of Utila's men going to sea to fish and to carry products to market coupled with their attachment to Anglo-America, made the transition from farming and fishing to maritime service a logical and easy step. Additionally, the labour intensive cash crop farming in the insect-infested bush and the poor market conditions of the "post bellum" economy ensured that fishing and agriculture would never again be more than a part time income source for most Utilians. Many of Utila's banana and coconut plantations by 1950 had been destroyed by disease and hurricanes *(ibid)*. Therefore, the maritime service industry, which began during the 1940s, became the primary economic institution on the island.

In Charles Wilson's 1968 work, he discusses the beginnings of the merchant marine service in the Bay Islands. He traced its origins to World War II, when the United States, in 1940, leased some of the larger and better equipped banana ships for emergency defence duty *(ibid)*.

By 1941, the United Fruit Company began sending representatives to Utila and the other islands to sign up men to work on their steamship lines. Shortly, some of the men found themselves working in the United States merchant shipping service. Neither Lord nor Wilson were clear on whether United Fruit was involved in the emergency leasing program or if they were simply training a reserve of sailors for their own use, nevertheless scores of Utilian men were acquiring marketable skills as the coconut industry dwindled. The remittance period in Utila's economic history was born out of necessity both for the Utilians and the United States. After World War II adult males ranging in age from 18 to 55, on regular basis left their island home to sail the open ocean. For periods of nine to twelve months, men would work for various shipping lines, sending their wages home *(ibid)*. These jobs were a dependable source of income for the men and their families. Additionally, the fringe benefits while on the ships secured this occupation as a lasting economic industry for Utila. During this time, Utila again oriented itself to the United States.

The USA became the land of opportunity for many Utilians. Children were sent to New Orleans for schooling and many families subsequently moved to the United States. New York and New Orleans have large Utilian communities today. As the merchant business of the 1940s took off, many locals realized that trying to make a living solely on agriculture and reclaiming the lifestyle before the introduction of the remittance system was unrealistic. This fact was reinforced in 1961 when Hurricane Anna struck the Bay of Honduras. Although the hurricane did not strike Utila directly, according to Lord, some 75,000 coconut palms were destroyed approximately one-third of the islands' total *(ibid)*. He also reported, for nearly two years following the event not a single plantain could be found growing on the island *(ibid)*. Subsequently, few men were inclined to repair the damage and hopes of reestablishing an agricultural market on the island were dashed. Utila settled into the remittance system that still exists in some form, but tourism has become of increasing importance.

Many traditional elements of Utila's society pre-adapted it for the remittance system and more importantly for this discussion, for the developing tourism industry today. These traditions include an emphasis on individualism, commercialism, and consumerism or non-cooperation. Lord suggested that these pre-adaptations are intimately interrelated and share equal importance in motivating the islanders into economic situations *(ibid)*. Since the Cayman Islanders first began farming on the island a shared attitude of independent economic, social, and political action has created the basis for the cultural trait of individualism *(ibid)*. The first farmers were generally independent of their neighbours. The lack of inter-family dependency allowed men to leave the islands to take part in the remittance system because families were so independent.

As tourism began to develop as a viable industry on the island very little cooperative effort was seen and businesses started, and continue to run, as family operations. Commercialism and consumerism follow along these same lines in that it is rare to see any sort of cooperative work ventures. This attitude is still present today, and is evident in the constant price wars between dive shops and hotel owners and the general skepticism that has occurred when ideas of creating regulations on prices are introduced by foreign owners. Additionally social and political actions tend to be more self-serving. Since the time of the original settlers, one's prestige and other accomplishments have been considered a function of individual effort, thus preserving the ideas of non-cooperation *(ibid)*. These traits can still be seen as islanders only get "up-in-arms" if their personal businesses are being effect by another's actions. More importantly for this discussion were the adaptations islanders made during the remittance period concerning attitudes of "rest and relaxation" for the men who returned home from sea. In total the economic history of Utila has had many peaks and valleys, from subsistence agriculture to commercial agriculture to the remittance period and now tourism. However, these endeavours have fostered certain traits that have helped the islanders to survive.

Tourism Development on Utila

The tourist development of the Bay Islands is a forgone conclusion. No area of such beauty and such accessibility can remain undiscovered and unexploited. To yield their full potential, however, careful planning is indicated...It would be most unfortunate if the beauty of the Bay Islands was not available to all visitors to—and residents of—Central America. Nature has not created comparable attractions along the Caribbean coasts of Guatemala, Nicaragua or Costa Rica. The Bay Islands are a truly regional resource. Before beginning a discussion of the history of the tourism industry on Utila, perhaps a note on tourist types is appropriate. Paul *Fussell (1980)* distinguished the tourist from three other types of people who take trips. His first classification is the explorer. Explorers seek the undiscovered and believe that no others have gone before. Christopher Columbus and his crew and the many other conquistadors who visited this part of the world during the colonial period are early examples. Travellers, Fussell's second type follow the explorers and attempt to learn about the newly discovered areas through study and experience. In the Bay Islands, people such as Mitchell-Hedges and his associates and William Duncan Strong, the first ethnologists and archeologists to visit the Bay Islands, are considered among this group. Travellers did not make it to the islands until early in the 20th century.

Fussell's definition of the tourist differs from the others because they seek areas already discovered by businesses and publicized by the media. People who want nothing to do with the mass stereotypical tourist destinations and seek only the most remote of places that they perceive to be more authentic Fussell labels the antitourist. These people, he believes, imagine themselves as travellers, however, the days of the explorer and traveller are long past because few places on Earth have not been visited by humans.

Fussell's typology lacks a category for the scoundrels, fugitives, and scallywags who visited the islands before they were developed by the modern Bay Islanders. Further, he does not suggest where academic researchers fit into this scheme. Still, utilizing his discussion, it is possible to determine when the first modern tourist reached Utila and that travellers came to the island well before tourism become a major economic component of the world market after World War II. The Bay Islands remained relatively remote until well into the twentieth century. Although they were accessible to wealthy explorers, scholars and the occasional fugitive, for the modern tourist, getting to the islands was difficult because the only transportation from the mainland was by small dories and fishing boats. Travellers such as Mitchell-Hedges gave accounts that portrayed images of a rustic, savage place with extensive reefs that held ship wrecks.

The possibility of pirate treasures hidden in the reefs lured the first major wave of tourists to the islands in the late 1970s. However, Utila's potential for tourism did not go unnoted by Rose in 1904, well before tourist began visiting the island. Ritchie, Davidson and Lord in the 1960s and 1970s, when an infant industry was beginning to develop on the islands, also noted the possibilities an economy based on tourism could bring to the islanders. Nevertheless, for Utila, it would be well into the 1980s before tourism became a significant component of their island economy. The conclusion of World War II brought a world boom in tourism and travel world wide. The Bay Islands and much of the western Caribbean, however, did not participate in the tourism explosion. Inadequate transportation, infrastructure, and boarding facilities were among the primary reasons for this lack of participation. The region also had acquired a reputation as being politically unstable.

In the late 1960s a diminutive modern tourism industry emerged in the islands as regular airline service from the mainland was initiated. In this same decade several popular periodicals suggested that the islands were perfect places for the adventuresome traveller who found sailing, diving and treasure hunting appropriate activities. Also fundamental in development of the tourism industry on the Bay Islands were the Honduran legislative actions taken in the 1980s to help the existing economic crisis. Additionally, the political unrest during the 1970s was resolved and a perception of peace throughout Central America contributed to the growing industry.

Though a modern tourism industry emerged in the 1960s it grew fairly slowly until the 1990s. Roatán had the largest number of hotels in 1960, while Utila and Guanaja each had only one. By 1989 Roatán's numbers had decreased by two leaving the island with only ten hotels while Guanaja's numbers had increased to four and Utila's to three. The inhibiting factors present during the 1960s, such as in adequate facilities and accessible transportation remained unresolved well into the 1980s.

Table 2 : Hotels on the Bay Islands from 1960-2001

	Roatan		*Guanaja*		*Utila*	
Year	*Hotels*	*Rooms*	*Hotels*	*Rooms*	*Hotels*	*Rooms*
1960-1969	12	81	1	H" 4	1	H" 2
1970-1979	11		4	H" 46	1	H" 5
1980-1989	10	168	4	46	3	34
1990-2001	59	953	18	178	28	330

A ferry service between La Ceiba and the island settlements of Utila, Oak Ridge, and French Harbour had been established but the transportation infrastructure on the islands improved very little. For example, Utila had no paved roads until the late 1990s aside from a small portion of Main Street that was paved in the early 1970s. In 1988 through international assistance, Roatán's small airstrip outside Coxen Hole was enhanced to handle jet aircraft *(ibid)*. In that same year, Honduras's airline Tan Sahsa began offering regular airline services between the mainland and the island, from several Central American countries, and from Miami, New Orleans, and Houston *(ibid)*. Service into the United States lasted only a few years because in 1994 the United States banned the airline because of safety violations *(ibid)*.

Utila's airport is the smallest of the three islands and is currently unpaved, therefore no international flights have flown into the island. As of 2001 only two airlines service Utila, Sosa and Atlantic.

Isleña Airlines recently discontinued services because the dirt runway was damaging the airplanes. Currently Utila has five daily flights, two in the morning, one at midday, and two in the early evening before dark. There are no scheduled flights after dark on the island because the runway is not equipped with properly lighted.

In 1974 approximately 1,000 tourist visited the Bay Islands, however by 1988 this number had risen to approximately 15,000. The 1990s has been the decade for the Bay Islands' tourism industry. In 1997 roughly 93,000 tourists visited the islands. This number was nearly quadruple the islands population total in the 1988 census.

In the early 1990s approximately 11% of the islands' total labour force was employed in service sector jobs *(ibid)*. By the end of the decade nearly 80% of the islands' population was directly or indirectly dependent on the tourism industry *(ibid)*. Most islanders were employed as service personal with little or no training and those in management or executive positions were mostly foreign *(ibid)*.

The number of tourist facilities from 1985 to 1996 also grew substantially from 17 to 80 for all the islands. Utila's proportion of hotels increased from 18% to 30%; total number of rooms increased from 34 to 199. Of course, Roatán still attracts the greatest number of tourist. Roatán also has the greatest price range for hotels; 10$ to $1500 daily. Guanaja has the highest mean price for daily lodging $94.25, and as might be expected Utila is the least expensive ($18.04). Since 1996 Utila has experienced an even greater spurt of development and continues to grow today.

Sea, Sun and Drugs: Factors that Attract Tourists to Utila

Utila's culture history prepared it well for a tourism industry. One of the most important cultural traits for the development of the tourism industry, which began during the remittance period, was the relaxing of laws and social norms for men returning from sea. Because of this, an atmosphere of "heavy partying and drinking" became a common occurrence on the island.

These relaxed social laws have been important in drawing tourists to the island. Women are free to walk around in swimsuits and men in shorts without being harassed by locals as might occur on the mainland. Alcohol and drugs are easily accessible on the islands and local law enforcement officials rarely make arrests for public drunkenness or drug possession. When they do, however, if the suspect can pay their fine, they are released within 24 hours. Utila has become so well known for its drug activity that an event was created to play off of this reputation. In August of 1998, Utilians hosted the first Sun Jam festival on Water Cay. In only four years the event has become the epitome of drinking, drugs, and partying on the island. People from all over the world visit Utila to take part in the festival. It has become so popular that the organizers feel having another in the spring could be financially beneficial for the island.

There are two main organizers (one local and one local foreign) although many others on the island participate. The organizers start receiving shipments of drugs weeks in advance as they prepare for the masses of tourists who are expected to participate (personal communications). These organizers also section off the small cay to local businesses who want to set up small booths to sell food and drinks (mostly alcoholic). At the centre of the cay is a large makeshift bar and D.J. booth where European "techno" and "trans" music can be heard playing well into the next day. Local boat owners ferry tourist to and from Water Cay for a small price (about 50 Lps or $3 US). They are usually packed well over their carrying capacity as was shown the year before when a boat turned over on its return trip. Advertising for the event occurs mainly by word of mouth between groups of tourists travelling through Central America although there is an Internet site set up especially for the occasion. Sun Jam has become a cult-like event as many "Sun Jamers" return each year to take part. The festival is not solely made up of foreign tourists as many Hondurans also visited Utila, "to see if something like this really takes place in Honduras." No matter how people came to know about the event, all informants had one thing in common, they wanted to take part in the drug activity.

Because Sun Jam is held on Utila, and is organized by locals, it appeared to be a moderately controlled environment. For example, it was reported that organizers had "taken care" of the police well in advance so that none were seen on Water Cay during the festival. This sense of security may also play a part in the popularity of Sun Jam as many informants expressed their reservation about taking part in drug activities in other places in Central America. However, on the Friday before the festival, an American military helicopter landed on the island. It was never confirmed why it had come and no one ever saw military walking around the island, but many suspected a major international drug bust. An attempt was made to determine the number of tourists on the island during this event. One local hotel and dive shop owner said that all rooms on the island were occupied so Many "Sun Jamers" where leaving for Water Cay the day before the event started to set up tents and hammocks. One estimate of the number of partiers was over 500. This number seems possible if all the hotel rooms were filled because at least 330 rooms are now available on the island and more than half of these are able to sleep more than one person. Additionally, a number of multiple occupant apartments are available. All included, the total occupant load of the island is well above 500.

The Sun Jam festival makes up a sizable portion of the summer tourism economy. There was no other time during the summer of 2001 that all the hotels were full and lines would form outside restaurants. Although it last only a weekend, the financial potentials for the local industry has become an important part of the summer tourism season.

The drinking and partying atmosphere is not the only draw for Utila. In fact before drugs were a major part of the Utilian allure, small groups of people were visiting the islands to explore, dive and fish the reefs. In the 1960s the islands' reefs and the possibility of "sunken treasures" attracted groups of American and European tourists to the island.Long before the local diving industry was established, fully equipped groups would visit the island and pay locals to take them to the reefs and lead them on underwater expeditions. On occasion these early divers initiated destructive practices when they removed objects hidden in the reefs. One diver reportedly used dynamite to reach the Spanish treasures that had been encased in the reefs. However, the Bay Islander's have also been accused of destroying the reefs.

Other tourists were more interested in fishing the still plentiful waters surrounding the island and discovering Utila's "pristine" island environment. By 1980 Utila had entered into its present economic phase.

Emergence of the Present Tourism Industry

From about 1960 onward a small but relevant tourism industry was beginning to form on the island. As early as 1965, in the report by Ritchie and his associates, Utila was recognized for its inexpensive appeal. The group wrote,

> *"The initial development of Utila should attempt to maintain a balance between the bargain appeal (the present boarding house charges $3 dollars per day American plan) and accommodations of quality that can be promoted by U.S. travel agencies...Design should be of high standards and in keeping with the architecture of the town. The objective is first-class comfort and housekeeping, without luxuries."*

These first tourists were made up of recreational sailors, fishermen, and SCUBA divers along with the occasional "hippie". In 1971, when Davidson carried out his survey of the Bay Islands tourism facilities, Utila had only one small hotel, the Jimenéz. A few years later, when Lord conducted his research on Utila he noted the presence of three local bars, including the most famous and the only one still in operation: the Bucket of Blood Bar. A handful of facilities existed before 1980. However, when the Honduran Government realized the islands' potential as a means to end the economic crisis of the 1980s, Utila, along with the other three islands, began to reap the economic benefits of new governmental legislation.

The periods of the most intensive growth can be linked to the establishment of these policies. The implications of these policies for landscape and cultural change have been important in this discussion. However, in this section, I will reconstruct the emergence of the industry on the island using dates acquired from locals and other documents from local tourism facilities.

Aside from Hotel Jimenéz, before 1980 Utila had one other family owned hotel, Hotel Trudy. A second hotel was begun sometime in the mid 1970s but was never finished. Its skeleton is visible on a ridge west of town. Locals say that an American named Duncan began the hotel. However, he ran out of money and left the island, "never to be seen again" *(Rafeal 2001)*. Now, the hill site is known by locals as Duncan Hill. As one of the few high outcrops of coral on the island the view is panoramic over the entire settlement of East Harbour. The hotel ruins are now home to ladino squatters. In addition to the two boarding facilities, Utila had one travel agency, (Morgan's Travel) (site unknown), two restaurants (site unknown), a general store (site unknown), three bars and an airstrip. As before 1980, tourism facilities on Utila were rare and the industry was still in its infancy. The situation changed during the 1980s.

As SCUBA diving became more popular worldwide after the 1970s the flow of tourist increased to the island. The first organized dive schools were established during the 1980s and included, Cross Creek Dive Centre, Utila Water Sports, and Utila Dive Centre. Three new hotels were also built, Cross Creek Hotel, Celena, and Blueberry Hill, and the first small resort was built in East Harbour (Utila Lodge). However, Utila Lodge was not advertised as a resort until the mid 1990s.

Cross Creek Hotel began a trend that has been followed in recent years, that is, dive shops build their own hotels or establish contracts with existing hotels for rooms. This arrangement allows the dive schools to advertise packages that give their clients cheaper rates on rooms. These arrangements have caused conflicts among locally owned dive shops and foreign owned dive shops. Cross Creek, along with its dive shop and hotel, also constructed a restaurant to complete its tourism complex.

Other restaurants were also built during the 1980s namely Mermaid's Corner, The Jade Seahorse, and Utila's first mainland-owned business, Las Delicias. Additionally, a second travel agency was built, as well as a bank, Hondutel telecommunications office, and two supermarkets. The decade of the 1980s began the escalation of the modern industry, with diving being its primary attraction.

Utila is known worldwide for being one of the "cheapest" places in the world to dive and thus attracts a certain type of tourist. The establishment of the first dive centres and the understanding of the type of tourist the island was attracting created a more coherent industry. Local businesses focused their attention and efforts towards building on this attraction. As each new diving school was built a hotel soon followed. With the exception of the three resorts, all of the other tourist related businesses stayed within the "unspoken" price parameters.

The 1990s brought the greatest changes to Utila's tourism industry and by the summer of 2001 Utila had developed into a thriving diving-oriented tourist centre. Today the island has 11 dive shops, reduced from a high of 14. Two dive shops, Sea Eye Dive Centre and Reef Resort Dive Shop, closed shortly after opening because of internal competition. After the Reef Resort Dive Shop closed in 1997 the owners converted the building into the Reef Cinema, one of two places on the island where films can be viewed. Within an eight year period eight dive shops have opened and are flourishing on the island.

As the diving industry continued to grow, an accompanying increase in the number of hotels and other related tourist facilities appeared to accommodate visitors. By the summer of 2001 Utila had 28 fully operational hotels and an addition five hotels were under construction. In addition, many islanders were renting extra rooms and empty houses to tourists who wanted to stay on the island for longer periods of time. Some 19 new restaurants, bars, and cafés were also constructed between 1990 and 2001. These new facilities were built especially for the growing tourist industry. In addition to the new dive shops, hotels and restaurants that were established in the last 11 years some 23 other tourist related facilities have also been built. These businesses include three internet shops, two bicycle rental shops, several souvenir shops, several laundry services, several boutiques, two community health centres, several household good stores and two bottled water businesses.

The bottled water business beginnings are in direct correlation with the escalating numbers of tourist to the island. Before the 1990s Utilians used well water and cistern water for drinking and other related needs. Imported bottled water was available for consumption on the island, however, when large numbers of foreigners start visiting the island locals saw the potential for personal profit. Therefore the two businesses began operation. Since 1970 nearly 49% of the tourist related facilities constructed, were built in the settlement of East Harbour on unoccupied land. While 51% of the facilities were placed in existing buildings or on land formally occupied. Of this 51%, 25% of the new facilities were housed in converted private dwellings. Although only 49% of the new buildings were built on unoccupied land the landscape and land-use patterns existent on Utila before tourism became an important economic factor were beginning to undergoing change.

Utila does not have the infrastructure that the other islands possess, such as 24-hour electricity or island-wide sewage disposal or plumbing. The island's electricity comes from a diesel powered-generator. In 1965 the generator ran only during the early morning and early evening, less than nine hours a day. Many islanders remember this time and joked that if the generator came on during the night it meant someone had died. A generator still produces the power on the island. It normally runs from six in the morning until midnight. Because of fuel shortages and frequent mechanical problems, neighbourhood outages often occur. Such inconsistencies required that tourist facilities have their own generators to guarantee their services.

New Trends in Development

Previous observers have noted a general pattern to the location of tourist facilities and the degree to which they alter the landscape. Until recently most of the tourist facilities that have been built on Utila have been concentrated in the settlement of East Harbour. Thus the islands' natural landscape, such as mangrove and tropical forests, had not been significantly altered.

However, the new trend to locate tourist facilities and residential areas away from the existing settlement of East Harbour has caused drastic changes to the natural landscape. These new developments have been constructed to cater to higher paying clientele and provide services beyond room and board. In the 1990s Utila acquired its first two resorts of this nature, the Laguna Beach Resort and the Reef Resort. Additionally, by the end of the decade two residential development projects had been started that have significantly altered the natural landscape.

There are two areas on Utila in which these developers have located: on the eastern tip of the island where the fragile iron shore is located and along the southwestern shore facing the cays. The development underway on the eastern tip of the island incorporates four different sites, including "Rocky Point Estates," "Paradise

Cove at Red Cliff," an unnamed site, and "Aquarium" hotel and residential lots. However, for the purpose of this discussion, this area will be referred to as one site. Both developments incorporate beach-front property in otherwise uninhabited parts of the island. It seems these developers bought large chunks of land for a relatively low price and then cleared the natural vegetation so that they could section the land off into smaller lots to sell to foreign tourists. We specify foreign tourists because, as many islanders explained to me, they can not afford to buy these lots from the developers. An estimated price of one such lot on the eastern tip was about $ 80,000 US dollars. These properties are being brokered through locally owned Alton's Real Estate, and American-owned Utila Island Properties.

The development on the southwestern section of the island was purchased and developed first, and already has attracted foreign buyers. Advertised prices for lots, including small houses, begin at $100,000 US dollars. The second development, on the eastern tip, came with the construction of the new airport. When the large machines were brought to the island to be used in the airport's construction, contractors soon realized the roads in the existing community were not strong enough or wide enough to allow passage. Therefore, a new road was cut beginning at the northern end of the old airport and wrapping around the northeastern coastline of the island. The real estate development began soon after this road was cut because, before, this area was virtually inaccessible except by boat. Essentially these areas will become foreign enclaves, well separated both geographically and economically, from the rest of the community on Utila. Additionally, if this development continues unchecked, a previously undeveloped area, close to mangrove habitant, tropical forests, and the delicate iron shore, may well suffer irreversible damage. During the summer of 2001, many locals became aware of the possible negative implications of these new developments. However, they soon discovered they had little say in the way in which land was sold and developed on the island. Therefore, fearing what had happened on Roatán, many local business owners petitioned the local government officials to create a Chamber of Commerce. This surge of local community participation was fueled by one of the owners of the sites on the eastern tip of the island.

An American man had begun developing land in this area, however, his land did not have direct access to the water because of the presence of the iron shore. Additionally, he had already sold the land near the iron shore and begun cutting paths to the beach without going through the proper channels and without acquiring the proper permits. Soon after he was fined and had to replace the coral he removed but the damage had been done. Many locals hope that by creating the Chamber of Commerce, unchecked development such as this will not continue to occur. If this new trend continues unabated, previously undeveloped areas of the island, which are close to important natural resources such as mangrove stands and iron shore, may suffer irreversible environmental degradation. The populated cays southwest of Utila are another matter.

Development on the Utila Cays

The two largest cays, Suc-Suc and Pigeon, have developed into a thriving fishing community separate from Utila. During the first surveys of the area in the 1970s, no tourism facilities were documented. However, since 1980 three small hotels have been constructed: Hotel Kayla, Lone Star Hotel, and Vicky's Rooms (found above Vicky's General Store). There is also a small house for rent at the west end of Pigeon Cay.

Many Cayens (This term is meant to distinguish those people who live on the cays fro those who live on Utila. It is a term that is used by Cayens and Utilians.) expressed that they serve as a day excursion spot for the tourists who are staying on Utila. One business owner expressed that much of her daily business comes from the diving boats. She said, "We are close to one of their favourite dive spots, so the instructors bring their divers here for lunch instead of going all the way back to Utila." Rarely, however, are the Cayen hotels full. It was suggested that their tourism lags behind the main island because they lack sufficient resources. For example, no fresh water wells exist on the cays and the closest well on Utila is not potable. Rain cisterns are present on the cays, which provide minimal water for washing purposes, but bottled drinking water has to be imported from the mainland or from the main island. Allowing large numbers of tourist onto the cays, many Cayens feel, could be detrimental to their water supply. Garbage disposal, which is already a problem, would also be magnified, if tourism were to expand. Many Cayens expressed their contentment with their tourism status.

The ten smaller, uninhabited cays, however, have become popular tourist spots. These include Diamond Cay, Jack O'Neil's Cay and Water Cay. Diamond Cay, just off the south eastern tip of Suc-Suc Cay, once housed the Utila Cay's Dive Shop and Hotel. Tourists can now rent or buy the abandoned structures. Jack Neil's Cay, Morgan Cay and Sandy Cay can also be rented (house included) for about 400 Lps a day ($27 US). Water Cay has become a favourite spot for tourists and islanders and has earned the reputation as being the "party island." To access the cay a caretaker charges one lempira a day. Hammocks are also available to rent from the caretaker's house for ten Lps. Utila's cays did not participate in the tourism boom found on the main island. Although, they do receive some business from the tourists that visit Utila, their economy has not become as dependent on this industry. Instead, this community continues to rely on the sea for its livelihood.

Defining Utila's Tourism Source Regions

The diversity of tourists that visit Utila is increasing. While discussing tourism issues with a few locals during the summer of 2001 this subject was broached. From their statements it seemed reasonable to infer that it was no longer just North Americans who were making up Utila's tourist population (or at least those staying in hotels).

This differs from documentation taken in the early years of the industry for the islands and especially the mainland. North Americans, more specifically those from the United States, have been documented as the major group visiting the North Coast and Bay Islands. However, today Europeans seem to make up the largest group on the island. Therefore, in trying to prove this shift I looked at several hotel records to try and determine places of origin for the island's tourists. By law each operating hotel on the island must keep a logbook that has all pertinent information about their visitors, such as, names, dates staying, place of passport issue, and where the tourist came from before arriving on Utila. I surveyed five of the local hotels ranging from the least expensive on the island to one of the higher priced hotels. It seemed important to do this to get an accurate view of the island's situation.

However, hotel owners either do not keep or would not divulge records any earlier than 1999. For each hotel it was necessary to make tallies of each person according to country. From the information gathered five categories seemed appropriate to get an accurate representation. The term "other" was used to group all persons not from Europe, North American, Central American, or South American because there were so few people not from one of the other categories. However, the diversity of this group is definitely increasing. The largest group visiting the island originated in Europe. North Americans were second. The stream of Central Americans is gradually increasing.

From the first travellers that ventured to the island, to the modern tourist, Utila's distinctive culture and impressive natural environment has spurred an economically prosperous industry. As the islanders realized this potential prosperity, tourism has become a significant economic factor. The most rapid phase of development occurred during the period from 1990 to 2001. The industry continues to grow, as is exemplified by the five hotels under construction.

However, until recently, development has been confined to the existing settlement of East Harbour and minimal landscape and land-use change has taken place. At the end of the last decade, Utila entered into a new phase of development that mimics the practices in other popular tourism sites such as Cancun and Jamaica. These practices include the building of larger more lavish resorts and housing developments away from the existing local community. In conjunction with the islands prosperity and as this new phase begins, large numbers of migrants have been flocking to the island seeking steady work. These groups bring cultural attributes that are different from those already in existence.

Island Tourism Development

When facing choices for economic development, island destinations share a number of common characteristics. These include:

* Small population

* Limited resources
* Insufficient capital to finance investment
* Little or no manufacturing
* High transportation costs
* Geographic isolation from markets.

Faced with these difficulties, there are few alternatives that island economies can pursue in terms of development. Most are dependent on one or several of the following:

* Agricultural exports
* Light manufacturing
* Export processing
* Fishing or other marine industry.

Tourism

The role that tourism plays in the economic development of small island economies is not unique to Hawaii or Okinawa. It is taking place in nearly every Pacific island destination at the present time. While the volume of tourism arrivals and the scale of tourism development may vary, each island destination is looking to tourism as its primary or at least one of the most important means to achieve economic development, and all destinations face common problems.

Importance of Sustainable Development

Sustainable development is a term often used to apply to tourism destinations and especially to small islands with limited resources. Sustainable tourism development emphasizes the need to achieve an appropriate balance between the economic, environmental, and socio-cultural aspects of tourism development and management. Due to their small size, island tourism destinations face a special challenge in achieving economic benefits for its people, determining the best use of its natural and environmental resources, and ensuring that development is appropriate to the socio-cultural characteristics of its resident or host community. Each of these aspects are summarized in this session and explored in greater detail in other sessions.

Economic Constraints

For many island destinations tourism is viewed as a means of economic diversification. In many destinations, agriculture or fishing was the major economic activity but increased globalization of the economy has put them at a disadvantage as the importance of export crops such as sugar cane production or fishery activity have declined. However, tourism is not an easy solution.

Because of the geographic isolation and limited resources of island destinations, they are most vulnerable to tourism-related economic costs that larger, continent-based destinations do not have.

Transportation is a key factor in terms of access of people and goods and in most cases poses a major obstacle for island destinations to achieve a successful tourism industry. The high economic costs of importing goods and services for tourists results in a high leakage factor from the gross tourism receipts or general revenues from tourism.

To the extent that goods such as food produce consumed by tourists and services required to support tourism must be imported, payments must flow out of the destination and profits must also be shared with outside investors. The extent of this leakage is quite high, and many island economies have tourism leakages of over 50% meaning half of the income from tourism flows out of the destination to pay for essential goods and services.

Environmental Constraints

Many island destinations are economically underdeveloped but have natural resources suitable for tourism. However, the conservation of the fragile ecosystems of these islands requires careful consumption of resources (water, energy) and factors such as waste treatment.

Islands also have limited fresh water resources and are more sensitive to sea level rises resulting from climate change. In terms of waste disposal, because of their size, islands also face environmental difficulties not found in larger continent-based destinations. If tourism is not well planned, developed and managed, it can result in negative environmental impacts such as: Water pollution-including pollution of coastal waters, rivers, and lakes resulting from improper waste management of sewage or solid waste system from hotels or other tourism facilities. In particular, coastal and marine environments are vulnerable to ecological damage caused by erosion and runoff which can endanger coral reefs Air, noise and traffic pollution-resulting from tourism activities and tourist vehicles and road congestion

Unattractive landscapes (visual pollution) – resulting from poor design of hotels and other tourism facilities, inadequate landscaping, obstruction of scenic views by tourism development Damage to historic and cultural sites – resulting from inappropriate development and overuse and misuse by tourists Ecological disruption of natural areas and wildlife – resulting from inappropriate development and overuse and misuse by tourists.

Socio-cultural Constraints

Although the economic benefits to the host or resident community may be substantial, the development of tourism facilities and services should also improve the quality of life for residents.

A major benefit has been the development of community infrastructure such as improved roads, water and other services for residents as a result of tourism development. When properly developed, tourism can also serve as a means to stimulate the practice and preservation of local cultures, folklore, traditions, arts and crafts, and cuisine while preserving historical, archaeological and religious monuments and sites.

However, at the same time, too rapid development or overdevelopment can often be detrimental to the host or resident community.

Destination Life Cycle

In understanding where an island destination is today in terms of tourism development, it might be helpful to review the concept of a destination life cycle. *(Refer to charts at the end of this section)* Historically, tourism destinations have tended to undergo an economic life cycle of four stages which may cover 50 to 75 years. This life cycle can apply to both the destination and to a specific resort. Each destination can be said to be at a different stage of the life cycle and faces different problems.

Exploration Stage

* Tourism facilities lacking
* Limited air transportation accessibility
* Destination relatively unknown.

Development Stage

* International class facilities available
* Better air accessibility
* Visitors increase, visible impact on local economy
* Government/residents welcome tourism
* Development is spontaneous and uncoordinated.

Maturity Stage

* Large number of tourists
* Loss of local decision-making power and control
* Hotels, airlines, tourism services dominated by international corporations
* Residents may develop hostile attitude toward tourism
* Competition for resources between residents and tourists.

Decline Stage

* Destination has well-established image but no longer popular
* Planning controls come too late
* Over-commercialized
* No sign of self-renewal.

While the destination life cycle may apply differently for each area, it can serve as a useful framework for policy makers to understand the development process for tourism and each destination's competitive position. Where the various destinations are on the life cycle scale is also of interest.

Most island destinations are in the exploration or development stages, while others such as Hawaii are well into the maturity stage and some may even say it is in a decline stage. Certainly, Waikiki, which is Hawaii's primary tourist destination, is now over 100 years old and much of it was unplanned and coordinated. Whether it can continue to rejuvenate itself and prevent decline is a major challenge.

Challenge to Island Destinations

While it is not surprising that so many island groups have chosen tourism as their principal means of economic development, most have encountered a number of difficulties. As each island destination has experienced more extensive tourism development, the common problems include:

* Increasing the number and type of tourism attractions
* Maintaining adequate air transportation routes and reasonable air fares
* Providing an appropriate level of accommodations and services
* Establishing adequate infrastructure including water, power, and sewerage facilities
* Providing effective government support for tourism planning and development
* Marketing and promoting the destination in competition with other island destinations
* Attracting outside investment capital for development
* Providing trained or skilled employees for the industry
* Among island destinations, Hawaii's development experience shares many similarities with Okinawa.

Historically, because both Hawaii and Okinawa were independent kingdoms, they had unique cultures which were brought under political and cultural domination through annexation.

Geographically, both Hawaii and Okinawa represent isolated island entities—Okinawa being the only island prefecture in Japan, and Hawaii being the only island state in the United States. Economically, the structures are similar with a dependence on tourism, military expenditures, and agriculture. Demographically, Hawaii and Okinawa have approximately the same-sized population, and their residents enjoy the highest longevity in their respective countries. In terms of tourism development, there are also many similarities.

Okinawa, like Hawaii is a warm weather destination with good beaches and ocean-oriented recreation which appeal to domestic tourists. Hawaii's largest number of tourists still come from the mainland U.S., and Okinawa's tourists are primarily from the main islands of Japan. For established tourism destinations like Hawaii and Okinawa, a major challenge is to maintain the ability to compete in the global tourism market place. Both must seek continuous reinvestment to support quality and freshness of appeal to maintain their respective market positions and avoid the possibility of decline.

In order to remain competitive, they must also continuously review and analyze their tourism markets and their products. The responsibility for tourism marketing and product development are largely a part of the government's role in planning for tourism development and management.

Market Analysis

An important challenge facing Hawaii and other island destinations is to widen the range of tourists both in terms of geographical origin and the type of activities they seek. This requires an understanding of the preferences of today's travellers based on their demographic characteristics including age, gender, income, marital status.

It is clear that because of the demographic changes, the attractions and activities offered by tourism destinations cannot remain the same year after year, but will need to adjust to the interests of different groups and preferences. The kinds of activities, accommodations and attractions which are popular today may not be popular tomorrow, and it is important for Hawaii and Okinawa to adjust to these changing market preferences.

Hawaii is currently reassessing its marketing strategy and looking increasingly toward market segmentation. It is looking at both new geographical markets but also special market segments. In terms of market segments, it has also developed new specialized tourism activities for selected markets in areas like ecotourism cultural tourism, sports tourism, and education tourism.

Product Analysis

As a tourism destination, Hawaii has many different tourism products to offer. In order to compete effectively, however, it is constantly examining these products which include the facilities, attractions, activities, and services to tourists and other visitors. The "image" or how Hawaii projects itself and how tourists see it is determined by its different products. Hawaii as an island destination projects an image of a sub-tropical beach resort destination with many ocean-related attractions and activities offering warm climate, friendly people and a unique historical and cultural heritage.

A large part of its image as a beach resort is projected through its recreational activities which are primarily water-oriented activities. However, these are not enough in today's competitive market. It is clear that if a beach resort destination is to succeed in today's global tourism market, it must offer other recreational activities besides its water-oriented activities.

In seeking new attractions, events, and ways of packaging its products, Hawaii is seeking ways to keep its repeat visitor market and attract new visitors.

Greater emphasis is being placed on improving visitor accommodations, facilities, and transportation systems. In particular, Hawaii is seeking ways to promote a greater role for its unique culture in enhancing the vacation experience for tourists. Increased emphasis is now being placed on protection, preservation, interpretation, and marketing of Hawaii's cultural and historic resources.

Role of Planning and Public Policy

Much of the success with which island economies like Hawaii and Okinawa will meet the challenge will depend on the public policies that will guide the development process and define the relationship between the public and private sectors. The government's interest is generally to develop a tourism industry, generate revenue, provide employment, and stimulate economic growth.

The private sector's perspective is to produce a profit and return on investment. But the success of tourism development also depends on a third important element and that is the partnership between the government, the industry, and the community. Community support is essential for any sort of development and the community perspective is critical to success.

Summary

There are many examples of the role that tourism plays in the economic development of small island destinations. It is taking place in nearly every Pacific island destination at the present time. While the volume of tourism arrivals and the scale of tourism development may vary, each island destination is looking to tourism as its primary or at least one of the most important means to achieve economic development and all face common problems. In the case of both Hawaii and Okinawa, the level of development is considerably higher than most other island destinations in the Pacific, but the level of competition and the changing trends in the visitor markets require a good understanding of the process of tourism development to ensure continuing success in global tourism.

6

New Trends in Health Tourism

The worldwide trends in trade of health-related services are looked at in detail in the fourth paper in The Lancet Series on Trade and Health, written by Professor Richard Smith, London School of Hygiene and Tropical Medicine, UK, and colleagues. In their analysis, the authors use the classification provided by the WTO for the General Agreement on Trade and Services (GATS): cross-border supply of health services, consumption of services abroad, foreign direct investment, and movement of health professionals.

Cross-border supply of health services does not receive much media attention, but many countries have invested heavily in this area. Teleradiology, for example, has benefited from the shift from hard copy to digital imaging. India, the Philippines, and Cuba are leaders in the exportation of medical-transcription services, telepathology, and telediagnostic services.

The authors say: "Demand for cross-border e-health is related to cost and, to a lesser extent, timing. For instance, the yearly salary for US non-specialised radiologists is \$300 000, but only \$20 000 for their Indian counterpart." But e-health brings its share of concerns as well as benefits. Who is legally liable when there are problems? And concerns have been raised about care becoming fragmented and disintegrated when e-services are used in this way.

Private patients seeking healthcare abroad "health tourism" is becoming big business. Thailand is the leading exporter at over 1 million patients per year and revenues of \$615 million, but India is predicted to have revenues of $2•2 billion, Singapore $1•6 billion, and Malaysia $590 million by 2012. The demand for services abroad is driven by domestic non-availability, often in specialised and niche or alternative treatment areas.

Low labour costs combined with high-quality medical professionals (many of whom trained in the USA or UK) give many developing countries a huge cost advantage. And it is not, as often thought, just cosmetic procedures that are 'selling'.

Heart-bypass surgery can be performed in Thailand for US$8,000, compared with $20,000 in the UK and $24,000 in the USA. The average cosmetic surgery comes in at around $3500 in Thailand, $10,000 in the UK and $20,000 in the USA. The potential for expansion of this trade is enormous.

The authors say: "The main constraint on trade is the scarcity of insurance portability. Many national insurance schemes restrict patients seeking foreign service providers when that service is available domestically. In the European Union (EU), for example, although there is portability across member countries for emergency care, elective care needs previous approval from domestic health authorities."

Foreign direct investment (FDI – mode 3), typically in new hospitals or clinics, has grown rapidly. Between 1990 and 2000, FDI from developed to developing countries grew from US$36 billion to $155 billion (over three-times that of official development aid) and FDI in services accounted for more than half of all FDI.

However, FDI in health remains small compared with other sectors, because of the nature of the services (many health facilities are publicly owned) and the existence of regulatory barriers. Developing countries are increasingly looking towards FDI as a source of capital investment in their health sector, as well as the potential for general infrastructure development, and investment in and transfer of technology and skills.

But concerns exist about foreign control of healthcare provision; increased privatisation of health (in mainly public systems); and associated concerns about the diversion of resources to curative and high-end procedures, domestic brain drain, and advantageous patient selection.

Migration has historically been the main pathway for health-services trade. Currently around 30% of UK doctors are of foreign origin, with India, Ireland, Pakistan, South Africa and Egypt providing the majority of these.

In the USA, Canada and Australia around 20% of doctors are foreign; many of whom are from the UK. Loss of doctors from poorer countries has a disproportionate effect on the national stock of skills in those nations.

For nurses, low- and middle-income countries provide the majority of foreign nurses working in the UK – in 2002, around half of the 25,602 work permits issued to foreign workers for nursing were to nurses from The Philippines or India. Job satisfaction, pay and career opportunities are among the reasons healthcare workers wish to migrate.

The authors say: "However, the effect of migration on human capital stocks (so-called brain drain) is a cause of concern. The ultimate destination of workers to rich countries, and often the private sector within these countries, has knock-on effects down the chain to public sectors within wealthy nations, private and public sectors in low-income countries, and ultimately the rural areas within poorer countries."

The authors conclude: "Perhaps because health care is fundamentally about people-health professionals and patients-that modes 2 and 4 of service delivery are the most prevalent and arguably most important areas of trade in health services is unsurprising." "No universal policy recommendation can be made concerning a country's involvement with trade in health services. Instead, every country needs to assemble the relevant information to assess how such trade can affect its key areas of concern... The stewardship of a domestic health system in the context of the trade environment in the 21st century needs a sophisticated understanding of how trade in health services affects, and will affect, a country's health system and policy."

Healthy Trade in Health Tourism

As food and oil prices rocket all over the world, consumers are getting a crash course in economics: when demand increases, prices increase. Although food and oil dominate the headlines, life's other essentials also obey this cast-iron law, including healthcare, which is threatening to bust government budgets all over the world. As with food, part of the solution lies in opening up trade and competition.

The Organization of Economic Community and Development estimates that world average healthcare expenditure last year accounted for 9 percent of GDP, up from just over 5 percent in 1970. The US now spends more than US$2 trillion per year on healthcare, eight times the amount in 1980. US healthcare costs are currently increasing by twice general inflation, a general trend in rich countries.

As populations grow older and more demanding, these inflationary pressures will increase. Politicians are finding cashed-strapped voters increasingly unwilling to stump up the large amounts of tax needed to fund government health systems, forcing them to deny treatments to patients in a bid to constrain costs. In the US, healthcare costs have become a major issue in the presidential election.

The last decade, by contrast, has seen very low inflation for other goods, partly because of a massive increase in global trade. The arrival of China and India as major new exporters has meant that most countries have been able to import goods cheaply, keeping prices down.

While the role of free trade in driving down prices and driving up quality has long been accepted by economists (and, to an extent, politicians), healthcare has been one area in which there has been almost no international trade. It is time for this to change.

Communications technology makes it increasingly easy for hospitals to outsource services such as diagnostics to laboratories overseas, cutting costs and treatment time. Patients can get treatment overseas where costs are lower. Open-heart surgery in India costs only one-sixth of the price in the US, including travel, accommodation and medicines. If only 10 percent of US patients went abroad for 15 types of treatment, they and insurance firms could save US$1.5 billion a year, including travel.

Patients are already voting with their feet. In 2006 alone, Singapore treated 500,000 foreign patients, India treated 600,000 and Thailand around 1.2 million. Other favourite destinations include Malaysia, South Africa and Cuba. Taiwan's Council for Economic Planning and Development believes it could bring in NT$7 billion (US$230.4 million) a year.

While the benefits of free trade in health are clear for rich countries, developing countries also stand to gain. Most obviously, there are opportunities for much-needed investment of foreign capital. These financial opportunities would also give developing countries' medical staff a far greater incentive to remain at home, reducing the debilitating "brain drain." As more money came into the health sector, some of the burden on government healthcare would be removed.

Despite the significant benefits, only two developed countries have ratified a WTO agreement on trade in healthcare – Iceland and Norway. While developing countries such as Gambia, Jamaica, Malawi and South Africa are prepared to liberalize, wealthier countries seem bent on protectionism.

This reluctance is largely down to lobbying by interest groups in developed countries. Public sector unions seek to protect their members and industries from competition. Non-governmental organizations ideologically oppose trade in healthcare, claiming that only governments can ensure "equity" and "universal" treatment – even though public healthcare in most of the world fails patients miserably.

This is a massive wasted opportunity. Free trade in healthcare could help rich countries keep the lid on healthcare inflation while helping poorer countries attract investment and skills and retain valuable medical professionals.

For this to happen, developed countries must encourage insurers to cover overseas treatment and open up their medical sectors to international competition. Developing countries need to standardize their qualification and licensing requirements in order to attract customers and improve skills.

Healthcare doesn't have to go the same way as food prices. Rich and poor countries should ignore calls for protectionism and liberalize their healthcare for the good of patients everywhere. Health tourism can be healthy for everyone.

Ayurvedic Tourism

Ayurvedic medicine is a form of unconventional medicine in use mainly in the Indian subcontinent. The word "Ayurveda" means the "Science of Life".

It deals with the therapies and treatments for the rejuvenation and renewal of mind, body and soul. Ayurveda is also one among the few conventional method of medicine involving surgery. Ayurveda is a knowledge of life so to know more about it, we must know what is life. Life according to Ayurveda is an amalgamation of senses, mind, body and soul. So it is clear from this description of life that Ayurveda is not only restricted to body or physical symptoms but also gives a wide-ranging knowledge about spiritual, mental and social health.

The Ayurvedic scaffold can be used to structure working models of the special state of each patient, and to project a vision or goal for a whole state of health, again unique to each case.

Ayurveda offers specific references to each individual on lifestyle, diet, exercise and yoga, herbal therapy, and even spiritual practices to renovate and maintain balance in body and mind. Ayurveda sees a strong link between the mind and the body, a huge quantity of information is accessible regarding this correlation.

History

Ayurveda is said to have been first conformed as a text by Agnivesha in the book Agnivesh tantra. Verses related Ayurveda are also mentioned in the Atharvaveda. In the earlier days of its formation, the structure of Ayurvedic medicine was orally transferred via the Gurukul system until a written script came into subsistence.

What is interesting is Ayurveda's utilization of herbs, foods, aromas, gems, colours, yoga, mantras, lifestyle and surgery. Consequently Ayurveda nurtured into an esteemed and widely used method of healing in India in ancient times. Ayurveda was marked out into eight definite branches of medicine. There were two main disciplines of Ayurveda at that time. Atreya (the school of physicians) and Dhanvantari (the school of surgeons). These two schools made Ayurveda a more systematically confirmable and classifiable medical structure.

Benefits

- eradicate toxins and toxic conditions from your body & mind
- refurbish your constitutional balance, refining health & wellness
- reinforce your immune system & become more defiant to illness
- repeal the negative effects of stress on your body & mind, thereby dawdling the aging process
- augment your self-reliance, strength, energy, potency & mental clarity
- Bring about deep respite & a sense of comfort.

Ayurveda provides both remedial and precautionary measures towards finest physical, mental and spiritual well-being. More than merely medicinal care, Ayurveda offers a viewpoint whereby one may avert unnecessary distress and live a long, healthy life. Ayurveda has undergone unremitting research, development and refinement over thousands of years.

Ayurvedic Medicare is based on natural and herbal procedures and appendages. Ayurveda does not consider antidotes and antigens, very seldom those techniques are used, Ayurveda works not to restrain the system of body, but to go to the origin and treat the basic disturbing element. In such treatments there are very small chances of side effect and the benefit of the body is everlasting. It gives you a absolute health treatment, which works on the full body system so it makes you feel healthier in your whole body.

Worldwide Popularity

In modern years, Ayurveda has achieved worldwide fame. People are looking for a medicinal system that allows lowest intake of chemicals, whose side effects and reactions are well identified. Thus, alternate health care systems are becoming more fashionable. Ayurveda, which is a total system including preservation of health, avoidance and curing diseases, can be the best exchange to today's medical sciences. A natural concord between Ayurvedic principles and the human structure is the main factor for its efficiency.

The present man-made lifestyle has led to many health hazards. The stress and tension of everyday life is a chief factor for many health problems.

Lack of exercise, tainted environment and climatically inapt menu further sap away energy. Ayurveda rectifies these health issues through therapy and massage. Ayurveda can lessen the problems created by the hectic lifestyle we lead today. Hence Ayurveda is a science that is gaining wide recognition and international fame today. With its innate remedies Ayurveda has grown into an absolute healthcare system without any side effects.

What is Ayurveda?

The word Ayurveda is composed of two Sanskrit terms— Ayu meaning 'life' and Veda meaning 'knowledge'. Therefore Ayurveda means the knowledge of life or science of life. It is defined as the science, through which one can obtain knowledge about the useful and harmful ways of life, happy and miserable types of life, conditions that lead to the above types of life, as well as, the very nature of life.

Benefits of Ayurveda

* Ayurvedic and herbal medicines ensures physical and mental health without side effects. The natural ingredients of herbs help bring 'arogya' (health) to human body and mind.
* According to the original texts, the goal of Ayurveda is prevention as well as promotion of the body's own capacity for maintenance and balance.
* Ayurvedic treatment is non-invasive and non-toxic, so it can be used safely as an alternative therapy or alongside conventional therapies.
* Ayurvedic physicians claim that their methods can also help stress-related, metabolic, and chronic conditions.
* Ayurveda has been used to treat acne, allergies, asthma, anxiety, arthritis, chronic fatigue syndrome, colds, colitis, constipation, depression, diabetes, flu, heart disease, hypertension, immune problems, inflammation, insomnia, nervous disorders, obesity, skin problems, and ulcers.

Promoting Ayurveda-Health Tourism in India

Ayurveda has gained a lot of global attraction. Being one of the main features of tourist attraction down south, many Ayurvedic centres are on a rise today. India is emerging as a great destination for medical tourism because it has several pull factors like Excellent medical treatment at low cost, easy accessibility, picturesque locations for excellent holiday, etc. The medical tourism market in India is expected to grow to $2 billion a year by 2012-13. South India is the preferred location and is the health capital of the country. In their quest to attract foreign patients, hospitals are opening up a wide of facilities like foreign cell for each country among the others. Hopefully, by the next few years, India will be the preferred location worldwide for good medical facility.

India Major Player of Health Tourism

Marketing Ayurveda as part of the 'health tourism' has brought a new definition to vacationing in India itself. Medical treatment combined with leisure activities, fun and fitness. India has originated as one of the most important hubs for medical tourism.

Top-class medical expertise and facilities: India has lot of tourists from other countries coming for the rejuvenation promised by yoga and Ayurvedic massage. Add to it, a nice blend of top-class medical expertise at attractive prices which is helping more and more Indian corporate hospitals to lure foreign patients, including patients from the UK and the US, for high end surgeries like Cardiac ByPass Surgery or a Knee/Hip Replacement. Indian corporate hospitals are well equipped, proficient and could measure up to or even outshine any hospital in the West, making the nation an attractive destination for health tourism.

Low medical costs compared to other countries: As the inflow of more patients from affluent nations with high medical costs look for effective options, are increasing, health care tourism in India is definitely on the cards for most of them and the fast growing Indian corporate health sector is fully geared to meet that need.

No waiting period: Not just cost savings or the high standard of medical care facility, but also the waiting time is much lower for any treatment in India than in any other country. Medical help is often an emergency and situations can turn worse if the treatment is delayed. While you might have to wait for several months to get a surgical operation done in the US, in India things can be arranged within a week.

Ayurvedic Centres in Kerala

1. Nagarjuna Ayurvedic Centre: Nagarjuna Ayurvedic Centre is part of the Nagarjuna group and are the pioneers in the promotion and treatment of Aurveda in Kerala. The centre is located on the banks of the river Periyar and offers the best of Ayurvedic treatments.
2. Kottakkal Arya Vaidya Shala: The Arya Vaidya Shala is a complete encyclopedia of ayurvedic procedures, including cultivation of medicinal plants, manufacturing of herbal medicines, publishing books and seminar reports on ayurveda and related subjects, and beyond obvious, encouraging a Kathakali Academy. The treatment is based on Panchakarma Principles.
3. Amrita Ayurveda Medical Centre, Cochin: Amrutha Ayurveda centre is in the heart of Kochi engaged in the traditional Ayurvedic treatment to provide mental and physical health to the needy. Its aim is to increase the health status of human beings and to make them aware of the same.

Ayurvedic SPa Tourism to Kerala, India

Kerala is the only state in India where ayurveda is practised with full dedication and knowledge. The main reason for this is the climatic condition here is much suited for this Indian traditional system of medicine. Especially the cool monsoon season and the green forests enhances this treatment much.

Though Ayurveda has been practised in India and Kerala for a huge number of years it is only a few years that it became a tourism promoting mean here. According to Ayurvedic specialists monsoon season is the best season for ayurvedic treatment as our atmosphere becomes dust free and cool. Many Spa resorts are available now in Kerala and they mainly aims tourists. Foreigners also now understood the positive effect of Ayurveda and are now coming here on a large scale for spa tourism and returns happily with freshness. Treatment plans ranges from Rs 2500 a day to Rs 65000 for 3 weeks are available and they are ready to pay what is asked.

In the changed condition of life people are suffering from a lot of pressure stress and tension in their day today life. Ayurvedic spa tourism is a best way to refresh you mind and body and to refill your spirit with freshness and peace. Ayurvedic treatments such as yoga meditation steam bath and massage have been proved to be effective for stress relief and also for a sound body. Though you are not suffering from such problems still you can opt this because it will give more freshness and health and also pleasure. And you can make it fully useful your holidays to Kerala.

10 Types of Ayurvedic Treatments in Kerala

1. Abhyangam: This is a type of oil massage treatment which takes a fourtnight length. It is a good treatment for problems like obesity and is done for 45 minute everyday.
2. Lepanam: The herbs are grind and is applied on the body parts. Mostly for allergies and inflammatory problems.
3. Thalam: A treatment for diseases related to head such as head ache, memory loss, hair graying, Insomnia etc. In this medicated oil is applied on the top of the head and is a very important one. I takes upto 40 minutes length.
4. Dhanyamla Dhara: This is a very useful treatment helping in curing diseases related to spinal chord and nerval system. This is found to be effective for curing diseases like spondylosis, rheumatism, paralysis, disc problems, back pain, asthma and arthritis. This takes a length of 14 days and 1 hour/day.
5. Dhara: Very effective for diseases promoted by vatha dosha and also for many skin diseases. In a special order and way medicated milk buttermilk and herbal oils are poured on the body and it takes upto 3 weeks for the treatments having periods of length 45 minutes/day.
6. Kizhi: Kizhi is for curing swellings and injuries. Diseases related to bones such as arthritis ans sports injuries etc. can be cured in this way. In this treatment herbal leaves

and powder immersed in warm oil is applied all over the body for 1 hour a day for 14 days.

7. Nasyam: For neurological diseases, skin diseases and also for diseases such as migrain nasyam is found to be much useful. In this the medical oil is applied through the nose fore one week.
8. Pizhichi: The treatment is used for problems like Paralysis sexual weakness and Nervous weakness. The method is applying luke worm oil all over the body in a special way by four skilled therapists.
9. Vasthi: Treatment for the curing of diseases such as Arthritis, *Hemiplegia*, Numbness and constant constipation. Herbal oils with other herbal medicines are applied through the rectum everyday. Treatment continues for periods upto 25 days.
10. Yoni Prakshalanam: In this herbal oils and other herbal extracts are applied through the vaginal route. It is very effective in curing gynecological disorders.

Ayurvedic SPA Resorts in Kerala

1. Coconut Lagoon, Kumarakom, At the shore of Vembanad Lake.
2. Marari Beach Resort, Mararikkulam.
3. Kairali Health Resorts, Palakkadu.
4. Somatheeram Beach Reasort, Kovalam.
5. Spice village, Periyar.
6. Taj Garden Retreat, Kumarakom.
7. Taj Garden Retreat, Thekkady.

Ayurvedic Tour

The Indian system of nature cure: Life is a combination of the body, the senses, the mind and the atma (spirit or the soul). They can't be separated from each other, and none can be neglected. From this combination ensues 'Ayus'- the span of life.

Ayurveda-the science of life is the knowledge of this association and of how to maintain it as long as possible. Ayurveda or the 'science of longevity' is the system of nature cure. It is known to promote positive health, natural beauty and long life. Although rooted in antiquity, Ayurveda is based on universal principles and is a living, growing body of knowledge-as useful today as it was in earlier centuries. It is said that Ayurveda is as old as the world itself. Its very basis is the spiritual knowledge of the ancient seers of India and the cosmic consciousness in which they lived. Into its ancient well profound healing wisdom, some of the greatest doctors and sages over time have poured their finest insights and discoveries, transforming it into one of the oldest systems with a consistent theoretical basis and practical clinical applications. Its strength lies in its broad, all encompassing view of all dynamic inter-relationship between organic philological processes, external factors including climate, life works and diet along with internal psychological and spiritual condition.

Very much like various other systems of cure based on naturopathy, Ayurveda believes that disease occurs not as an arbitrary phenomenon but for definite reasons which if correctly understood could help to cure and, more importantly, prevent recurrence of the disease. Ideally human being and nature should be in perfect harmony. Disease occurs when the equilibrium between these two is disrupted. Restoration of this fundamental balance, through the use of nature and its products, is main goal of this medical system. "The object of Ayurveda", said Susruta the famous physician some 2600 years ago, "is the restoration to health of those who are afflicted with diseases and preservation of sound health of those who are well".

Evidently Ayurveda believes in the treatment of not just the affected part, but also the individual as a whole. The stress is on prevention of bodily ailments and not just curing them. There are no distressing side effects and it has, today, become an internationally acclaimed form of healing, rejuvenation and healthy living.

Trends in Health Industry

In the rapidly changing health care industry, technological advances have made many new procedures and methods of diagnosis and treatment possible. Clinical developments, such as organ transplants, less invasive surgical techniques, skin grafts, and gene therapy for cancer treatment, continue to increase the longevity and improve the quality of life of many Americans. In addition, advances in information technology continue to improve patient care and worker efficiency with devices such as hand-held computers that record notes on each patient.

Information on vital signs and orders for tests are transferred electronically to a main database; this process eliminates the need for paper and reduces recordkeeping errors.

Employment Outlook

Job opportunities should be excellent in all employment settings because of high job turnover, particularly from the large number of expected retirements and tougher immigration rules that are slowing the numbers of foreign health care workers entering the U.S. Wage and salary.

Employment in the health care industry is projected to increase 27 percent through 2014, compared with 14 percent for all industries combined. Projected rates of employment growth for the various segments of the industry range from 13 percent in hospitals, the largest and slowest growing industry segment, to 69 percent in the much smaller home health care services.

About 545,000 establishments make up the health care industry; they vary greatly in terms of size, staffing patterns, and organizational structures. About 76 percent of health care establishments are offices of physicians, dentists, or other health practitioners. Although hospitals constitute only 2 percent of all health care establishments, they employ 40 percent of all workers.

Trends & Emerging Issues

Macro Trends

- The population of the United States is expected to grow 29.2% between 2000 and 2030, from 282,125,000 to 363,584,000.
- Rates of all cancers for men declined between 1990 and 2001 (almost 1% per year), while for women the rates increased (an average of 0.4% per year).

- The prevalence of overweightness and obesity among adults has dramatically increased.
- The number of persons covered by employer-based health insurance decreased steadily between 2000 and 2004, and during that period the total number of uninsured adults increased by 6 million.

Market Trends

- 8 out of 20 occupations projected to grow the fastest are in health care.
- More new wage and salary jobs – about 19 percent, or 3.6 million – created between 2004 and 2014 will be in health care than in any other industry.
- Most workers have jobs that require less than 4 years of college education, but health diagnosing and treating practitioners are among the most educated workers.

Forecasts

- Researchers have found that by electrically stimulating certain nerves they can influence human movement, and possibly create better prosthetics.
- A California biotech company expects to begin trials of a treatment for spinal cord injuries next year.
- New drugs that target the brain's nicotine receptors, without the addictiveness of cigarettes, might help memory impairment in Alzheimer's disease and schizophrenia.
- Researchers predict significant health and cost benefits from linking data from individual biomonitors, as well as community health monitoring, to encourage healthy behaviour changes.
- Accenture is developing a talking medicine cabinet to help the elderly manage their medications and keep track of their vitals.

Health Care Industry Trends

Health care industry trends manifest an upward growth but several areas need to be attended to for enhancing health care services for the common man. Different countries like Indonesia, Russia, Mexico, Brazil, India, Turkey and China comprise approximately 1/5th of the worldwide health care sales.

Health care industry trends also suggest that the medical related conditions in the developing countries which are chronic in nature, will be similar to the ones existing in the developed countries. In order to meet international standards, the existing health care industry is required to alter the mode of operation for generation of higher revenue and greater contribution to the Gross Domestic Product of the country.

Facts about the health care industry trends:

- The cost related to health care was seen to rise in the 90s. Americans not possessing any health care coverage or any kind of health insurance attained the 42 million mark.
- It has been anticipated that the elderly sick people will impose considerable stress on the health care sector of US.
- The total number of different health care programs and different health care insurance coverages are likely to increase in the coming years. There has been an escalation in the medical plans from 42.5 million in the year 2006. The health care industry trends also show that it is likely to attain 70.2 million in the year 2025.
- The health care industry trends also indicate that the expenses for preventive measures is negligible as compared to the amount spent on treating chronic diseases which accounts for 70% of the fund used for health care.
- Trends suggest that there are very less Americans (around 23%) who make an effort to prevent any lifestyle diseases by consuming the optimum level of vegetable and fruits.

Health care industry trends suggests changes in the following spheres:

- The companies manufacturing medicines provide health care plans
- More stress is to be laid on prevention than treatments

- Sufficient supply of the essential health care products should be made available to the consumers to meet the demand of the health care industry.

Health care industry trends manifest an upward growth but several areas need to be attended for enhancing health care services for the common man.

Introduction to the Health Care Industry

Health Expenditures and Services in the US

Health care costs continue to rise rapidly in the U.S. and throughout the developed world. Total U.S. health care expenditures are estimated to have grown from $2.39 trillion in 2008 to $2.50 trillion in 2009.

The health care market in the U.S. in 2009 was made up of hospital care (about $789.4 billion), physician and clinical services ($539.1 billion), prescription drugs ($244.8 billion), nursing home and home health ($213.6 billion), dental care ($101.9 billion) and other items totalling $611.2 billion. Registered hospitals totalled 5,708 properties in 2008, containing 945,199 beds serving 37 million admitted patients.

Net federal spending on Medicaid and Medicare accounted for about 22.3% of all federal government expenditures in fiscal 2009. Medicare, the U.S. federal government's health care program for Americans 65 years or older, provided coverage to 45.5 million seniors in 2009 (up from 44.8 million the previous year). Federal Medicare costs for fiscal 2009, net of premiums paid by beneficiaries, were projected to be $430.8 billion. By 2030, the number of people covered by Medicare will balloon to about 78.0 million due to the massive number of Baby Boomers entering retirement age.

Medicaid is the federal government's health care program for low-income and disabled persons (including children), as well as certain groups of seniors in nursing homes. The federal government incurred Medicaid expenditures totalling $180.6 billion in fiscal 2006, $190.6 billion in 2007 and $201.4 billion in 2008. This amount was projected to reach $262.4 billion in 2009, but the actual amount may be higher due to temporary spending. At one time or another during 2007, 61.9 million people (about 20% of all Americans) were enrolled in Medicaid, and average enrolment for the year was 49.1 million. State governments incur large expenses for Medicaid benefits as well. For example, in 2007 alone the states spent $149 billion on Medicaid, over and above the federal expenditure.

The Great Recession devastated the budgets of most of the 50 states. Tax revenues plummeted while demand for many state services rose. For example, as of October 2009, unemployment remained at a very high rate in the United States, just below 10%. This pushed more people into poverty, which increased the number of people eligible for Medicaid by several million. Federal stimulus spending included a temporary, $87 billion increase in Federal support for state Medicaid spending for the period October 2008 through December 2010.

Health spending in the U.S., at about 17.6% of Gross Domestic Product (GDP) in 2009, is projected to grow to about 20.3% by 2018 unless drastic reforms take place. Health care spending in America accounts for a larger share of GDP than in any other major industrialized country. Despite the incredible investment America continues to make in health care, 15.4% of people in the U.S. (46.3 million people) lacked health care coverage for the entire year of 2008.

For some, insurance was unavailable or unaffordable. In other cases, a lack of insurance was due to a personal decision not to pay for it. For example, a significant number of the uninsured, about 8.2 million, were in households with annual incomes above $75,000. A large number of the uninsured, approximately 8 million, are illegal immigrants. According to the Centre for Immigration Studies, about 64% of illegal immigrants were uninsured in 2006. The actual number may be much higher today. A Kaiser Family Foundation study, "Medicaid and the Uninsured," dated February 2007, estimated that one-fourth of the uninsured are eligible for public programs but are not enrolled. These are largely low-income children, and in some cases their parents.

Clearly, the large number of people with no coverage is a problem, but there is little-to-no agreement as to what to do about it, if anything. As of late 2009, a sweeping health care reform and expansion of coverage was being pushed by the White House, to the extent of universal health care for nearly all Americans. Agreement among members of Congress as to the advisability, method and funding of such care is far from certain. At the same time, large numbers of Americans are relatively well satisfied with their current payors and methods of coverage.

Likewise, many Americans and their legislators are extremely reluctant to see government take a lager role in the health care system, fearing runaway costs, bloated bureaucracies and less competition in the marketplace. Some feel that it is not the role of government to penalize patients or employers who do not purchase coverage.

Others are reluctant to see America follow in the footsteps of nationalized medicine in neighbouring Canada, where patients for many types of common treatments are on extremely long waiting lists or find it next to impossible to receive certain types of advanced therapies.

Yet another concern is that expensive treatments or drugs may be made off limits under a national system in order to restrain costs.

As of October 2009, the Obama Administration was pushing an agenda of health reform based on federally-mandated universal coverage. If such a bill is passed by Congress, it will likely contain some or all of the following elements:

1) Roughly 25 million of the current 45 million will remain uninsured. This includes 8 to 10 million illegal immigrants who will not be covered. (A small number have already obtained health coverage independently.) Among citizens and residents who reside in America legally, many will remain uninsured because they cannot afford even subsidized insurance, they make a personal choice not to participate (and thus face potential tax penalties) or otherwise fall through the cracks.
2) To help pay for a large portion of the federal cost of universal care, the government will attempt once again to cut waste and fraud in Medicare and reduce Medicare expenses overall.

3) Private health insurance companies, makers of medical equipment and other health industry firms will face higher taxes or fees to help pay for the new system.
4) Individuals who receive particularly generous work-related health insurance plans, or the companies that provide these plans, may be charged an excise tax. High income individuals who incur large medical expenses may receive lower tax write-offs for health care costs.

Health Expenditures Globally and in OECD Developed Nations

A comprehensive study published by the OECD (Organization for Economic Cooperation & Development), covering 33 nations with the world's most developed economies, found stark contrasts between health costs in the United States and those of other modern nations. In 2006 (the latest data available), the average of 33 OECD nations, such as France, Germany, Mexico, South Korea, Australia, etc., including the U.S., spent 8.9% of GDP on health care. The highest figures were in the U.S. with 15.3% of GDP, Switzerland 11.3% and France 11.1%. Health expenditures per capita for these 33 nations in 2006, on a purchasing power-adjusted basis (PPP), averaged $2,824.

Globally, the total prescription drug market was in the $600 billion range in 2009. Total health care expenditures around the world are difficult to determine, but $5 trillion would be a fair estimate for 2009. That would place health care at about 8% of global GDP, with health care expenditures per capita at about $800. This $5 trillion figure breaks down to approximately $2.4 trillion in the U.S., $2.3 trillion in non-U.S. OECD nations, and $0.3 trillion elsewhere around the world. (Outside the U.S. and the rest of the OECD, that would allow $50 per capita per year in lesser-developed nations.) Clearly, there is vast disparity in the availability and cost of health care among nations, as there is with personal income and GDP.

Health Care Costs in the US

Particularly in the U.S., continuous increases in the cost of health care, growing at rates far exceeding the rate of inflation in general, are hammering health consumers and payors of all types. Insurance providers continue to struggle to contain costs.

Meanwhile, employers are hit hard by vast increases in the cost of providing coverage to employees and retirees. In 2009, employer-provided health care insurance coverage for a typical family cost an average of $13,375 for the year (up from $12,680 in 2008), according to a study conducted by the Kaiser Family Foundation, and $4,824 for single coverage for the year (up from $4,704). Employees were required to pay $3,515 of that cost for families and $779 for single coverage in 2009, on average, with employers picking up the balance. According to Kaiser, premium costs for family coverage rose 131% from 1999 through 2009, while the employee contribution rose 128%.

Many major employers are utilizing unique new programs in efforts to reduce employee illness, and thereby reduce costs. For example, the use of preventive care programs is growing, as is the use of employee education aimed at better managing the effects of diseases such as diabetes.

Smart employers are showing their employees how to use the Internet to obtain better information about diseases and prevention. Insurance providers are jumping on the Internet bandwagon as well. Some employers are even hiring in-house physicians and nurses to provide primary and preventive care in the work place.

Patients and insurance companies are also dealing with sticker shock over the nation's prescription drug costs. Other factors edging costs upward include expensive new medical technologies and patients' demands for greater plan flexibility in choosing doctors and specialists at their will. At the same time, hospitals and health systems write off massive amounts of revenues to bad debt, which increases costs for bill-paying patients.

In the wake of the tremendous growth of all aspects of the health care industry from the end of World War II onward, efficiency, competition and productivity were, regretfully, largely overlooked. Much of this occurred because employers plus federal and state governments paid such a large portion of the health care bill.

Physicians are caught between the desire to provide quality care and the desire for cost control on the part of payors, including PPOs, Medicare and Medicaid. The cost versus care debate has spawned an energetic movement to improve the quality of health care in the U.S., much of it centred on patients' rights, disease management, preventive health care and patient education. Nonetheless, wellness programs, preventive medicine and health education remain woefully inadequate.

A study released by the Milliken Institute in 2007 found that during the year 2003 (the year on which the study focused), 109 million Americans suffered from one or more of the most common, chronic diseases, including cancer, diabetes, heart disease, pulmonary conditions, mental disorders, stroke or hypertension. This means that more than one-third of all Americans had these conditions to one degree or another.

The study estimated one year's cost of treatment of these conditions at $277 billion, but estimated lost economic productivity to be vastly higher at $1 trillion. In other words, lost work and lost output due to these illnesses reduced the nation's GDP by about 10%. These burdens could be vastly reduced through better consumer health practices and better preventive medicine. For example, obesity, lack of exercise and cigarette smoking are immense contributors to these diseases. The Centres for Disease Control and Prevention reported that medical costs for obesity-related diseases rose as high as $147 billion in 2008, compared to $74 billion in 1998.

Meanwhile, technology marches ahead relentlessly. Be sure to read our descriptions of such innovations as HIFU, Proton Beam Radiation Therapy and the newest biotech developments later in this chapter.

The American health care industry faces more challenges than ever, due to a number of significant factors:

- While the advent of managed care appeared to tame health care cost inflation during the early and mid-1990s, costs have been rising very rapidly since then.
- The number of Americans who are underinsured or are without any type of insurance coverage at all remains staggering at more than 45 million.
- The U.S. population is aging rapidly. At the same time, the life expectancy of seniors is extending. Senior citizens will place a significant strain on the health care system in

coming years. America's 76 million surviving Baby Boomers begin turning 65 in 2011.

- The future obligations of Medicare and Medicaid are enough to cause vast problems for the federal budget for decades to come. The number of seniors covered by Medicare will continue to grow at an exceedingly high rate, from 45.5 million people in 2009 to 78.0 million in 2030.
- Likewise, costs for Medicaid, which is administered at the state level, have grown so rapidly that they are decimating state budgets and causing cuts in education and other vital state-provided services.
- The pharmaceuticals industry faces continued financial challenges. Pharmaceutical costs have created a large backlash among health consumers and payors. Patents for money-making, blockbuster drugs are expiring at a rapid rate, increasing competition from makers of generic drugs. At the same time, the drug industry remains under intense public scrutiny and is facing continued calls for increased government regulation.
- We are now entering what will long be remembered as the beginning of the Biotech Era. Breakthroughs in research for drug therapies are occurring at a rapid pace, creating financial and ethical challenges along with opportunities. Personalized medicine is beginning to emerge, but it remains to be seen who will be the early beneficiaries and who will pay the costs.
- Due to rising health care costs, employers large and small are straining under the financial burden of health care coverage expenses for current employees and retirees.
- Physicians, other care providers, pharmaceutical manufacturers and insurers face daunting pressure from litigation and potential claims regarding malpractice and denial of care. Lawsuit reform legislation has recently been enacted in many states with very promising results.
- Few Americans focus on leading healthy lifestyles that would prevent disease and cut both the amount and the

cost of medical care. Obesity-related illnesses are adding an immense amount to the nation's health care costs. A 2005 study led by researchers at Michigan State University estimated that 76% of Americans do not smoke, but only 40.1% maintain a healthy weight and only 22.2% exercise for at least 30 minutes, five times per week. Likewise, only 23.3% were found to eat the recommended amount of daily fruit and vegetable servings.

- The three biggest causes of death in the U.S. are heart disease, cancer and stroke. Nearly one-fourth of America's annual health expenditures go for treatment of these three killers.
- While only a relatively modest amount of money is spent on preventive medicine and health education, about 70% of health care funds are spent on chronic disease.

Health Care Industry Trends and Issues

Summary of Findings

While intense debate continues to swirl nationally around fundamental issues of equity and cost in the U.S. health care system, there seems little serious room for debate around a more narrow issue; e.g., the importance of health care to the local New York City economy and labour market. This FPI labour market update shows that:

1. The health care industry employs approximately 375,000 people in New York City, making it the city's number one sector in terms of employment, as well as the number one sector in every borough except Manhattan. Further, the industry overall has exhibited a growth pattern that persists through the ups and down of the wider economy.
2. The health care industry involves an extraordinarily wide array of occupations, including both direct service and non-direct service occupations. Many of these occupations are open to people with associates degrees or less. For example, according to the 1998 occupational data analyzed in this update, some 66,000 people were working in New York City as nursing aides, home health aides, and licensed

practical nurses. An additional 46,000 or so people were employed in one of several health-related clerical support occupations, while some 16,000 worked as janitors, housekeepers, or food service workers.

3. The health sector labour market is both highly regulated and highly unionized, making for relatively well-paid jobs. In addition, certification requirements and terms of collective bargaining agreements on the direct patient care side of the labour market tend to create unusually well-defined career ladders.
4. The New York City health sector labour market is heavily female, and heavily non-white. For example, Equal Employment Opportunity Commission data on operations with over 100 employees (mostly hospitals) shows black females as the single largest employment category (at 28% of the work force), followed by white females (at 25%).
5. While employment growth in health care overall has been relatively steady, the decade of the 1990's produced substantial shifts in the internal composition of the health care work force. Employment growth moved away from large hospitals and toward outpatient, home care, and long-term care settings. At the same time, employment growth moved away from the public sector and toward the private/voluntary sector.

Employment Shifts: Steady but Uneven Growth

The decade of the 1990's saw pronounced shifts in the structure of the health care industry both nationally and locally. Just a few of the most important health care "megatrends" included the overall health system's shift toward managed care, hospital consolidation, cost containment in the Medicaid and Medicare programs, and deep funding and personnel cutbacks for New York City public hospitals.

The overall results of these shifts. Stated simply, employment growth moved away from large hospitals and toward outpatient, home care, and long-term care settings, and at the same time away from the public sector and toward the private/voluntary sector. Among major subcategories of employment, public hospitals were hardest-hit with a 33% decline, while home health care services saw the greatest gains with a more than 75% increase.

Despite the uneven employment growth, however, the overall health care sector grew by 14.1% over the course of the decade (from some 329,000 workers to some 376,000 workers). In comparison, overall New York City employment (private & public) grew only 3.3% between 1990 and 2000.

Moreover, total health care employment continued to grow even through the sharp regional recession of the early 1990's that saw the loss of hundreds of thousands of jobs citywide.

Health care is particular important as a stable anchor for the economies of the four boroughs outside Manhattan, as Note that many additional home care workers are counted under the Standard Industrial Classification code for social services.

Fiscal Policy Institute

At the peak of the year 2000 boom, the business services industry briefly eclipsed the health care sector as New York City's single largest private sector employer. Recent downsizing in the business services sector, however, has vaulted health care back into its traditional leading position.

What's most unique about health care, however, is the importance of the sector to the economy of every borough. The health care industry is the top private sector employer in the Bronx, Brooklyn, Queens and Staten Island. The public health care sector by itself would be the third largest employer in the Bronx if it were incorporated into Compared to other industries, the health care sector is unusually regulated, monitored, and structured.

This is true in at least four general senses:

First, on the direct patient care side of the industry, employment ladders are defined by an extensive and legally binding system of professional certifications. This characteristic makes pathways for advancement more clear than in most other industries, and places an emphasis on the importance of educational institutions granting the certifications. The system also seems to have the general effect of both raising and buffering wage levels.

Second, the industry as a whole is highly unionized. Unionization tends to formalize employment and wage levels, and makes health care unions important institutional players in the labour market.

Third, health care costs and reimbursements to providers are regulated. This is especially true of Medicare and Medicaid reimbursements. Finally, health care providers themselves must be licensed by the State's Department of Health.

The State provides operating certificates to (and also reviews any service provision or facility changes carried out by) the following entities: diagnostic and treatment centres; certified home health care agencies; hospices; hospitals; residential care facilities (nursing homes); and long-term home health care programs. In addition, there are "licensed" home health care agencies, which are regulated by a separate branch of the Department of Health.

Fiscal Policy Institute

Labour market demographics: a heavily female and minority work force 1997 Equal Employment Opportunity Commission (EEOC) data shows that health care workers in New York City are majority female and majority non-white.

The specific ethnicity/sex breakdown of New York City private sector health care workers. Black females represent the single largest category, followed by white females. Note that since the EEOC data used for this table only covers entities over 100 employees, it may be best interpreted as a reflection of large institutions like hospitals.

Befitting its size, the health sector includes an unusually large array of distinct occupations. These occupations include both direct service and non-direct service work. They also include work that requires different kinds and levels of qualification and training – jobs from surgeon to stock clerk. All in all, the State Department of Labour lists exactly 300 separate occupations connected in some way to health care. More than 50 of these occupations involve 1,000 or more industry workers. The occupational matrix for the health care sector involves a lot more than doctors and nurses (though note that RN's are the single largest employment category and that substantial opportunities exist in this field given the current nursing shortage). For example, according to the OES data, some 66,000 people were working in New York City as nursing aides, home health aides, and licensed practical nurses in 1998. An additional 46,000 people were employed in one of the several clerical support occupations listed, while some 16,000 worked as janitors, housekeepers, or food service workers.

The list could go on, but the point remains that the health care labour market is highly diverse, and includes large numbers of low to moderate skill-level occupations.

Occupational Wage Scale: Many Middle-income Jobs

According to 1998 Occupational Employment Survey data, the vast majority of NYC health practitioners and technicians on the direct service side of the industry are earning at least $15 per hour. Some of the highest paid positions include physicians and surgeons ($48.58 per hour) and registered nurses ($28.95 per hour). Licensed practical nurses earn a median hourly wage of $16.25 in comparison. Pharmacy technicians are the lowest paid direct service health care workers, earning a median wage of $10.27.

Getting a bead on wage levels in the non-direct service side of the industry is somewhat more difficult, as the OES data lists median wages for individual occupations on an all-industry basis only. So, for example, while we know that the median hourly wage for food preparation workers citywide is $7.67, it is difficult to determine without further research whether health care food service workers get paid more or less. We can say as a generalization, however, that high unionization levels would tend to point to higher wages relative to the same occupation in non-unionized industries.

Occupational Projections

While a detailed discussion of occupational projections would be beyond the scope of this update, it's worth noting that the New York State Department of Labour projects significant growth in nearly all direct health service occupations. Such projections – always a tricky proposition – are perhaps more reliable in health care than for other more cyclical industries.

A particularly important issue, with quite substantial public health as well as economic implications, relates to growth in the number of registered nurses versus nurses aides. In our State of Working New York report, FPI has already pointed out a statewide trend toward substitution of nurses aides for higher paid and higher-skilled registered nurses. While the current "nursing shortage" may signal that this worrisome trend has for the time being played itself out, official employment projections show much faster expected growth rates for job classifications such as home health aides, nursing assistants, and medical assistants than for RN's.

Medical Market Overview & Industry Trends

Growing Population & Healthcare Spending

The worldwide healthcare market is influenced by a number of demographic trends, including the following:

- Growing and Aging Population: The U.S. Census Bureau predicts that the majority of the U.S. "baby boom" population (28% of the total U.S. population) will begin to turn 65 between 2010 and 2020.
- Consumer expectations for improved healthcare are increasing in both developed and developing countries.
- Reimbursement and coverage of medical expenses by insurances companies and employers are on the decline—customers/patients have to contribute more money.
- Technology is giving rise to new clinical therapies, which in turn are addressing more and more medical ailments and aiding in earlier diagnosis and prevention of diseases.

Healthcare spending per capita has gown significantly across the world. In the U.S., it has increased from $144 per capita in 1960 to almost $4,400 by 1999. The U.S. per capita spending is projected to grow to $7,500 by 2008. Equipment suppliers understand that in order to be successful in the medical market they have to be focused and successful in the U.S.

Technology Fuels Healthcare Productivity

In the next 10 years, the healthcare market will focus on early diagnosis, digitized patient information that can be accessed from numerous locations, and "total solution" selling that contributes to healthcare productivity gains. Early diagnosis and prevention is enabled by emerging diagnostic technologies. For example, positron emission tomography (PET) is used to detect many kinds of cancer with great accuracy.

A "paperless" hospital is another emerging trend. Digital patient records enable doctors to access patients' records—wherever the doctor is. In a digitized hospital, healthcare providers do not have to wait days for an x-ray to "come back from the lab" because the x-ray machine is digital and the image is instantly available.

Hospitals are also moving away from purchasing point solutions and toward buying equipment from different vendors that is interoperable and that has a uniform user interface. Hospitals are developing internal networks that connect all diagnostic equipment that feeds all patient information (e.g., computed tomography (CT) scans, x-rays, positron emission tomography (PET) scans) over a network to data storage servers for instant access. This drives medical equipment vendors to develop interoperable equipment that has a uniform user interface. In effect, vendors are beginning to sell complete solutions that include not only the diagnostic equipment but also the data storage servers as well as the interface software.

All these trends lead to an increase in healthcare productivity—this means more patients can be put through the healthcare system by using better, faster diagnostic equipment, which leads to early ailment diagnosis and treatment. When the paperless hospital becomes a reality, productivity is further enhanced because of instant patient test results and records access.

Programmable Logic Advantage

Majority of medical products have some type of semiconductor in it. In fact, the semiconductor content continues to increase in these myriad of products. Programmable Logic Devices (PLDs) continue to see a much higher rate of adoption than other semiconductor types. PLDs offer a viable and powerful alternative to both ASICs and ASSPs in medical equipment development. PLDs eliminate the up-front non-recurring engineering (NRE) costs and minimum order quantities associated with ASICs, and the costly risks of multiple silicon iterations through the capability to be reprogrammed as needed during the design process. When compared to ASSPs, PLDs provide the design flexibility and board integration opportunities to differentiate against competing medical equipment manufacturers. Additionally, PLDs can be upgraded in the field as standards evolve or requirements change. Also, the ability to re-use a common hardware platform allows designers to create differentiated systems which support a variety of feature sets with one basic design, resulting in reduced manufacturing costs. Whether designing a CT machine or patient monitoring equipment, programmable logic is a flexible, low-risk path to successful system design—offering optimum cost efficiencies while providing value-added differentiating capabilities versus other medical equipment manufacturers.

Last but not the least, PLDs have a very long life cycle and protect customers against product obsolescence, which is very critical in the medical industry because of long product cycles.

Medical Applications for Programmable Logic

By using programmable logic, engineers can cost-effectively develop leading-edge equipment for many applications in the medical space, including:

- Diagnostic imaging: X-ray, ultrasound, CT, magnetic resonance imaging (MRI), and nuclear/PET.
- Electromedical: Patient monitoring, life support, and anesthesia equipment.
- Cardiac Rhythm Management (CRM): Pacing systems, implantable cardiac defibrillators (ICDs), and automatic external defibrillators (AEDs).
- Life Science & Hospital Equipment: Lab instrumentation, radiation equipment, and various hospital equipment.

The Altera Advantage

Altera gives medical electronics equipment manufacturers a competitive edge. Altera's solutions are currently found in various medical end-applications worldwide; they combine a wide range of PLDs with optimized intellectual property (IP) cores, hard and soft microprocessors, powerful design software, and a variety of development kits to create a complete, easy-to-use design platform.

Altera's PLDs, including the Stratix® II, Stratix GX, and Cyclone™ II FPGA families, which include a rich feature set of logic, memory, dedicated digital signal processing (DSP) blocks, and I/O standard support, which give medical equipment designers all the tools they need to win in this highly competitive market.

Altera® PLDs offer medical electronics equipment manufacturers a flexible, cost-effective, obsolescence-free path to successful system design. Some of the opportunities that Altera offers manufacturers are:

- Cost reduction by avoiding ASICs' extensive NREs and minimum ordering costs,
- Time-to-market advantage by avoiding the lengthy and risky ASIC development cycle,
- Cost reduction and differentiation by integrating multiple ASSP functions into FPGAs,
- Reprogrammability during the design process and after equipment is in the field,
- Reusability of one hardware platform for various systems with one basic design,
- Adaptability to multiple industry standards and protocols.

Intellectual Property

Off-the-shelf IP cores that have been optimized for Altera's products can reduce engineering costs and shorten time-to-market. Standard interfaces and IP cores are available from Altera or approved Altera Megafunction Partners Program (AMPP℠) partners. Prior to licensing, the OpenCore® evaluation feature allows users to evaluate Altera MegaCore® functions and AMPP megafunctions at no cost.

Altera designs, supports, and sells Altera MegaCore functions. All MegaCore functions have been rigorously tested and optimized for the highest performance and lowest cost in Altera PLDs.

Development Kits

Altera and its partners offer a variety of development kits to support the development and verification of system-on-a-programmable-chip (SOPC) designs.

Emerging Trends in Health Care Industry – Medical Tourism

It has often been said that "medical tourism 'is nothing new. This is true. It is also true that since man has been a nomad he, or she has always been looking for greener pastures and a better life, quality of life or services than they have presently available. So is it with medical care.

The "baby boomer" generation is ending. So is or has the birth rate in industrialized countries. Who will physically provide the service? Who will pay to it? Medical or home care is a labour and attention intensive service. In Italy now – once now for large families – people pay to "rent "grandparents. There certainly are no valued, privileged children, who in many societies are given the revered task and privilege of caring for aged parents. Never mind the money involved, in most of the wealth, industrialized countries there will not be the staff to care for the aged, or the ill. It is not as if an electronic chip or even robots can ever do these tasks. Each situation is different, each unique.

Hence it is no startling fact that medical tourism will grow and grow and will become a major growth industry. More and more baby boomers, many with means, some with benefits and lesser means. It is estimated that these numbers, within North America, – US and Canada, Europe, Australia and New Zealand will approximate 250 million people. The health care system – and overall budgets of these countries – whether they provide health care universally by the government purse – such as Canada or privately – as in the USA – will not be able to provide either the resources – labour or funds for quick, prompt, quality health care. What makes more sense than medical tourism – both from a cost and logistical standpoint where treatment and labour is available and at a reasonable cost?

The Issue: Emerging Outsourcing Trends in the Healthcare Industry

As the scope of potentially outsourced functions and processes in the healthcare industry continues to expand, EquaTerra anticipates market growth could be even faster than some project. Buyers across the healthcare industry are facing acute cost pressures that make business as usual impossible. Thus, they must accelerate efforts to gain greater process efficiency and effectiveness. These efforts are facilitated by improved and consolidated IT systems, greater automation and selfservice capabilities, and some amount of labour cost reduction. This involves changing the service delivery model for back-office functions as well as core healthcare administration and operational functions and processes.

Healthcare Provider and Payer Market Trends

Healthcare providers are hospitals, nursing homes, long-term care facilities, physician and other professional services groups, and specialized therapeutic enterprises. While outsourcing is occurring in this market segment, it is not doing so at the scale or scope seen in other segments of the market, given its more fragmented and decentralized nature.

On the provider side, outsourcing is more likely to occur at the corporate level around back-office IT and business process functions and processes.

The healthcare payer segment of the market is becoming more aggressive in its pursuit of new service delivery models for core business processes. Healthcare payer organizations include commercial insurers, government insurer programs, not-for profit insurers and benefit management firms.

The commercial payer segment has recently experienced consolidation, primarily due to competition for bargaining leverage with providers, as well as a focus on the scale associated with consolidated operations.

Additionally, the rapidly evolving nature and complexity of health plan product lines are changing in response to increases in healthcare service expenses, and support and customer satisfaction requirements. These and other factors have produced the following conditions:

Merger, acquisition and divestiture activity has increased demands on technical and support infrastructures, further driving the need for change.

- The costs and infrastructure to update and maintain these systems is driving the requirement for innovation and transformation. Many of the larger payers have remained with legacy hardware and proprietary or internally developed applications that no longer meets their needs. They are looking for ways to reduce costs and minimize expenses for all sales, general and administrative (SG&A) processes.

- The growing complexity of offerings, and government and regulatory changes, have increased delivery and support requirements.
- Governmental payers have moved much faster than commercial payers in sourcing their operational support requirements. This should encourage a "follow the leader" mentality.
- Confidentiality and privacy issues around personal health data has caused an increase in expenses associated with the delivery of services.

Overall, the healthcare industry is characterized by older systems that did the job a decade or so ago, but have not kept up with the times. Consequently, payer organizations have taken a "we will patch it now and fix it later" approach. But they are now starting to look at functions and processes that are less core to their business and are thus more viable candidates for outsourcing, like broader elements of policy maintenance and claims administration. Additionally, they are assessing speed-to-market and cost reduction in those areas that offer value and payback to the organization through an outsourcing lens.

The operating model of many large healthcare firms can complicate their back-office outsourcing management efforts. According to one EquaTerra advisor:

> *"Healthcare firms are very driven by cost reduction and capital avoidance, even though most say they want to make the back-office more strategic. It is all about the money." Said another EquaTerra advisor: "Cost structure in healthcare has shifted radically, and governmental regulations, the ability for consumers to become and remain informed, the Internet, new health plan creation and execution, price controls and real-time adjudication are all putting pressure on margins."*

Get to What Matters. How are Healthcare Buyers Responding?

The healthcare industry is now facing a wake-up call in terms of slumping stock prices, additional competition, regulatory pressure and an informed consumer that is demanding the best service at the lowest possible cost.

For these reasons, payers must become more competitive and cost effective. Given their experience in forging and managing complex business partner relationships, they should view outsourcing as another example of this type of partnership-oriented relationship.

The healthcare industry faces unique outsourcing challenges, however, because of application and system integration challenges exacerbated by the highly regulated nature of the market.

First, firms typically have older systems and applications in place.

Second, there is overstaffing in back-office functions.

Third, the industry has gone through change, and many of the firms have not adapted to the evolving business climate.

Fourth, healthcare buyers are facing more financial challenges and need to continue to innovate and transform.

Outsourcing is a catalyst for changing behaviour and reducing "the fat."

EquaTerra recently polled the top outsourcing service providers in the U.S. healthcare payer space and, coupled with its own direct market experiences, mapped the level of buyer demand across functions and processes specific to the healthcare payer space.

The demand level ranking is based on a one-to-10 scale, with one equating to low buyer demand and 10 indicating high demand levels. Process areas that exhibited the greatest level of buyer demand included claims and enrolment data entry and claims adjudication.

Further, there was growing demand in a variety of other functional and process areas including emerging knowledge services, such as reporting, planning and related analytics.

EquaTerra and the outsourcing service providers also assessed the market maturity of providers delivering services into these areas. Characteristics of market maturity on the supply side include the size of the installed client base, the depth, sophistication and standardization of the service offerings, and the degree to which the offerings are formalized as opposed to assembled and delivered on an ad-hoc basis. These maturity levels, as well as the gap between buyer demand and supplier maturity.

Overall, we see that buyer demand is outpacing supplier maturity, which is characteristic of an outsourcing market in more of a demand-pull than a supplier-push mode. This is due to the recent increase in buyer demand levels, coupled with a supplier lag in developing and expanding service offerings as a result of historically weak demand for outsourcing services in this market sector.

EquaTerra also polled healthcare outsourcing service providers on the leading drivers for growth in outsourcing, particularly around emerging BPO areas. Not surprisingly, cost reduction was the leading driver. However, citation levels in healthcare were even higher than those usually found in other industries, scoring 90 percent among service providers polled.

This reflects the cost pressures facing U.S. healthcare payers today. Process improvement as a driver ranked second. Interestingly, cost avoidance scored near the bottom, as did access to new technologies.

The low scoring for accessing technologies is in part a function of assessing BPO versus ITO drivers. While achieving cost reductions is obviously critical to U.S. healthcare payer organizations, they should not lose sight of ancillary and complementary opportunities to improve process performance, or overstates on pursuing levels of cost reduction that compromise the integrity of the business processes involved.

How are Outsourcing Service Providers Responding?

Leading outsourcing service providers that target the healthcare industry are generally in sync with EquaTerra relative to outsourcing trends. These providers focus on how to enable broad, global outsourcing efforts and place strong emphasis on moving beyond traditional "lift and shift" efforts to those that embed transformation and process improvement into the initiative.

Healthcare outsourcing service providers that have traditionally targeted the ITO and back-office BPO market segments have, in many cases, been slow to expand offerings into emerging BPO and KPO areas.

Or, their efforts in these areas have not been leveraged or made repeatable across their client portfolio. Recently, however, legacy multi-national outsourcing service providers have become more proactive in targeting these areas, and the leading Indian service providers that focus on the healthcare payer space have also been aggressive in pursuing these newer areas.

EquaTerra polled healthcare outsourcing service providers on what they believed to be the key attributes required to effectively compete in the emerging healthcare payer BPO space.

As expected, industry knowledge was cited as the key attribute to compete in this market. EquaTerra also appreciates and supports the citings of the importance of cultural fit between the buyer and service provider and the need to take a collaborative approach to the BPO effort. Highlighting the increasing global nature of the healthcare services market, the requirement for offshore and global service delivery capabilities also ranked high.

While past positive client experiences ranked lower, EquaTerra attributes this to the fact that, for deals in emerging BPO areas involving multi-national service providers, buyers have typically worked with these same providers in prior ITO engagements. Most Indian service providers in this market segment also have previously performed ITO work for the buyers.

In both cases, buyers have a positive track record with the outsourcing service provider used in the new areas. EquaTerra feels this past experience is an important aspect to account for when entering into emerging and more complex BPO efforts. Overall, outsourcing service providers in the healthcare and healthcare payer markets are more aggressively investing in and expanding their outsourcing – especially their BPO and KPO – offerings. They must, however, remain sensitive to some of the specific challenges healthcare buyers face. Mis-steps in outsourcing deals are always problematic, but can become even more so when healthcare services and patient care and information are involved.

The Advisor Perspective – critical Points to Consider

Healthcare organizations that have not recently done so should update and reassess their strategy and action plan for use of alternative service delivery models for both back-office and core operating functions and processes.

Emerging areas of BPO, if successfully executed, can play a positive and growing role in helping healthcare organizations address the serious challenges they are facing today. While buyers should use caution when exploring and assessing emerging BPO areas, the market is expanding and rapidly maturing, and what was premature in the past could be ready for primetime today.

Healthcare buyers should also view the increased use of emerging BPO and KPO services as part of a service continuum. Some of this work will always be performed internally.

Some activities are or will become more suitable for a shared services or offshore captive environment, and others are best suited for outsourcing. Buyers need to have a flexible global sourcing delivery model and framework that continually assesses the best delivery model for different services.

For further insights, follow this link to access the EquaTerra Perspective "How to Design and Optimize Global Services Delivery Models." Operationally, buyers must focus on the critical, but often misunderstood or under-supported, areas of outsourcing transition and governance. As the number of outsourcing efforts and relationships grow, buyers must adequately invest in their outsourcing governance capabilities and strive to take a portfolio approach to managing these efforts. Outsourcing service providers must also become more sensitive to the governance needs of their clients, and better support relationships that can span multiple service providers.

Conclusion

The healthcare industry around the world, and especially in the United States, is under extreme pressure to reduce costs while also expanding services and maintaining high service levels.

Addressing inefficiencies in delivering both back-office as well as core operational services can play a key role in addressing these challenges. While the healthcare industry has historically lagged other industries in its uptake of alternative service delivery models, this has begun to change.

Healthcare payers, in particular, are more aggressively pursuing a broader outsourcing agenda that includes emerging and strategic business and knowledge process outsourcing services. Outsourcing service providers targeting the healthcare space – both legacy multinational service providers and India-based firms moving beyond IT into business services – are starting to develop more targeted and compelling outsourcing offerings.

While there are alternatives to outsourcing, as well as many complexities to consummating it successfully, healthcare buyers are heeded to carefully reexamine their outsourcing strategy and plans in light of prevailing industry conditions.

Bibliography

Benefice, Brian G, and Cooper, Chris: *Geography of Travel and Tourism*, The, London, Heinemann, 1987.

Bernthall, R. : *International Conference for Tourism Educators*, Guildford, University of Surrey, 1988.

Bolshevism, Germy: *Coping with Tourists: European Reactions to Mass Tourism*, Oxford, Berghahn Books, 1995.

Broggi, M. : *Sanfter Tourismus: Schlagwort oder Chance Für Den Alpenraum?*, Vaduz, Commission Internationale pour la protection des Regions Alpines (CIPRA), 1985.

Burkart, A and Medlik, S: *Management of Tourism*, The, London, Heinemann, 1975.

Chambers, Erve: *Native Tours: The Anthropology of Travel and Tourism*, Prospect Heights, Waveland Press, 2000.

Chandler, Harry and Carter, John: *Chandler's Travels: A Tour of the Life of Harry Chandler*, London, Quiller Press, 1985.

Clark, Mona: *Interpersonal Skills for Hospitality Managers*, London, Chapman Hill, 1995.

Cukier, J. : *Tourism Employment in Bali: Trends and Implications*, London: Thompson, 1996.

David L: *International Tourism Policy, New York*, Van Nostrand and Reinhold, 1990.

Donald E. : *Public Personnel Management: Contexts and Strategies*, Upper Saddle River, NJ: Prentice Hall, 1998.

Donald M.: *Customer Service in the Hospitality and Tourism Industry*, Englewood Cliffs, Prentice Hall, 1994.

Douglas C: *Practical Tourism Forecasting*, Oxford, Butterworth Heinemann, 1996.

Eberts, Marjorie: *Careers in Travel, Tourism, and Hospitality*, Lincolnwood, VGM Career Horizons, 1997.

Eckel, Peter J.: *College & University Foodservice Management Standards,* Westport, AVI Pub. Company, 1985.

Fesenmaier D., Klein, S. : *Information & Communication Technologies in Tourism,* Springer-Verlag, Wien-New York, 2000.

Foster, Douglas: *Travel and Tourism Management,* London, Macmillan Educational, 1985.

Graham M S: *Language of Tourism,* The, Wallingford, CAB International, 1996.

Harrison, Lyndon: *Tourism Means Jobs,* Chester, Lyndon Harrison, 1996.

Judi Radice: *Restaurant & Food Graphics,* Glen Cove, PBC International, 1994.

Judy A: *Tourism: Management of Facilities,* London, Pitman: M & E, 1993.

Kotler, Philip: *Marketing for Hospitality and Tourism*: New Jersey, Prentice-Hall, 1998.

Larkham, P J: *Building a New Heritage: Tourism, Culture & Identity in the New Europe,* London, Routledge,1994.

Leivadi, S: *Sociology of Tourism, The: Theoretical And Empirical Investigations,* London, Retailed, 1996.

Lucas, Rosemary E.: *Managing Employee Relations in the Hotel and Catering Industry,* London, Cassell, 1995.

Madhukar Manoj : *Hospitality Industries in Next Millennium,* Rajat, Delhi, 2001.

Marcussen, Carl H. : *Internet Distribution of European Travel and Tourism Services,* Research Centre of Bornholm, Denmark, 1999.

Margaret Wade: *Medieval Travellers: The Rich and Restless,* London, Hamish Hamilton, 1982.

McNicol, B.J. : *Views of Residents, Developers and Government Planners About Tourists and Tourism Resort Developments in Canmore, Alberta,* The University of Galgary, Alberta, 1996.

Murphy, P.E. : *Tourism: A Community Approach,* London: Methuen, 1985.

Nancy, N.: *Choosing a Career in Hotels, Motels, and Resorts,* New York, Rosen Pub. Group, 1997.

Paajanen, M. : *Assessing Local Income and Employment Effects of Tourism: Experience using the Nordic model of tourism*, Wiley, 1999.

Pearce, Douglas: *Tourism Today: A Geographical Analysis*, Harlow, Longman, 1995.

Peters, M: *International Tourism*, London, Hutchinson, 1969.

Richards, G. : *Culture, Crafts and Tourism: A Vital Relationship*, Tilburg: Atlas, 1999.

Rocco, M.: *An Introduction to Hospitality Today*, Orlando, Educational Institute, 1998.

Rosenzweig, J. E.: *Organisation and Management*, New York, McGraw Hill International, 1963.

Sabharwal Rajiv : *Tourism and Hospitality Management in Liberalised Era*, Pacific, Delhi, 2011.

Scottish Tourist Board: *Visitor Attractions: A Development Guide*, Edinburgh, Scottish Tourist Board, 1991.

Sharma Sunil : *Planning and Development of Tourism and Hospitality*, Rajat Pub, Delhi, 2007.

Shrivastava Atul : *Modern Hospitality and Tourism Management*, Centrum Press, Delhi, 2010.

Slinn, Judy A: *Tourism: Management of Facilities*, London, Pitman: M & E, 1993.

Stear, L. : *Design of a Curriculum for Destination Studies*, Annals of Tourism Research, 1981.

Swarbrooke, J. : *Tourism and Leisure Education in the United Kingdom*, Tilberg, Netherlands, Tilberg University Press, 1995.

Thomas, F.: *Introduction to Management in the Hospitality Industry*, New York, Wiley, 1995.

Timothy R.: *Cases in Hospitality Management: A Critical Incident Approach*, New York, Wiley, 1995.

Tribe, J. : *Community and Commercial Interests in Tourism*, Developments in the European Tourism Curriculum, Tilberg, 1998.

Tribe, John *Corporate Strategy for Tourism, London*, International Thomson Business Press, 1997.

Index

A

B

C

E

G

H

I

W

❑❑❑